BAD GROUND
INSIDE THE BEACONSFIELD MINE RESCUE

TONY WRIGHT
WITH TODD RUSSELL
AND BRANT WEBB

PIER 9

CONTENTS

THE RUSSELL WEBB LEGACY

A donation from the proceeds of each copy of Bad Ground will be made to the Russell Webb Legacy.

The Russell Webb Legacy was established by Todd Russell and Brant Webb as a way of providing assistance to the youth of Beaconsfield and surrounding areas, who continue to feel the effects of the disaster. for more information on the Russell Webb Legacy, see page 348

PROLOGUE

SWEAT OF THE SUN

Gold is that most treacherous combination: beautiful and rare. It drives humans – the only beings on Earth vainglorious enough to wish to adorn themselves with metal – to risk everything and wipe out entire civilisations in their lust for the stuff.

If you were to gather together all the gold ever mined in history – all the jewellery, all the treasures ancient and modern, all the gold coins ever minted, the reserves held in government vaults, the gold visors on astronauts' helmets, the tiny connections in computer chips, the fillings in teeth and the reflective coatings on high-rise office buildings – you would find yourself with a cube measuring just 20 metres at each edge.

In other words, all the gold taken from the earth would sit comfortably within two tennis courts, though it would be 20 metres high.

You would be able to cram it into three decent-sized

houses or carry it across the ocean in a corner of a container ship.

It would, however, weigh almost 150,000 tonnes. And in the second half of 2006, with gold worth more than US$600 a troy ounce, the raw value of this pile would be around US$3 trillion, give or take a billion, or A$4 trillion. Which is around five times Australia's entire gross domestic product, or more cash than any right-thinking mind could get a handle on.

The mythical King Midas, who turned anything he touched to gold, and King Croesus of Lydia, who is said to have minted the world's first gold coins (giving us the term 'rich as Croesus') would have been green with envy at today's amount of the yellow metal. There wasn't all that much gold around in the ancient world – about 80 per cent of that 20-metre cube has been dug up only since 1848 when the Californian Gold Rush got underway, followed by the rushes in Australia.

Gold by its nature is ethereally beautiful. Its deep yellow appears to glow with a promise beyond words and can drive men and women mad with desire for it. The bones of disappointed treasure hunters lie mouldering in deserts, jungles and oceans across the world, yet hardly a month goes by without another expedition setting off in quest of legendary reefs and lost El Doradoes. Even science is driven to poetry in its use of the letters 'Au' to denote gold's chemical symbol. It is short for the Latin word 'aurum', which means 'glowing dawn'.

It is one of only two pure elemental metals with its own colour, but it is the only one that doesn't tarnish. The other, copper, reacts with the atmosphere and finally takes on a bilious green. Bury gold in the earth for as long as you wish, or drown it in a lake or an ocean, and it will lie waiting to be found, perfect, unchanged, for it is inert – it will not rust or react at all with most chemicals.

You can do almost anything you wish with the stuff and it will still be gold. According to the World Gold Council – to which we are indebted for all sorts of esoterica about the precious metal – a goldsmith can hammer a single gram into a sheet more than half a metre square, so thin that light shines through it. If you were to stretch this same gram into a thin wire – and you can, because gold is the most stretchable of metals – it would measure 3.2 kilometres.

The Incas revered gold as the 'sweat of the sun' (and silver as 'tears of the moon'). They were more accurate than they could have known.

Sweat and tears were certainly shed, and rivers of blood, too, as Spanish conquistadors, crazed by craving for the treasures that gave meaning to Inca culture and spirituality, laid waste to the great kingdom. The golden wedding bands we still bestow to symbolise the hope of everlasting love are as likely to have come from the metal the Spaniards stole and melted down as from a modern mine; or possibly even from an Egyptian tomb looted centuries ago. All the gold ever ripped from the earth is still with us somewhere, much of it recycled.

But modern astronomers have gathered enough evidence from the heavens to suggest that gold is almost literally the sweat of a dying star – though a star several billion times as powerful as our sun.

Every gram of gold on Earth began its cosmic journey billions of years ago with the explosion of a giant star in the galaxy we call the Milky Way. Stars begin their lives as massive balls of hydrogen. Hydrogen 'burns' in a nuclear reaction known as fusion to produce helium. In massive stars, when all the hydrogen is consumed the helium burns to produce carbon, which in turn burns to produce heavier elements. Eventually the core of the star becomes iron, compressed to a density and temperature beyond our imagining. Iron is the final frontier of the nuclear process and the star collapses inwards, resulting in a titanic supernova explosion that tears it apart. The apparent chaos that follows in the next few seconds hurls hyperactive atoms together, and some of them combine to forge gold.

In the last moments of its existence, the supernova that interests us blew most of the material from which it was constituted into the vast maw of space. Some of the element-enriched gas it spawned entered the large collapsing cloud of gas from which our Sun and its planets were created. Thus gold became – in microscopic quantities – part of the material that formed the earth.

Here and there, gold concentrated in substantial quantities in some areas of the earth's crust. To do so, it required superheated water with precisely the right chemical qualities to dissolve it out of the surrounding bedrock. The right conditions were often found in water flowing under immense pressure deep underground, near volcanic vents and along tectonic plates or fault boundaries. The fluid containing the dissolved gold migrated wherever fractures in the rocks allowed it to. Eventually, over tens of thousands of years, the water cooled and the gold within it became insoluble, creating a reef. It crystallised, often surrounded by masses of white silicon dioxide, or quartz. And there it stayed, waiting to be found and mined.

This is essentially what happened beneath what would become Beaconsfield. Neither Australia nor Tasmania at that time looked anything like its current form, however. It was around 500 million years ago, during the Ordovician Period – the second period of the Palaeozoic Era. The area at that point was part of Gondwanaland, a super-continent that included the landmasses of Africa, South America, Australia, Antarctica and the Indian subcontinent, joined together and extending from the South Pole to the tropics.

The reef of gold-bearing quartz, held within immensely hard conglomerate, siltstone and sandstone, sat there as the great landmasses shifted, broke apart, experienced ice ages, drowned, bucked free of the oceans, and saw the coming and going of all manner of large and small species of animals, the arrival of human beings, the separation of Tasmania from the mainland, the flooding of the Tamar Valley and finally, in the early 1800s, settlement by Europeans.

Alluvial gold – traces of the yellow metal weathered away from the cap of the reef and washed across the surface – was found as early as 1847, but the gold rush to Cabbage Tree Hill and the settlement then called Brandy Creek did not begin until 1877, when the cap to what would become known as the Tasmania Reef was discovered.

Within three years a rough township had sprouted at the foot of the hill and census takers counted the population at 1,520, a few more than today, many of these hardy souls living in tents and lean-tos. There were by then 32 companies with claims on the field and another 21 a few miles south. A tramway was built and shafts were sunk in every direction. Two steamship companies ran daily services along the Tamar River from Launceston.

Growing civic pride persuaded the authorities that Brandy Creek was not a suitable name for a town that considered itself Christian and had a substantial population of temperance-propounding Methodists, despite the presence of several hotels and sly-grog shops. In March 1879, the town was renamed Beaconsfield after the former British Prime Minister Benjamin Disraeli, the First Earl of Beaconsfield.

Water proved the miners' biggest enemy from the very start. Shaft after shaft flooded and expensive steam-pumping machines were brought into the battle. Some mine owners were outraged that water from other mines that didn't have pumps was flowing into their workings. One outfit, the Tasmania Gold Mine Co., gradually emerged as the most powerful miner, buying out many of the smaller enterprises.

By 1898, the Tasmania Co. celebrated its 21st birthday by announcing it had won 434,857 troy ounces, or a mighty 13.5 tonnes, of gold from the ground below Beaconsfield. It was Australia's richest gold mine. But it would also prove to be the most expensive water-pumping operation.

The scale of the pumping remains awe-inspiring. Massive steam pumps brought in from England drove steel-encased pitch pine pump rods more than 300 metres into the shafts, plunging and sucking at the water. These rods were designed to move between six million and eight million gallons of water every 24 hours. They were still not enough. By 1906, there was no larger or more extensive de-watering plant in the world.

Costs rose, the labour force began agitating for better pay and conditions, yield decreased, the world price for gold stagnated, the company paid expenses for two boards of directors – one in England, the other local – and water continued to flow in.

By 1914, with World War I looming, Beaconsfield's great Tasmania Co. conceded defeat. It switched off its pumps and closed the shaft, allowing the workings beneath the town to flood.

The company had mined 854,000 troy ounces of gold, or 26.6 tonnes. The average yield was 24.7 grams of gold to a tonne of ore, a fabulously rich haul unmatched in the nation. But the company had not shown a profit since 1908.

The town of Beaconsfield, which had reached a population of more than 5,000, began fading. Gaps began appearing in the streetscape as houses were loaded on to bullock wagons and hauled 40 kilometres away to Launceston, where they became workers' cottages in new suburbs.

But those who stayed on in increasingly quiet little Beaconsfield believed there were still great riches to be had beneath their town. Eighty years after the old shafts had become watery graves for ancient dreams, a new venture began.

Beaconsfield Gold NL and Allstate Explorations NL joined forces to create the Beaconsfield Mine Joint Venture and began pumping out the primitive workings in the mid 1990s. By 1999, ore was once again being extracted from the Tasmania Reef, and in September of that year the first gold bar of the new era, a 13.5 kilogram ingot, was poured.

The quest for the sweat of an exploded star was underway again in a town few Australians knew existed. Soon after the mine reopened, Todd Russell, Brant Webb and Larry Knight were recruited to work underground, down in the deepest dark.

Until Anzac Day, 2006.

CHAPTER 1

ANZAC DAY IN A SMALL TOWN

The little Tasmanian town slept beneath a waning crescent moon as Colin Smee began his morning ritual. He rolled up his flags of Australia, New Zealand and Tasmania, climbed into his car, flicked on the headlights and the heater against the quiet chill, and headed for the main street. It was a bit before 5 am, three hours earlier than his usual morning foray. This was a special Tuesday.

The one feature of the town visible through the dark – a great triangle of steel with a wheel at its peak, up on the shadowy ridge above the town that is Cabbage Tree Hill – blazed under a battery of floodlights. The structure viewed from a distance appeared to float free of any moorings to the town or even to the earth, but it was an illusion – it is more *of* the earth than most other buildings anywhere. There is a dainty name for this rather brutish arrangement: poppet head.

Beaconsfield is a town that goes to bed early and rises gradually, but under that triangle, deep in the ground, a secret city hummed and roared and never slept. As Colin Smee crept through empty streets, a kilometre beneath his tyres the dog-tired men of the night shift of the Beaconsfield gold mine were swinging themselves into trucks and light four-wheel-drive vehicles to climb their way up a spiralling subterranean road they call the decline, the motors of their vehicles bellowing and echoing through the black tunnels at the one-in-six gradient. Colin Smee could not hear anything of this activity; nor could anyone else who might have been awake in the town at that hour. What happens underground stays underground, the hard-rock miners of Beaconsfield will tell you.

It wasn't quite true. The miners fire high-explosive charges into the rock to get at the gold that gave Beaconsfield, once a wild and lawless place called Brandy Creek, its reason for being. The explosions regularly shook houses on the surface, cracking plaster and concrete driveways and driving some of the citizens to distraction. But this day, there would be no firing. The mine management had promised it a few months previously at a meeting of angry homeowners. No firing on Christmas Day, Good Friday or Anzac Day.

Smee, a man in his sixties with a shaggy white beard, took it upon himself to be the keeper of Beaconsfield's flags after cancer stole his wife Diane a few years ago, leaving him alone with a Jack Russell terrier named Benji. Every morning since, he has ventured out to hoist his standards on flagpoles all up and down Weld Street, the main road through town, and every evening he takes the flags down again before sunset. Smee wears short pants most days, socks pulled up almost to his knobbly knees. Even when the Tamar Valley delivers frozen winds and icy rain fresh in from the troubled waters of Bass Strait, he simply pulls his leather Overlander bushman's hat tighter over his bald head and declares it is a well-known principle that if you insulate the roof of your house, the heat doesn't escape.

On 25 April 2006, however, he wasn't wearing shorts. He had a date with the dawn and it required a certain level of formality.

Colin Smee is president of the Beaconsfield sub-branch of the Returned Services League and this was Anzac Day. He donned long slacks and shrugged into a sports jacket, slipped a flask of Captain Morgan into his pocket and pinned on his medals. He spent his working years as a Navy man. He was aboard HMAS *Quickmatch*, a fast anti-submarine frigate when, accompanied by HMAS *Vampire*, she steamed up the Mekong River to Saigon in January 1962. *Quickmatch* and *Vampire* were the first Australian warships to reach Saigon since World War II and their surreptitious job was to explore a safe route for the troopship HMAS *Sydney* to ferry Australians into what would become the long and hopeless conflict known as the Vietnam War. The Australian Government insisted the journey was nothing more than a goodwill visit and it still rankles with Smee and his fellow sailors that they never got a Vietnam War campaign medal. 'They said nobody shot at us,' he says. 'In that case, they must have been bloody big mosquitoes.'

Anyway, he had his memories and no one could take them away. Especially on Anzac Day, a time of remembering wars, lost lives, heroism and injustices that stretch back a long way before Vietnam. On 25 April 1915, naïve boys from farms and towns and cities all around Australia and New Zealand, out for a grand adventure, splashed into a hail of bullets on a little beach beneath the cliffs of the Gallipoli Peninsula in Turkey. The Australian and New Zealand Army Corps, a separation from the old British Empire, was born that appalling, bloody day and the acronym Anzac has lodged deep in the consciousness of the two nations. Australians aren't much given to using words like 'sacred' about anything, but Anzac Day comes close. From Gallipoli on, more than 100,000 Australians have died in wars across the oceans.

Thus Colin Smee would hoist his flags around Beaconsfield at half-mast on 25 April: the Australian and New Zealand national flags at the Beaconsfield cenotaph where the Anzac ceremonies would be held; Tasmanian flags outside the Club Hotel and the local doctor's surgery; an Australian flag at the Beaconsfield health clinic; and right in the centre of town, outside the newsagent and across the street at the post office, two more Australian standards. Up Weld Street to the north, the service station owner hoists two of his own flags of Australia. Beaconsfield is a modest little place of weatherboard homes housing just 1,490 souls, but no one there could plead they don't know the state and the country they live in.

Smee had the job done before dawn and as Venus and the fingernail moon began fading he bustled in to the Tamar Valley Wholefoods and Coffee Shop across the road from the newsagent for a coffee, no milk. John and

Penny Farrar open their shop around 5 o'clock on Anzac morning and the coffee is free for the first few hours. Smee produced his flask and tipped a couple of nips of Captain Morgan into his steaming cup. The rum would fortify him when it came time for him to recite 'The Ode' down at the cenotaph. He wasn't the only returned military man warming up in this manner – just down the street the Exchange Hotel had also unlocked its doors at 5 am, and a few of the town's stalwarts had slipped in for a rum and milk.

Directly across Weld Street from the coffee shop on the corner of West Street, in the house attached to the rear of the Beaconsfield Newsagency, Lorraine Kramer, a pretty dark-haired woman with sad eyes, was overwhelmed with memories of her own. The day before, she had received word of something that had been coming for a long time. Her father, Syd Sweeney, had finally given up the ghost.

A hard-rock miner since he left school aged 13 in the mid 30s, Sweeney's mining days came to an end when he drilled into a stick of gelignite left carelessly in the rock nearly 400 metres down in the Rossarden tin mine in the Fingal Valley, about 130 kilometres south-east of Launceston. It was July 1981 and Sweeney, the father of seven, crawled out barely alive. The explosion blinded him and caused fearful injuries to his throat. Lumps of rock worked their way out of his neck and his eye sockets for the next 25 years of his shattered life. He knew the risks – he left school early because his own father had died of injuries he received in an underground accident on Tasmania's west coast. Underground mining in Tasmania sometimes seems akin to a war and families all across the little island state are left with nothing more than recollections and stories of the victims.

When it came time for Syd Sweeney's daughter Lorraine to marry, it was to Mark Kramer, who started his working life at 16 in the Rossarden mine. But the Kramers got away from the life: Mark became an electrician, did his apprenticeship at the mine, and he and Lorraine moved away from the Fingal Valley to take over the Beaconsfield Newsagency. They renovated the rooms behind their shop. Hardwood floors shine and a log fire burns in a grate all winter. Step outside their door, though, and look up the West Street hill and there, not 200 metres away, is the great steel windlass of the Beaconsfield gold mine.

While Lorraine Kramer wrestled with her private misery, remembering a father who would come home parchment-white, starved of oxygen after a day drilling vertically rising shafts deep in the earth to keep food on his family's table, Colin Smee put away his flask of rum and made his way down Weld Street to the cenotaph, an obelisk half-enclosed by a curving stone wall bearing the names of the Beaconsfield boys – a lot of them gold miners – who went off to wars and never came home. Tunnelers, some of them, up on the heights of Gallipoli and fair devils at the business of digging deep trenches in the mud of the Somme.

A lightening of the sky to the east across the Tamar Valley signalled the approach of the dawn. A small crowd, maybe 100, began gathering, collars turned up. A piper named Fraser Murray warmed the reeds of his bagpipes, Ray Veevers prepared to play the 'Last Post' on his bugle and Colin Smee silently rehearsed

'The Ode' – the fourth stanza of Laurence Binyon's poem 'For the Fallen': 'They shall grow not old, as we that are left grow old; / Age shall not weary them, nor the years condemn. / At the going down of the sun and in the morning / We will remember them.'

What a beautiful morning, Colin Smee thought. A peaceful, perfect morning. No wind. Gold shooting through orange and pink into the violet depths of the sky. This is the reason he and Diane quit the mainland back in the 1980s. Drove through Beaconsfield in a motor home and just knew this was the place to retire. Wouldn't go back to Sydney for quids.

Up the hill, the windlass whirred and the men of the night shift, B crew, rode the cage up the shaft and came blinking into the dawn. They would have 12 hours to rest, eat and mooch around before they returned to the depths of the strange world in which they do what men have done since before the age of the Pharaohs: claw through the earth in a fevered quest for gold.

The men climbed out of the cage and swung through the safety gate. Their white hardhats fitted with lamps, their navy blue overalls, orange shirts and jackets slashed with glow-in-the-dark tape stripped away any sense of individuality. They were unmistakably miners, back from the underworld.

A lot of them wore circular beards, a form of goatee where the moustache extends all the way around the mouth and joins the growth upon the chin, though it eschews the concept of the full beard – the facial growth does not extend up the jawbone to the ears. It is a style popularised over the past decade by bikers, rock musicians, football players and labourers, often teamed with close-cropped hair or shaven heads, and it lends the wearer a tough, outlaw appearance as if it were intended to intimidate. If you were to dress these men in leather jackets and denim, they could be mistaken for a chapter of the Hell's Angels. Drape them in chain mail and sit them upon horses and they would be Hollywood's vision of medieval crusaders. This morning, though, they fitted their surroundings. Miners clomping along in Wellington boots.

Their moment of arrival on the surface required ritual. The men gathered around a large painted board dotted with little hooks standing next to the head of the mineshaft. One side of the board was painted red, with the words 'In U/Ground' printed at the top. On the hooks below hung the identification tags of each of the 17 men of the night shift. One by one, the men retrieved their tags and placed them on hooks on the opposite side of the board. This side was painted green and headed 'Out – Safe'.

Out. Safe. The men tramped in their gumboots up to the row of demountable huts that serves as offices, headquarters and service centre for the Beaconsfield Mine Joint Venture.

There is a transitory sense to this gold mining enterprise made stark by its surroundings. The steel poppet head and its windlass above the mineshaft and the demountable huts sprout from the ruins of old mines built in a time when craft had importance beyond the mere business at hand. Sprawled around are elegant buildings of red brick that once housed giant, belching steam-driven pumps and engines. The designer could simply have thrown up cheap sheds to accommodate these monsters of the industrial revolution. Instead, the façades of the old mine buildings constructed during the late 1800s employed the aesthetic notions of the neo-classicists. Builders who paid heed to form set graceful arched windows and fanlights into the symmetrical brick walls as if, somehow, the hand of the Italian architect Palladio had been at work.

What remains of one group of these buildings has become a museum: the Grubb Shaft Gold and Heritage Museum, where the visitor can learn about the early gold-mining operations of Beaconsfield that finished in 1914 – crushed by cost, mismanagement, greed, flooding and mad dreaming – just in time for its miners to rush off to war and become Anzacs. Diggers from Beaconsfield; Diggers of World War I.

Next door is the equally handsome Hart Shaft Winder House, which has been appropriated and spruced up by the new mine to house its massive cable winding mechanism. No hiss and thump of steam engines these days, though. A visitor can peer through knotholes in the big wooden doors to spy the winder's drum, which spools out cable to the wheel atop the new triangular steel structure to raise and lower the cage down the Hart Shaft. The winder these days is driven almost soundlessly by electricity.

The men of the night shift hung up their helmets and their lamps, pulled off their overalls and gumboots, and showered away the rock dust and the grime and the sweat of their labour. They didn't talk much; the efforts of the night had stripped them of energy and even though they were shift workers it always felt a bit weird to arrive at the surface at dawn. It wasn't natural and gave them that strange sense of dislocation that you get when you walk out of a cinema after a matinee and are hit with daylight and people going about their ordinary business in the street.

Todd Russell and his father-in-law, Alan Bennett, climbed aboard Todd's Toyota ute and rattled away down the hill, heading for Russell's home hardly 200 metres from the mine. Bennett, a truck driver in the mine, lives with his wife Jill at Port Sorell near Tasmania's northern ferry city, Devonport, but he had decided to stay with his daughter Carolyn that night to avoid the wearying trip there and back, almost an hour each way. Bennett lay on the couch in Todd and Carolyn's lounge-room to catch the sleep he needed, the TV tuned to *Sunrise*. No bed was available. Todd had been planning for a long time to buy a block out of town and build a new home with four bedrooms. He and Carolyn had three kids and the two boys bunked in together. Todd wanted space and bushland around. It would take planning, because funds were tight even though Todd earned good money underground and Carolyn also had a job at the mine. She was assistant to Rex Johnson, head of occupational health and safety and chief of the mine rescue crew.

Brant Webb pointed his Holden Commodore north for the 6-kilometre trip to his home in Beauty Point, a pretty town perched on the western bank of the Tamar River. A couple of kilometres out of Beaconsfield, the river spread out on his right, wide, still and silver as an ocean bay on this crisp morning. Come the weekend, Brant and his wife Rachel would be out there bending a sail in the breeze. This morning the river was empty, though steamships once hauled up and down its waters and wharfies lined up in the mornings hoping for a day's work. The big cargo sheds on the old wharves at Beauty Point that decades ago housed millions of export apples have been converted to tourist businesses: Seahorse World, boasting more seahorses drifting around in its aquarium than any other single place in the world, and Platypus House, where visitors ooh and ah at the bizarre duck-billed creature that English scientists once thought was an elaborate hoax. Maybe 5 kilometres across the water, over at Bell Bay, a power plant belched steam, spoiling the postcard perfection of the scene.

Larry Knight had a longer drive ahead of him. He lived in Launceston, more than 40 kilometres of winding road, forests and roadkill in the opposite direction, away down the Tamar Valley.

Their fellow miners spread out across Beaconsfield and its district, all of them ready for breakfast and the embrace of sleep. They had been working for 12 hours, all night, and most of them were to be back before nightfall.

Down at the cenotaph, the dawn service was underway. Todd Russell and Alan Bennett could hear the pipes and the bugle when they got home – the service was just around the corner from Todd and Carolyn's house. Brant Webb clean forgot to attend the service. He had been in the habit of dropping in on the Anzac Day dawn observance, but the cenotaph had been moved from its old site in a park on West Street below the mine to a new spot around the corner in Weld Street, and it wasn't on his route. Anyway, he wanted to crawl into bed with his wife Rachel and breathe in the scent of her golden curls.

Colin Smee and his mates from the RSL and their families – maybe 75 people – had breakfast at the Exchange Hotel in the main street after the early service, hoeing in to bacon and eggs, swapping war stories and topping up with beer and rum chasers. The handsome two-storey hotel – one of the town's three remaining pubs from the old ripsnorting gold-mining days when there were up to seven pubs in the main street – shone beneath a coat of cream paint and a new roof thanks to a grant of more than $20,000 from the Federal Government for the restoration of historic buildings.

The Exchange is from the same vintage as the old mine workings up the hill. It was built in 1890 on the burnt-out ruins of an earlier pub, also called the Exchange because the horses for the coach service that ran between Launceston and Beaconsfield were exchanged there, and passengers lined up outside the hotel to board. The hubs of the coach's wheels, it is said, were regularly crammed with gold filched from underground by some of the craftier mine workers.

All across town, families prepared for the main event of the holiday – the Anzac march down the main street and the 11 am service at the cenotaph. The West Tamar Band formed up behind the old Diggers from the RSL, and the Girl Guides, the Boy Scouts, the local Sea Rescue members and most of the students from the Beaconsfield primary school turned out. 'We had hundreds of people there,' Smee says. 'It just gets bigger every year.'

Right across the street from the cenotaph, Todd Russell's mother Kaye sat on the steps outside her home and watched the service, enjoying the sunshine. Townsfolk smiled and waved to her, recognizing her shock of white hair. There wasn't a person in town who didn't know the Russells. Beaconsfield born and bred. Kaye's husband Noel, a grey-bearded man known to everyone as Nobby, had already attended the dawn service and had gone on to the RSL breakfast afterwards at the Exchange Hotel.

Noel hadn't missed an Anzac service for 40 years. Started attending when he was a little kid and his father used to play the 'Last Post'. Noel is not a returned man himself, but years ago when he was a boy and had just got his driver's licence, he turned up to a dawn service and was buttonholed by one of the RSL men who had cut himself shaving and had blood on his shirt. He asked young Nobby to drive him home so he could change into a clean shirt before the RSL breakfast.

'So I took him home up the back here and got him a clean shirt and I took him back down,' Nobby remembers. 'And he said, "We better give you some breakfast". "No" I said, "I'm not a returned man". He said, "Oh, if you're good enough to come to the dawn service, you're good enough to come to the breakfast", so I've been going ever since.'

Tradition runs strong in Beaconsfield. Today, one of the Russells' grandchildren, Monique, the child of Todd's sister Lisa, would lay a wreath.

Todd's wife Carolyn took her three children to the service and, later, most of the town's population turned out to lunch at the Senior Citizens Hall, where the Girl Guides – Todd and Carolyn's daughter Maddison among them – served hotdogs and raised $946. The RSL put on a barrel of northern Tasmania's most popular beer, Boags. It was quite a day.

Beaconsfield has always liked a parade and a picnic. In 1880, just three years after it was reported that a Mr William Dally had found 'a very rich quartz reef' with gold showing in the stone at Brandy Creek, the fledgling town was able to turn on a Boxing Day outing that would shame a lot of much larger communities today. At the time there were five rollicking pubs in the town, newly renamed Beaconsfield, but the strength of the religious and anti-alcohol forces meant there would be no barrel of beer at this shindig. One of the early movers and shakers provided the money to build the town's first church. He is remembered still on a plaque in the red-brick Uniting Church right in the centre of town: 'Frederick John Layton: Pioneer of West Tamar Methodism, 1877'. No alcohol would pass this pious and powerful gentleman's lips, and early Beaconsfield mining rules meant that habitual drunkenness, a court conviction or crime of any kind would find a miner out of employment. Bad language was discouraged. God-fearing was the fashion in Beaconsfield, whatever might happen in the saloons. Historian Jan Critchett describes the 1880 Boxing Day parade in *Beaconsfield Gold:*

> A procession was formed composed of the Sons of Temperance, Daughters of Temperance, Invincible Lodge of Good Templars, Crystal Spring Lodge of Good Templars of the World, Odd Fellows, Band of Hope and Juvenile Templars. This procession numbering about 300 people with banners flying and other insignia of office displayed, headed by the Beaconsfield Brass Band, paraded the main street and then marched on to Jamieson's paddock for a picnic.

One hundred and sixteen years later, the Anzac Day commemorations wound down by late afternoon and Beaconsfield and district began to settle in for an early night. The air chilled as the sun sank over low hills and wood smoke rose lazily over the town. Most homes in the valley have open fires or slow-combustion stoves and the afternoon was punctuated by axes chopping away in back yards. The forests and bush blocks of the West Tamar make firewood cheap and easy to obtain. Anzac Day, everyone agrees, is the first day of the year you really need an open fire. The day when autumn starts turning its face to winter. The scent of burning box and eucalypt was the signature of evening.

At Beauty Point, Brant Webb's wife Rachel cooked up Asian chicken noodles for lunch and Brant liked them so much he had her pack a container for his night shift. For crib. Miners speak an arcane language, and down in the mine, the meal-room carved out of the rock is called the crib room. Old-timers spent their meal breaks playing cribbage, or crib, and eventually the word's meaning was extended. Labourers take smoko, but miners eat their crib in the crib room. Mine bosses claim there is an extra meaning: the crib-room is where the wilier fellows crib a bit of extra time from their break.

Todd Russell organised his own crib – a frozen pack of six chicken curry pies. A big man weighing in at 114 kilograms and standing a bit over 185 centimetres in his socks, he didn't much like working night shift. He'd rather sit down to a meal of steak and chips and vegetables in the evening and then head out into the bush in his ute to shoot a few kangaroos to feed the four hunting hounds he kept in a wire enclosure in the back yard. The ute was all set up for such expeditions. It had spotlights fitted and a platform above the cabin with soft foam where he could rest his body and take easy aim. But Carolyn and the kids – Trent, 12, Maddison, 10 and Liam, 6 – secretly enjoyed the evenings when Todd went off to the mine. 'Todd's a meat and three veg sort of person, but the children like to eat something a bit different; pasta and that sort of thing,' Carolyn says. This was to be Todd's last night down the mine before he got a five-day break.

Down the road in Launceston, Larry Knight almost forgot the most important item in his crib bag. He kissed his partner Jacqui goodbye and was in the car before he remembered and rushed back inside. The newspaper with its crossword puzzles. The men rely on more than food to keep them occupied during their midnight break in the crib, and Larry Knight's pleasure was working on crosswords, both cryptic and plain. He was the quietest of men, silent for hours on end as he drove the mine's grader up and down the long kilometres of the decline. Larry was a man of slight build but he was known as Horse – the men had seen him in the showers and agreed that in one stand-out respect, he was built on equine proportions. Among the babble of conversations in the crib, Larry Knight occupied a serene space known only to him, absorbed by the mysteries of words on a page linked by riddles.

Todd played chess. The method in the game contented him. He was a competitive man, known throughout the Tamar as a fierce Australian Rules full-forward who had regularly kicked 100 goals in a season. He approached chess with the same explosive passion he applied to football. His colleagues in the mine considered it splendid sport to surreptitiously move a pawn or a bishop across the board if he left the room briefly, just to see his rage when he returned.

Brant's amusement was sudoku. The happy-go-lucky jokester, his round, pleasant face always creased by laughter or threatening it, was captivated by the challenge of patiently figuring out how to place numbers in logical patterns.

If any of the other men found anything a bit incongruous about a wordless man addicted to words, an impatient man captivated by chess and a carefree spirit enthused by the logic of numbers, nobody said anything. A mine wasn't the place to search out consistency, anyway – everyone there worked in the dark, but there wasn't a man among them who wasn't keen on the outdoors. In the crib room, way beneath the earth and the cares of everyday life, you found whatever turned you on to get you through the slow hour.

Besides, there was another game that got a lot of the blokes involved; a card game they called 'Grass'. It's a novelty game that invites the player to 'unleash your inner hippie' in the pursuit of 'the fine art of growing pot plants'.

In short, it's a game about growing dope – the cards, instead of displaying aces and spades and kings and queens, feature pictures of marijuana plants, police, dandelions, weed killer and hippies. A player wins by growing a 'crop' despite all the dangers from cops, hippies that smoke your stash, dandelion infestation and thieves.

And so, on any given night below Beaconsfield, a visitor to the crib room might find large men in overalls and safety helmets, their faces streaked with rock dust and sweat, fairly whooping it up over a card game that was very likely invented by a bunch of stoned, long-haired university drop-outs in San Francisco. On such nights, you could hear Brant's high cackle ricocheting off the stone walls of the crib or Todd's snort of disgust when a player dropped a dandelion into his happily growing crop.

There seemed an easy camaraderie to it, but there was also an unspoken hierarchy underground. The jumbo operators – who used massive drilling rigs to pierce rock faces – received the biggest money, maybe $100,000 a year or more, and were at the top of the pile. The air-leggers – those skilled in manhandling heavy hand-operated drills balanced on an expanding leg driven by high-pressure air – were the 'guns' and stood apart in status from the men who drove trucks and graders, who were paid perhaps $50,000 or $60,000 a year.

The fitters worked on the mine's machinery in a cavernous workshop at the 375-metre level where the shaft terminated, far from the depths where those involved in the actual getting of gold laboured.

And there were the charge-up crews who placed explosives into the holes drilled by the jumbo operators; the electricians who took care of the power that drove just about everything in the mine; the offsiders learning various mining skills; the bogger operators, who drove roaring front-end loaders; and the remote operators, who used a contraption similar to a large PlayStation control pad to run their ore-loading machines, manoeuvring them by wireless into areas too dangerous for a man to venture.

Like any high-pressure environment where men are thrown together, the miners formed their own small social groups and friendships. It was a bit like a boarding school.

Brant and Todd may have worked in the same mine for six years, often on the same shifts, but they weren't friends. They weren't enemies, either. They were simply so different in personality, so divergent in their interests and pursuits, that they had never found the common ground that welds men together. They inhabited the same galaxy, but they swung in separate orbits. Down the mine, Brant was a jack of all trades and Todd's specialty was the charge-up, loading holes with explosives. In all their years in the mine, the two men had never worked on the same task together. And when Brant, Todd and Larry rode the cage up the shaft after their shifts, they went their own ways.

Brant's gladness outside the mine was to be found on the waters of the wide Tamar River down in the valley, or out on Bass Strait. He had a small aluminium dinghy for laying nets for shark, a speedboat for water skiing, and he and Rachel crewed an Etchell class yacht, a highly strung racing vessel owned by their local doctor, Tony Lyall, a laid-back man of middle age with a ponytail. The yacht is around 10 years old but Lyall and the Webbs gave the sailing community from up the river at Launceston a lesson or two when the breeze was up. Brant began sailing as a little kid and by the time he was 19 was captain of a fishing trawler in far north Queensland. He was a man of the sea.

Todd had little time for boats and water. He was a hunter and the forests were his domain. Kangaroo, wallaby, possum, rabbit, deer. If it walked or hopped, needed culling and could be eaten by dog or man, Todd hunted it. His father Nobby had taken him out in the bush with a gun when he was nine years old and the outdoors had captured him. The most treasured month in his calendar was March, when Tasmania permitted its hunters to shoot adult male deer. Todd took his deer rifles to the state's Midlands during that month and the walls of the lounge- and dining-rooms at his neat brick home in Beaconsfield sprout his trophies – the antlered heads of fallow stags, side by side with soft-focus photographs of Carolyn, at 34 still the prettiest girl in town.

Todd and Carolyn met at Exeter High School, 20 minutes away from Beaconsfield towards Launceston. She was 15 and he was 14 and he still ribs her about cradle snatching. He made clear his opinion about boats and fishing and his intentions towards Carolyn when, a few weeks after their first meeting, he turned up at her family's home at Kayena, a village on the banks of the Tamar River. Todd had been talked into going fishing with his father and uncle, but the boat broke down. Disgusted, he quit the fishing party and walked to Carolyn's house. She was in Year 10 and he was in Year 9.

Larry at 44 still liked the sun on his back and the breeze in his face. He had a big Harley-Davidson for blasting around the twisting roads of Tasmania and a shed full of bikes he had bought over the years and couldn't bear to sell. Years ago, before he took up grader driving at the Beaconsfield mine, he travelled around Australia with a mate, Justin Stevenson, known inevitably as Stevo. They had a big old Valiant station wagon with a trailer on the back to haul their bikes. Larry and Stevo worked in mines in Victoria, the Northern Territory and Western Australia to pay for their odyssey and when they got home to Launceston about two years after they left, Larry met Stevo's sister, Jacqui. Jacqui already had a son, Addison, and when she and Larry partnered up they had a son together, Thomas. Larry had been married as a young man but it didn't last. He had fathered a daughter, Lauren, and they had kept in touch as she grew, even though she moved to Queensland and took the surname of the man her mother met and married and who raised her as his own child: Kielmann.

Larry, his mates thought, finally had life figured. Family, bikes to blow away the darkness of the mine, and in the shed out the back a perfectly preserved 1966 two-toned HR Holden owned since new by his late grandfather. There were days when Larry would stroll out the back, sit in the old Holden, close his eyes and just rest up. For hours. No one knew what he was thinking. He was an easy-going bloke, was gentle Larry.

CHAPTER 2

A DAY AT THE OFFICE

Gavan Cheesman left his small, grey, concrete block apartment, dropped in to the IGA supermarket, grabbed a couple of pies and strolled across Weld Street and up West Street, dusk settling cold over Beaconsfield. He would be shift boss for 16 men and he liked to get to the mine early to read the mail and check the circulars and any safety alerts that might affect the night's work.

Cheesman appears a lot younger than his 50 years. He speaks softly and has soulful dark eyes that appear to be constantly measuring up his surroundings. He wears his black hair close-cropped and he has a goatee, the favoured facial fashion of the men at the mine. When he drags on a cigarette you notice his fingernails are perfectly clean. His mates kid him about spending ages in the mine's shower after work scrubbing away at his nails with a little brush, but the joke has grown so old he ignores it. He hasn't had anything to prove for a long time. Cheesy – nobody calls him anything but Cheesy – went down his first Tasmanian mine in 1973, and he's done it all. Jumbo operator, air-legger in tight tunnels, explosives. He was married for 18 years until things fell apart in 1992. There was a daughter from the union, Renee, grown now and spending time in Ireland, and Cheesy missed her.

His existence in Beaconsfield had an impermanence about it. His flat contained a few chairs, a TV, a table with his papers stacked carefully in aligned piles, and a calendar, a year out of date, hanging from a wall. A friend from Sydney, an Irish wag who was best man at Cheesy's daughter's wedding, dropped in one day, cast an appraising eye around and declared straight-faced that he loved what Cheesy had done to the place.

Funny how life turns out, says Cheesy. He was raised in Mildura, a fruit-growing town on the Murray River near the junction of Victoria, New South Wales and South Australia. 'The Sunraysia district', the good burghers of Mildura call their place in the world, as if no other place could be so blessed. Cheesy went to a Catholic school and figured he didn't fit the sort of future laid out by the priests for most of the boys – off to university or into the safety of a bank teller's cage. He took off for the lights of Melbourne and signed up for a short course in hairdressing.

The first job offer that came his way was from a hairdressing salon in a West Tasmanian town he'd never heard of. Rosebery. A purely mining town of 1,300 people sprawling up and down a hillside, dominated by a zinc mine, rainforests all around. Cheesy arrived in the middle of a wet night. The hairdressing salon's owners had arranged a bed in the mine's single men's quarters. In the morning, Cheesy dressed himself in platform boots, flared jeans, a snappy jacket with zips all over it and, hair cascading down his back, walked into the dining hall. Every man there was dressed in overalls and mud-encrusted work boots. The whole place went silent. As Cheesy approached the servery, a single hissed word followed him. 'Pooftah.' It became a chant. 'Pooftah, pooftah.'

A few weeks later, he hung up his hairdressing scissors, pulled on work overalls and went down the mine.

Thirty-two years later, here he was, donning overalls on Anzac night and preparing to oversee his crew underground at the Beaconsfield mine.

First he had to complete the ritual of the changeover with Brett Cresswell, boss of the day shift. Cresswell laid out photocopies of the day's doings, showing where all the big machines were, the jumbo drilling rigs, the trucks, and the location and quantity of stockpiles of dirt that had been dumped in tunnels. The two men chatted easily about tasks that needed completing: holes to be drilled, areas that needed reinforcing with mesh and bolts, and the location of ore to be bogged out with loaders. Here was the rhythm of the mine: the day shift straggles out and the night shift trails in. Six o'clock in the morning, six o'clock in the evening. The changeover. On and on.

Four crews, each with their own shift boss, rotated underground. A, B, C, and D crew. There are, of course, only two shifts every 24 hours, which means that effectively the men worked only half the year. The men worked a confusing array of rosters, but a relatively typical roster had a man working four night shifts end-to-end followed by five days off, then five day shifts in a row followed by four days off. There were other permutations, but the men all recognised that no one could tolerate the hot, dark underworld for long stretches.

Cheesy met up with Todd Russell at the cage above the shaft. Todd always arrived early. He was conscientious, a member of the mine rescue team for all the five years he had been underground and always on the lookout for the edge that might lead to promotion. His ambition was to get on a high-paying jumbo drilling rig, but he had not reached farther up the chain yet than charge-up.

Lately Todd had begun worrying about his personal safety. A few months previously his oldest friend, Michael Piscioneri, who runs a hotel in Western Australia, visited Beaconsfield for Christmas. Todd and Piscioneri went to primary school in Beaconsfield together, and when Todd married Carolyn 13 years ago, Piscioneri was his best man. After the buck's night at the Beauty Point Hotel was called off early because a few of the boys had got to brawling, the two mates handcuffed themselves together, slung a couple of cartons of beer on their shoulders and staggered singing beneath the moon down Bowens Jetty Road, a track out of Beaconsfield to the shore of the Tamar River.

Todd's the sort of country man who veers away from confiding much of his inner life, but he could tell Michael Piscioneri pretty much anything. At Christmas, he told his old friend that he was thinking of quitting work underground. You can get killed easily down there, he said. You can be run over by a machine, blown up, caught in a rock fall. A wrong step could be the end and you wouldn't know about it until the last second.

There was too much seismic activity in the mine for Todd's liking, too. There'd been cave-ins, one of them in a tunnel he'd worked in just a shift before. Maybe a job with the security team upstairs would be a better life.

The idea had kept gnawing at him, doing battle with the knowledge that he still had to pay a mortgage, dreamed of a bigger home and there was no job around Beaconsfield that paid as well as underground. Nevertheless, he had undertaken some of the study necessary to become a security man and was seriously planning to make the transition. Soon. But there he was, heading down the hole on Anzac night, a pack of chicken pies and three cans of soft drink in his crib bag.

The laid-back Brant was never in a hurry to abandon the day and would be along a bit later. 'Afternoon shift's here,' teased one of the drillers, Darren Geard, when Brant wandered in, last as usual. No one minded – Brant was always laughing and horsing around at the start of a shift and shift bosses figured it was good for morale. Besides, he was sharp and never slacked off in the mine – he was one of those blokes who always appeared to have a good sweat on him by crib time. Sharp all right. He'd found a dripping pipe in the crib washroom and sometimes stepped under it. Made it look like he'd been sweating.

Cheesy rang the bells, opened the gate and stepped into the cage, rang the bells again and Pete Goss the winder driver, over in the Hart Shaft Winder House, lowered away. The cage disappeared into the earth, the ears of the men popping with the rapid change of altitude. They streamed 375 metres through the black rock to a great cavern 6 metres wide, 15 metres long and

8 metres high. The Plat, the miners called it, where diesel fuel was stored in pods, ore bins waited for trucks, four-wheel-drive utes were parked and fitters worked on heavy machinery. By the time the men had reached the Plat – shorthand for platform – they had travelled about as deep as the Empire State Building is high, though this was the mere start of their journey.

Everything that goes in and out of Beaconsfield's mine rides the shaft to and from the Plat. Gold-bearing ore rides up in bins shackled beneath the cage, to be whisked away on a conveyor belt up the hill, ready for milling and the release of the yellow metal from its entrapment within quartz.

Trucks, troop carriers, drilling rigs and loaders are wrenched apart at the surface, slung in bits below the cage and lowered down the shaft to be reassembled by the fitters at the Plat. It's tedious, but Beaconsfield township has grown around the mine, squeezing its available space, and there is no alternative. Most underground mines these days have a road leading straight from the surface, but not at Beaconsfield. Its shaft spoke of the ages. The big rigs down in the mine were a bit like old-time pit ponies. Once they were below ground and bolted together, they stayed there and would not see daylight again until they were decrepit and crippled.

The Plat also houses one of the two crib rooms in the mine. As the men stepped out of the cage in twos and threes, they skirted around the machinery and took a side path to the crib. They sat around waiting for Cheesy to delegate their tasks for the night.

Brant was chirpy. He expected to be assigned to a silo above ground in the backfill plant. It was the easiest job.

All he would have to do was watch the monitors as computers controlled the mixing of cement and sand to create a slurry that was then pumped into the mine. The sand and cement mix, combined with rockfill, is used to fill open stopes – empty voids as big as cathedrals left in the earth after gold-bearing ore has been blasted out and carted away.

In the backfill plant, a worker was safe and dry and there was a TV to keep him entertained.

Brant valued the idea because, like Todd, he knew a bit about the hazards of the underworld that could take your life away quicker than a thought.

A few years ago, Brant got his gumboot tangled in a metal tap protruding from a length of poly-pipe being towed behind a ute down in the mine. Helpless, he was dragged on his back for 150 metres across the hard, rough, dark dirt of the decline, his buttocks stripped of skin before the ute driver knew anything was wrong. A fellow miner, Ray Digney, ran panting alongside Brant, grabbing his body and heaving it away from the sharp, angled corners of walls when the utility roared around bends. Digney saved Brant's life that evening, for the rock walls would have smashed him into the next world.

Another time, Brant hoisted himself aboard a front-end loader, kicked it into gear and very nearly broke his neck. The loader runs on hydraulics and a valve normally reduces the start-up power from its full operating strength of 1,500 pounds per square inch to a more manageable 300 psi. But the valve stuck, giving the machine so much brawn it was flung forward with the sort of jolt that could fracture a mountain. Brant was off work for weeks suffering whiplash.

Yes, thought Brant. An easy night in the backfill plant sounded good.

Cheesy had different ideas. The backfill plant wouldn't be working just yet. He began detailing the jobs his men would be required to tackle.

Darren Geard, a jumbo operator, and his offsider Phil Walters were to go down to the 980-metre level and finish rehabilitating the walls and the ceiling of a tunnel.

Dave Johnson ('Johnno', a young man built like a mountain) and Trent Clayton were to accompany Geard ('Geardie', of course), and Walters into the 980-metre level and re-tension and replate some old cable bolts drilled and grouted 6 metres into the roof to keep the rock stable. Then they were all to head way down to the farthest reaches of the mine at 1080 metres and begin preparing the area for future blasting.

Mick Borrill, a chunky, highly skilled miner of the old school, was to drive a Simba – a drilling rig normally used to drill long holes vertically into the roof, often for ventilation or drainage – into an old tunnel at the 630-metre level.

Glen McCarthy, one of two blokes in the mine known as 'Macka', was given the job of driving one of the front-end loaders, a heavy, low-slung machine known as a bogger, down to the 900-metre level and loading dirt to replenish a stockpile at the 925.

Waste dirt, known as mullock, graded from the decline and blasted from drives, is stockpiled in holes all through the mine for all manner of uses, but the material dumped in the 925 level was needed for a bund – a wall dividing the end of a tunnel and the yawning cavern of the stope.

Once he had dealt with the stockpile, Macka was to take the bogger down to the 1080 level and begin loading trucks with ore already blasted out of the walls by previous shifts. Three trucks driven by Alan Bennett, Theo Visser and Don Walters would haul the ore away back up the decline.

Three fitters – Ian Pillon, Brad Newett and Kingsley Nankervis – would be employed in the workshops on the Plat at 375 metres and another at 700 metres, and electrician Scott Waddle would take care of power.

That left Todd, Larry and Brant. Cheesy told them he needed them to work in a level known as 925 west. Almost a kilometre below the surface. In an area of the mine known among many of the men as 'bad ground'.

'Yeah, it's bad ground in there,' says Geardie. 'Shit ground.' Indeed, Geardie had worked in 925 west the previous night, guiding the manoeuvrable arm of the jumbo to bore eight boltholes into the walls.

'It was real drummy, the ground was drummy. You put the drill into the rock and you hear it drummin'. It sorta feels hollow. It means the rock is loose back there somewhere and it's soft . . . the rock isn't holding too good. All this fine dust was drifting down. There was mesh all hangin' off from the previous firing and I put a bolt in the footwall to hold it and I thought the ground was too shitty – it just didn't feel good. So I pulled back a bit from where I was supposed to put the boltholes and I put 'em in better ground. I told Cheesy later I didn't put the holes for the pins where he wanted because the ground was too shitty.'

Miners work in an odd environment and have their own language. Most of us walk upon the ground, but miners are inserted within it. The ground to them is all that surrounds them: rock underfoot, overhead and to the sides. They don't speak about the 'roof'. The ceiling is known as 'the backs', as if there is the yearning knowledge that everything above them leads back to the world. In fact, it's an old Cornish mining term that refers to the area above a drive where the lode or metal-bearing ore resides. In the old days, miners worked in low, narrow tunnels, hunched over or even crawling along on their stomachs. The lode above was at their backs.

In the late 19th century, one in six miners in Beaconsfield was a Cornishman. They brought with them a yearning for the beautiful river that divides Cornwall from Devon. It is called the Tamar, and its wooded English valley is strewn with the detritus of two centuries of mining. Perhaps the early Cornish settlers in northern Tasmania gained some relief from their homesickness to discover themselves in the Tamar Valley of the south, its largest town named in honour of Governor Philip Gidley King, who was born in Launceston, Cornwall.

The writer George Orwell wrote of a journey into a coal mine in England in a 1937 essay he entitled simply 'Down the Mine'. It was not a hard-rock gold mine like that at Beaconsfield, of course, and machinery has taken much of the drudgery out of the work since 1937. But his description of the underground remains apt, even half a world and three-quarters of a century away. The time to go down a mine, Orwell wrote,

> is when the machines are roaring and the air is black with coal dust, and when you can actually see what the miners have to do. At those times the place is like hell, or at any rate like my own mental

picture of hell. Most of the things one imagines in hell are there – heat, noise, confusion, darkness, foul air, and, above all, unbearably cramped space. Everything except the fire, for there is no fire down there except the feeble beams of Davy lamps and electric torches which scarcely penetrate the clouds of coal dust.

As miners blast their way through the earth, they have a name for every surface that is revealed. There is the 'hanging wall' that follows the slope of the seam that holds the precious ore. At Beaconsfield, the ore body slopes at around 60 degrees. Think of a drive as a corridor. The wall on the left side of a drive that travels to the west – as did the 925 where Geard had inserted his bolts – is the sharply angled hanging wall following the ore up to 'the backs', the ceiling. The opposite wall, on the right, runs vertically to the roof and supports the drive. It is known as the footwall.

Hold now, landlubbers, while we explore the Beaconsfield gold mine.

The town above perches upon a subterranean world so honeycombed with shafts, passages, drives and tunnels that if they were all to collapse at once the houses and shops would simply disappear. A regular warren of workings down to around 500 metres lie dormant, just as they have since 1914 when the old mine closed and groundwater was allowed to flood in for 80 years before the latest venture got underway.

Having ridden the shaft to the Plat at 375 metres we have hardly dipped our toes in.

Leading down from the Plat is the mine's highway, the decline, pronounced in the American way: DEE-cline. It is a one-lane passageway maybe 5 metres high and around the same in width. It is the main artery for everything down here, travelling in a spiral to the depths, falling away at a grade of around 1 in 6. In short, for every 6 metres you travel, you drop another a metre below the surface. Thus, to reach 1 kilometre vertically you must travel 6 kilometres; or you would if the decline were a perfect spiral tilted at a constant grade, which it is not. It is flat in some spots, a little steeper here, a little shallower there. The entire trip down the decline to the bottom of the Beaconsfield mine is closer to 10 kilometres.

The miners travel in four-wheel-drive utilities when they leave the Plat, and the first stop is at 700 metres to stow their crib meals. Here is another vast cavern: the main crib. There are pie-warmers, microwaves, a refrigerator, an iced-water dispenser, a few tables and chairs. A rough dining room. Nearby is a workshop where the loaders get their daily mechanical service. There is an office for the shift boss to map out his 'plods' – the personal log of duties for every miner underground.

The crib has the rare mercy of electric lighting, lending it some semblance of normalcy in an abnormal environment. There is nothing so dark as the belly of a mine. Walk down a tunnel, turn out your cap lamp, and you could hold your hand in front of your face and see nothing. Nothing at all.

The only light in the decline comes from the headlights of utilities and trucks and any bogger or drilling rig that is grinding up or down the road.

The headlights wash eerily over rough walls of hard rock laced with reinforcing mesh.

Intersecting with the decline is a confusion of tunnels, spokes on a wheel, leading off horizontally into total darkness where gold-bearing quartz ore awaits in its ancient seam.

The tunnels appear random, but they are not. Each gives access to a particular level at which the mining of ore occurs.

The levels for much of the reach beneath the 375 crib are spaced 20 metres above and below each other, but at Beaconsfield, as one travels deeper than 840 metres, the horizontal rock pillars between each level are only 10 metres apart. Put out of your mind the picture of a pillar as most of us understand it, a structure standing upright to hold up the roof of a house or a temple. In a mine, a pillar lies horizontally, though its purpose remains that of support. If you were to think of an equivalent in a building, you would come up with a roof beam or a truss. But that would hardly be a reasonable comparison either, because as the mine went deeper, all these natural pillars of quartz were blown up, removed and replaced with a hard-set mixture of waste rock and concrete.

Many of the miners underground worried about the fact that pillars were being progressively mined out, regularly voicing concerns that the narrow shelves of natural rock should be retained to support the great stresses within the earth at such depth.

They were miners, though, and they were philosophical because they also knew that the ore from 880 metres down to 925 metres was particularly high-grade gold-bearing quartz, and that every metre of it was increasingly prized by the mine management, particularly as world gold prices rose and rose during 2006. Around $20 million worth of gold had been pulled out of the Beaconsfield mine in the first three months of 2006. The pillars of ore were simply too valuable to be left alone.

In some areas, once the ore had been blown down, stockpiled and washed of dust, the miners could actually see the deep yellow traces of gold glowing in the quartz. It is possible to work in gold mines all your life and never see such a thing. Those loading the ore on trucks were told by their bosses, 'Don't be spilling any of this on the decline – it's too expensive to be roadfill.' Trucks could be hauling hundreds of thousands of dollars' worth of metal in a single load of ore. Not surprisingly, trucks get precedence on the decline.

Any small vehicle that comes head-to-head with a truck must extinguish its lights and quickly back up until its driver finds a side tunnel or any other hole in the wall into which he can reverse, allowing the larger vehicle to trundle by. Drivers mostly know where the other vehicles are because everyone is linked by squawking radios, but there is only one decline and confrontations are inevitable. The lights-out rule on the submissive vehicle is a courtesy and an acknowledgment that a driver could find himself blinded in that deep gloom.

This courtesy with light extends to the miners' cap lamps. Every miner has his own cap lamp, connected by cable to a battery on his belt. It emits a powerful, thin, white light when flicked to full power (there is a dim half-setting) that naturally follows a man's line of sight if his helmet is balanced properly on his head. Protocol requires that every miner avoid shining his headlamp into the eyes of another. A mine is alive with dangers and there is no one down there who wants to spend even a few seconds blinded simply because someone looked them full in the face when they were talking. The result is that conversations have an awkwardness about them, almost a shiftiness. Men stand at an angle to each other or tilt their helmets and look sideways at their interlocutors.

With Cheesy's briefing over, the men set off to fetch the equipment needed for their tasks. Most of them boarded Nissan utes to journey down to the workshop and parking station at the 700 crib.

Larry's grader was undergoing a mechanical service. It would prove to be the greatest misfortune in his life. Instead of spending the night smoothing down the surface of the decline, he headed off from the Plat on a telehandler, a muscled-up cherry-picker machine with two prongs sprouting from a boom arm extending from the rear to the front. Larry roared away down the decline to a temporary store at the 680 level where he fitted the prongs to a steel-framed basket. Brant, driving a ute, collected wire cable, shackles, eye bolts and reinforcing mesh.

Todd picked up a front-end loader, a bogger, from the 700-metre level and drove directly to the 925. He set to the task of building the bund Cheesy wanted constructed at the end of the drive, scooping mullock from a stockpile and dumping it on the spot designated for the wall.

Todd's journey into the drive in which he was to build his bund – and that of Larry and Brant when they turned up later – involved turning left off the decline into an access tunnel. About 30 or 40 metres down the tunnel he came to the crosscut – a T-intersection where those who had blasted the access passage had met the seam of gold-bearing ore. Here the miners of the blasting crew had followed the seam both left to the east and right to the west. Todd turned right. Around 30 metres along, the drive ended, disappearing into a spooky black void. This was the open stope, where ore had been blasted clear up to the next level, removing the pillar above. It was not a place to venture. A rock falling from the roof of the void, perhaps 18 to 20 metres above, would kill a man.

Todd's task was to build an earthen wall at the end of the drive, just short of the opening to that great hole. It would form a barrier when, later, thousands of tonnes of waste rock were to be dumped from the level above to fill the void. The bund would prevent the waste from bouncing and spilling back into the drive.

This, then, is how mining at Beaconsfield progresses. Backwards. Tunnels are driven west into the seam of gold-bearing quartz. Then the end of the tunnel is blown up, literally, and the whole pillar above, 10 metres of it, collapses. The shattered ore is scooped up and hauled away, leaving an immense open hole. Waste rock is dumped in from the level above to replace the natural ore and a slurry of concrete and sand is pumped in to set it hard. Then the process is repeated further back in the drive to the east. Again and again, until the whole level of ore is removed and there is nothing but a man-made pillar supporting backfill, loose rock hard-packed, replacing what had been an ancient seam.

The end of the cramped drive in which Todd was working – around 5 metres high and 6 metres wide – was raggedy. The rock ceiling, known as the brow because it stopped dead at the entrance to the void, was held together by wire mesh and scores of bolts drilled deep into the rock and held in place by square steel plates. Every few metres steel straps curved from the walls across the roof. When you're in bad ground, you need all the ground support you can get, but some miners wondered openly whether you could reach a point at which there was too much support. In the 925 west drive, it sometimes seemed there were more bolts, steel straps and mesh than actual rock.

Todd had finished his bund by the time Brant Webb and Larry Knight arrived. He had dumped 22 bucket-loads of mullock, each weighing around 6 tonnes, and the wall rose more than half the height of the drive. He backed his loader down the drive and parked it in a hole in the wall at the crosscut.

To complete the job, Todd and Brant were required to string a net of wire cable from the top of the bund to the ceiling, threading it through eight expanding bolts they would fit into the holes Geardie had drilled into the footwall and the hanging wall the previous night. The two men would be hoisted in the steel basket balanced on the arm of the telehandler that Larry Knight had driven into the drive. Brant had arrived in a Nissan ute and parked it behind the telehandler.

The drive seemed eerily stable to Brant Webb when he arrived. No rocks popped from the ceiling or the walls; no sound of cracking or fizzing disturbed his ears. It was peaceful. The calm, as it turned out, before a storm.

Fifty-five metres below, in the 980 level, Darren Geard wasn't having it quite so easy.

Standing on the platform of his rig and twitching levers, he used the boom arm of his jumbo drill to 'scale down the backs' – scraping away loose rocks from the roof of the tunnel. Then he and Phil Walters drilled and fitted six chemical bolts into the roof – long split pins anchored in place by the insertion of a powerful resin goo. 'There was a bit of a bang and a spurt of rock at one stage,' Geard recalled later. 'I just told it to shut the fuck up.' The men at Beaconsfield are accustomed to the walls talking to them, and they talk right back. Such a nonchalant term, the walls 'talking' to you. It means the sound of cracking rocks; the pop of stone spitting from the roof; the high corners of walls 'fretting', dribbling dust and fine rocks. It is the sort of thing that terrifies visitors from the surface, but miners in the deep earth below Beaconsfield had grown accustomed to it.

Once they had attended to the misbehaving 980 tunnel, Geardie and Walters pulled out their rig, a large tractor-like machine with an operating platform for the drilling boom, and travelled right to the bottom of the mine at 1080 metres to pin sheets of reinforcing mesh to the roof and the walls and to prepare to drill into the rock face, driving the mine even deeper. Johnno and Trent Clayton stayed in the 980-metre level to finish the reinforcing job.

'You'd better check to see that Geardie isn't getting too hot down there,' Cheesy told Macka before the bogger driver headed below to load ore.

The mine becomes hotter the deeper you go, and in the confines of the tunnels and the stopes, the energy and belching exhausts of giant diesel motors in trucks, boggers and drilling rigs stew the atmosphere. It might be near freezing on the surface, but down deep temperatures of

35 degrees Celsius and higher are common. Add the evaporation of water seeping from the walls and you may as well be working in a tropical jungle.

There is an ice machine in the crib and every miner carries a polystyrene container of iced water. It's not uncommon for a man to drink 7 or 8 litres during a 12-hour shift. Sweat pours from the body. Fans the size of jet engines at the surface suck air out of the mine, creating an atmospheric depression that drags fresh air from ventilation shafts into the deepest recesses, but it merely keeps working conditions survivable. The air returns to the surface through a hole drilled away in the bush up Cabbage Tree Hill. It pukes clouds of steam shot through with diesel fumes, visible from all over Beaconsfield.

Flooding plagues the mine. Water streams through the walls, often falling like rain even in the decline. Mick Borrill would discover a pool of water at the entrance to the 630 level too deep to traverse, and Cheesy would later help him to set up a new pump line to drain it. A fast-flowing underground creek tumbles through the earth around the 630 level and its waters seep and bubble down through the rock, finding paths along fissures and through the very ore itself, answering the call of gravity.

The mine plunges way below the level of the Tamar River and is essentially an aquifer sitting within the sediment of ancient seabeds. Water infiltrates limestone and pours from the surface through the old mineshafts dotted around Beaconsfield and on the slope of Cabbage Tree Hill. It is the wettest mine in Australia, and it was ever thus. As far back as June 1879, a shaft at Beaconsfield called Dally's United – the predecessor to the current mine – suddenly began flooding. The miners clawed their way out, but within 35 minutes the level had risen so far that water was surging out of the mouth of the shaft. According to accounts from the time, a steam pump running flat out to remove 10,000 gallons of water an hour made little impression on the problem.

Huge electric pumps work constantly to keep the modern Beaconsfield gold mine from flooding. There are lakes down there in the blackness. Five 30-metre tunnels have been allowed to fill with water, creating settling dams. Each of the dams is placed strategically between 655 metres and the bottom. They allow sediment to drift from the water, preventing the pumps from chewing themselves to death.

The water is propelled vertically from sump to sump, lifting it from 1030 metres to 905 metres, then up to 790 metres, to 680 metres, to 375 metres and finally to 180 metres and up out to the surface and down the hill to holding dams in the valley before emptying back into the Tamar. Some is pumped back up to the backfill plant and the mill.

It sounds simple enough, but most of the shafts drilled for water evacuation were done the hard way, by a method known as air-legging. It means a driller climbing a steel ladder, balancing an expanding monopod – the 'air leg' – of his 40 kilogram hand-operated machine on a rung and sinking the long tungsten-tipped bit into the rock above him, dirt falling around his head, the air-leg pushing the drill high. Up and up. Blasting a vertical tunnel. This is known as rise-mining and it's hot, exhausting, oxygen-depriving work requiring the balancing skills of a gymnast, the strength of a weight-lifter and the tenacity and courage of a bulldog. It is what caused the long, slow death of Lorraine Kramer's father, and miners lower their voices and speak with respect about rise miners. 'Guns', they call them. In mining districts, air-legging competitions are a drawcard at agricultural shows. Without rise miners, the Beaconsfield mine would be nothing but a water-filled sinkhole.

Each pumping station has four big pumps, two of which operate at any given time, the others ready to kick in should one fail. Each pump is capable of dealing with immense amounts of water, but for the past few years they have steadily drained around 69 litres a second. In other words, about 6 million litres of water is expelled from the Beaconsfield mine every 24 hours; enough to fill two Olympic swimming pools.

Down in the 925-metre level on the evening of Anzac Day, the walls were not only silent, but dry. It seemed a blessing.

With Todd's bund completed, Larry Knight set the telehandler's basket on the floor so Todd and Brant could climb aboard, and hoisted them above the dirt wall. Todd screwed expanding eye-bolts into the holes bored by Geardie and together he and Brant began stringing steel cable from hanging wall to footwall, right up to the roof. Brant used a wire-straining device called a Tirfor to tighten the wire and the two men shackled it, taut as the strings on a violin. The next step was to stretch wire mesh over the cable frame. Combined with the bund, the arrangement would seal off the tunnel from the void ahead. When it came time to blow the roof of the tunnel, the wire wall would alert those miners bogging out the shattered ore that here was the end of the drive, and the loaders should not proceed beyond it.

Todd and Brant were happy with their work. As they completed their cable net, Cheesy drove in to check on their progress. He spent much of his shift cruising the underground inspecting all the different jobs, assessing safety, making sure stockpiles were topped up, gauging temperatures and diverting the miners to tasks that might need attention.

'I often stop and have a smoke with the blokes,' he says. 'I don't know why I didn't that night, but everything seemed fine and I just gave them the thumbs up, said "good job" and drove away.'

Todd needed a drink. Larry lowered the basket on to the bund, turned off the telehandler and slung Todd's water bottle up. The men had stowed the wire mesh for the next phase of the job back down the tunnel, and Larry set off to fetch it.

Both Todd and Brant had been leaning over the basket's steel edge to tighten dog clamps holding the ends of the cable together. They were sweating and decided to have a spell. Todd leant down in the basket to pick up his water bottle. Beside him, Brant stood, stretched and prepared to light a cigarette.

The atomic clock used by government agencies across the world to calculate the precise time for moments of significance ticked at that very second to 11.26 Coordinated Universal Time. It was therefore exactly 9.26 pm in Beaconsfield, Tasmania. We know this because at that moment a seismograph monitored by Geoscience Australia, a client of the atomic clock, suddenly became agitated.

CHAPTER 3

DO YOU COPY, LARRY?

■ ■ ■

A shock of wind hit Brant hard as a hammer, blowing his cigarette clean out of his lips.

Crazily, Brant snatched a single thought: all the tyres on the telehandler have blown. He had been standing next to a truck in the mine one day when a tyre exploded. The wind blast almost blew him from his feet. But this was far more violent.

And then there was blackness.

Todd felt the wind, too, but it was nothing compared with the noise. It was as if someone had stuck a detonator in a stick of explosive and fired it right above his head, a hundred times louder than a shotgun going off in his ear. BANG! The convulsion of raw energy tore through his body. Todd was on his feet, leaning down, and a microsecond later he was mashed on the steel floor of the basket, laid out contorted on his left side.

He was buried. Crushed beneath rocks. The roof had come in. He knew it; couldn't believe it. He could not move. His shoulders, legs, arms. Head. He strained to shift even a millimetre. But not one part of his body would answer the strain of his muscles. He was bound tight, helpless. Hard, sharp rock covered his entire body. There was no sound. He was deaf. His brain screamed at him. *This is not happening. This is not happening.*

Larry. Larry would come and get him out. 'Larry!' he bellowed. 'Larry!' Silence. 'Larry, for Christ's sake.'

Brant. Shit. Where's Brant? 'Brant, you gotta help me. Brant. You there? Brant, Brant.'

Each time Todd drew breath to yell, the weight around his chest became more crushing. As he exhaled, the great weight of rock pressing on every surface of his body shifted and settled, making it even more difficult to get air into his lungs. He strained against it and the effort of it forced his system to demand more oxygen. Every breath was an agony.

Todd was beginning to die. A deep melancholy drifted upon him, numbing the panic that threatened to overwhelm him. A vision floated into his head. Carolyn and his three children, Trent, Maddison and Liam. He had never given them enough of his time. The very morning after his wedding he had bounced out of bed early. Going out the bush hunting. You'll never change me, Carolyn. Get used to it. And now he wouldn't be able to make it up. The kids would grow up without him. Carolyn would be alone. He hadn't listened hard enough to his own fears about going down the mine and here he was, utterly helpless, sinking into a red mist. Todd forced air into his lungs and screamed.

Brant struggled into half-consciousness. His ears rang and sizzled and from somewhere there was a voice calling his name. He drifted away and when he came back, the voice – a hoarse, panting urgency to it – was still there. Brant felt around him and his hands scrabbled at piled rock. His knees pressed against his chest and his head was pushed down somewhere near his knees. He could move only his arms. He could not understand where he was, what had happened. And why was that voice calling his name? Todd? Brant's thoughts swam slowly out of their muddle. Pain gave him focus. His knees felt on fire.

He felt around and found his cigarette lighter in his shirt pocket. He flicked it, and the little flame revealed the setting for a nightmare. His brain whispered low and guttural at him, or perhaps it was his real voice. *This is bad. Really, really bad.* Not an obscene word came to his lips. It was too awful for that.

Smashed rock everywhere. Jagged chunks, some twice the size of footballs, others smaller, shattered, piled within the basket, half filling it. Most of Brant's body was down there among the rocks. He had been driven as if by a pile-driver from a standing position to a painful squat. His head and part of his chest were free, but there was no space above to allow him to sit upright. A small sheet of steel mesh, rock covering it, pushed down on the back of his head. The roof was not worthy of the name. It was a crazed jumble of stone, separate rocks all jammed together, each somehow supporting the other. Any one of them – possibly every one of them – was a keystone. Just as in a carefully constructed arch, the removal of a keystone means the whole thing collapses. But this wasn't carefully constructed. Many of the rocks wedged above the basket were splintered shards, sharp as daggers. They looked to Brant like swords suspended. And it wasn't simply this precarious balancing act that horrified him. It was the insignificant space over which the light from his flame danced, muted by swirling dust. Small stones continued to rattle down and crushed sediment dribbled from crevices above.

Todd's voice was coming in gasps now. 'You've gotta help me, Brant. I. Can't. Move.'

The basket was no larger than a small kitchen table, but Brant couldn't see Todd. He couldn't move either. Both men wore webbing belts around their hips, and connected to the belts were bulky oxy-boxes containing their emergency breathing gear and batteries attached by cords to their cap lamps. These essential items, wedged down among the piles of rocks, were anchoring them. 'Hold on, just fuckin' hold on,' Brant cried. Frantic now, adrenaline kicking in, Brant managed to slide his hand between his body and the rocks and freed a Stanley knife he kept in a pouch on his miner's pants. He used it to hack through his webbing belt and wriggled out of it. He pushed stones aside and toppled forward but his feet, clad in heavy gumboots, remained trapped. Determined, he pulled his right foot clean out of his boot. But there was too much weight bearing down on his left foot – he couldn't extract it. He twisted around and used the knife again, slicing the rubber from behind his calf down to the heel. He pulled himself over the bed of stone and found Todd's nose poking out of the mess.

Brant clawed rocks, tossing them in all directions, exposing Todd's face. The big man was struggling so hard for breath he sounded inhuman. 'Unnnnh, unnnnh, unnnnh.' Sediment spilling from above was settling in among the rocks and each time his chest heaved the constriction became tighter, as if he were being crushed by an anaconda. His stomach contents were being squeezed into his throat, foaming out of his mouth and across his beard.

The only light within the cavern was a weak glow at the top of the basket. Todd's cap lamp had been ripped from his head as he was struck down and it was crushed between fallen stone and the basket's upper rail. It was failing fast. Brant had ripped his helmet and lamp off his head when he sawed off his belt with the lamp battery attached and he had no idea where his light was. He kept flicking his lighter to check that Todd was still alive. Todd's eyes had rolled so far back that the whites shone in the flame. Every now and again he roared, veins popping on his forehead. He was a footballer who could explode through a pack of players, their bodies cannoning off him, and soar high to grab a mark. He was trying to use his strength to burst out of his entrapment. 'Aaaahunnrrrh.' But his body was held tighter than a vice. Todd's desperation lent Brant a fierce blast of strength and he ripped at the tangle of rocks. He couldn't, wouldn't let this bloke die. He didn't want to be alone. Not in this place.

Brant tossed aside enough rocks for Todd to free his arms, and the two of them began tearing at the stone, slowly, piece by piece easing the weight on Todd's chest. Both of them were heaving for breath and their hearts thudded. Gradually the weight upon Todd's chest eased and his breathing became more or less under control.

He had no gloves; had taken them off to use the shifter to tighten dog clamps on the cable wall. The skin on his hands tore as he helped Brant shift the fractured stone. A measure of purpose slowly replaced the panicky effort to dig. But most of Todd's body was still covered. Pain in his legs, his back.

The biggest immediate problem facing the men was the lack of space in their basket. There seemed nowhere to put the rocks they were removing from Todd's body.

The basket measured 1.45 metres wide, 1.25 metres from front to back and just 1 metre high. In the old imperial measurements, it was around 5 feet at its broadest width, 4 feet from front to back and 3 feet 3 inches high. However, these were the exterior dimensions. Inside was even tighter, reduced by upright steel posts and mesh that gave it strength. The foot space beneath an office clerk's desk is larger. If you were to cage a dog in an enclosure that size, you would be charged with cruelty. But here were two large men crammed together in such a space, and half the height of it was already gone, filled with rockfall. The roof was no more than 600 millimetres, or two feet, above the basket's upper rail, though most of it hung lower even than that. Brant could not sit up – he was forced to lie on his stomach as he tried to deal with around three-quarters of a tonne of stone that was crushing Todd.

The rockfall, the cause and extent of which were unknown to the two men, had wrapped around the front and back of the basket, and the hanging wall had collapsed from the left. Brant's lighter revealed that on the right was a small void between the basket and the footwall. Each side of the basket had an opening of

400 millimetres, or nearly 1 foot 4 inches, secured with chain, to allow occupants to board and alight. The two men decided their only option was to squeeze as much rock as they could through the opening to the right into the empty space beyond. The void was no more than 800 millimetres or around two and a half feet high, and about the same wide, but it was all they had. Wheezing and sweating, they began pushing rocks out of the basket, Todd using his forearms to flick boulders from his body and Brant rolling them to the opening.

Brant's every instinct, however, shrieked in conflict. There seemed to him no way that fresh air could penetrate the jumble that had entombed him and Todd. What if the only path for air was through that little void? What if his efforts to save Todd by rolling rocks into that space were blocking the airflow and cutting off their only chance at life? Their oxy-boxes, buried somewhere now, offered no more than 45 minutes of breathable air. Yet there was no choice. They had to ease the weight on Todd's body.

But as they continued shifting rock, they quickly got to the point where they had used every square centimetre of space within the basket. There was nothing for it but to continue rolling stone through the opening, filling whatever space existed outside their steel confinement.

■ ■ ■

The concussion was so great Gavan Cheesman thought it would blow in the windows of his four-wheel-drive. In all his years of mining he had never heard an explosion like it. Two immense bangs, as if giants had slammed sledgehammers into a steel door the size of a mountain.

He felt the shockwaves in the pit of his stomach. He knew instantly what had happened; didn't want to believe it.

Cheesy had driven a bit up the decline after leaving Larry, Todd and Brant and had veered into the 900-metre level, a tunnel that dipped to the west down to 915 metres because part of it had collapsed months before. He was only 10 metres higher than the tunnel in which Larry, Todd and Brant were working, but maybe 60 metres to the west. As the din from the two gigantic thuds died away, he jammed his ute into reverse and spun the wheels up the ramp back to the decline, snatching the radio mike from the dashboard.

'Have you got a copy, Larry?' he shouted. 'Larry Knight, have you got a copy?' Nothing came from his radio. Not even static. 'Larry, have you got a copy?' Cheesy knew there was a radio in the telehandler's cabin. Why couldn't he raise Larry? He knew also that neither Todd nor Brant would have a radio in their basket. Desperately, he tried calling them anyway. 'Do you copy, Todd? Have you got a copy, Brant?

He kept calling as he raced his ute down the decline. Again and again, with no response.

All up and down the mine, men could hear Cheesy's increasingly distressed radio transmissions.

Mick Borrill had returned to the 700-metre workshop next to the crib. He felt the shock of two colossal thumps coursing through his body. The walls rippled. Just as if a truck had smashed into the other side. The sight of it imprinted itself on his brain. Walls of solid rock, undulating.

Unbelievable. Borrill knew exactly what had happened. Somewhere down there, ore had exploded. Yeah, a rock burst. Two years previously, Borrill and another Beaconsfield miner, Ray Digney, had been working in the 790 level when the roof came in. They had seen the walls shimmer then, too, flowing like a mirage. He and Digney had dug themselves out. This felt and sounded worse. Borrill looked at Kingsley Nankervis, the mechanical fitter, and his eyes were wide with dread. The radio began blaring Cheesy's plea for a word from Larry, Brant and Todd.

Way below at the mine's farthest depth of 1080 metres, Darren Geard was juggling the levers on his jumbo, drilling a hole deep into the roof to pin an extra sheet of mesh. His offsider Phil Walters and bogger operator Glen 'Macka' McCarthy were standing by, watching the process. The heat was oppressive and Macka, following Cheesy's instructions, wanted to know whether Geardie would mind if he used his loader to bog out a stockpile, even though the motor would drive the temperature higher.

Suddenly the ground reared. It slammed into the feet of the three men, buckling their knees. The walls and the roof shivered. The two biggest bangs Geard had heard in his life.A shower of small rocks blew from the roof and sand streamed from the top of the hanging wall to the left. 'Fuck!' Geard bawled. The men wanted to run. Anywhere. But they didn't move. The shift boss controls every action in the mine. They stood, shocked, waiting for Cheesy's voice to light up their radios. In seconds, they heard Cheesy screaming for Larry, and they heard the silence that followed every call.

Cheesman skidded his ute to a halt at the access to the 925. A cloud of dust boiled from the passage into the decline. He leapt from the vehicle and ran down the access tunnel, almost blinded. Choking, he reached the crosscut. The loader Todd had used to build his bund was parked next to the mullock stockpile across the intersection. It was almost covered in rock. Fractured slabs of the hanging wall hung askew. Cheesy had only a few seconds to take in the scene of chaos before the earth shook again and rocks cascaded, smashing into the floor a few metres ahead of him.

He retreated to the decline and grabbed his radio mike. As calmly as he could, Cheesman ordered every man in the mine to find his way up to the crib at 700 metres. 'Make your way up, get out of there,' he relayed. He waited for each of them to copy his call, counting them on his fingers as their voices checked in. He ordered the truck drivers to park in any available drive off the decline and to catch a ride in any light vehicle that was passing. The last thing he wanted was lumbering trucks blocking the single lane to safety.

Cheesman radioed Pete Goss, the winder driver up on the surface. 'An emergency down here,' he said. 'Rock fall at 925. It's bad. We're gonna need the mine rescue crew. Call Rex Johnson and Pat Ball.' Johnson was the mine's chief of occupational health and safety and head of the rescue team. Pat Ball was the mine's underground manager.

* * *

Cheesy couldn't stay still. He had to get back into the tunnel; try to find Larry, Todd and Brant. He was responsible. He'd sent them in there. He was shift boss. Had to assess the damage.

The noise in the access passage was frightening. At the crosscut and around the corner in the westbound drive it was terrifying. The walls cracked like pistol shots, rocks dropped from the roof and spat from the walls. Cheesy pressed on, creeping past the light vehicle Brant had parked in the drive. Dust churned, blotting the beam from his cap lamp and suddenly the roof caved in right in front of him, roaring. Cheesy had no option but to hightail it out, running for his life.

* * *

Geard, Glen McCarthy and Phil Walters bolted into action the moment they heard Cheesman radioing that everyone should get to the crib. Macka reversed his bogger out of the drive, fast, parked it in the decline and the men ran to their ute. 'Yeah, we didn't walk; we fuckin' ran,' Geardie said later.

One hundred metres above them, Johnno Johnson and Trent Clayton needed no second order, either. Still working on the cable bolts in the 980 level, they were only 55 metres below the catastrophe that had overwhelmed Larry, Brant and Todd. The explosion of cracking earth had deafened them and the shock of it had rattled them clear to the core. Soon as Cheesy hit the radio, they were in their ute and out of there.

A few hundred metres up the decline they hit dust. Thicker than any fog. Black. Dense as the depths of a swamp. It consumed the headlights, just gobbled up their beam.

Geardie was at the wheel and he couldn't see beyond the windscreen. Couldn't see the walls. He'd been up and down the decline a thousand times and he was lost, floating in darkness, heart pounding. Hit the wall and you'd never get out. You'd choke to death down here. Another explosion in the earth and they'd be buried. The three men said not a word. Didn't need to. Each knew what the other was thinking because there was no possible way you could think anything else.

It took little more than 3 minutes to creep through the dust, but it seemed hours.

Cheesy had forced himself back into the 925 drive for the third time by then. This time he slid past Brant's ute and advanced 15 metres beyond it. Ahead through the black mist, the shaft of light from his cap lamp washed over two high piles of shattered rock, the farthest from him filling the tunnel. He could see no sign of the telehandler Larry had been operating. Again the earth boomed, and more rock blew from the roof. Cheesman got out of there.

As he returned to the decline, the headlights of the ute carrying Johnno Johnson and Trent Clayton emerged from the dust cloud, followed by the vehicle with Geardie, Macka and Walters. Cheesy instructed them all to keep going. Get up to the 375 and get the ambulance ready, he told Geard. The ambulance was nothing but a four-wheel-drive troop carrier with a canopy and space for stretchers and first-aid equipment. *Christ knows what good it could do tonight,* Cheesy thought. But he had to go through the drill, make sure everything was done right. At least no one had needed to take refuge in the big safety chambers. Fire was the biggest danger down here. If a truck overheated and caught fire in the decline, the flames would devour all the oxygen in minutes and men could do nothing but race to one of the chambers, steel air-tight containers with their own supplies of air, food and water, each big enough for 20 men. No need for them tonight. His radio told him all the men had reached the crib. All but Larry, Todd and Brant.

Cheesy sat alone in the dark. Nine hundred and twenty-five metres below the surface. The earth rumbled around him, the roof of the decline cracked and creaked and every now and then a stone fell to the roadway. Dust filled his nostrils and stuck to the sweat running into his beard. He prayed silently for a light to emerge from the 925 access, but he knew it wouldn't happen. *Those three men are dead,* he thought. No one could survive what had happened down here.

CHAPTER 4

THREE MEN MISSING

Colin Smee dozed in his easy chair, his little dog Benji in his lap and the TV murmuring. Boom! The house shuddered. Smee's windows rattled. Benji whined, jumped to the floor. 'Bugger that,' Smee hissed. Anzac Day. They promised. No explosions today. He grabbed the phone, dialled the number for the mine. *Gonna rip skin off their ears up there.* He got an answering machine.

Carolyn Russell had turned in early. Her three children were asleep. The Anzac march, the picnic, a long afternoon of mucking around with their friends in the autumn sunshine had tired them all. Carolyn climbed into bed, flicked on the TV. Luxuriating.

The shock wave hit the house like a train. The bed jumped. The Russell home is little more than a couple of hundred metres from the southern gate to Beaconsfield's mine and the tunnels are almost right under it. Carolyn had felt explosions and seismic shifts before, but this was the most violent of them all. She looked at the clock on her bedside table: 9.26 pm. *That's not right,* she thought. The crew wouldn't be firing so early in the shift. Anyway, not today. Everyone knew there was no firing today.

The phone rang. It was Carolyn's sister Melanie Harris from Cornwall Street a bit across town where a lot of houses had suffered damage to their brickwork and plaster from the underground works. Colin Smee lived in Cornwall Street, too. 'Did you feel that?' Melanie asked. 'It's not normal,' Carolyn replied. 'Maybe they've had a seismic.'

A 'seismic' had become shorthand around Beaconsfield. It meant a mini-earthquake when immense stress within the rock underground had shattered gold-bearing quartz, bringing tonnes of rock smashing into tunnels. Blasting with high explosives caused the ground above to shake, too, but seismic activity was a much greater concern. Several residents had taken to recording the whoomp and thump of mining activity, and Phillip and Judy Batchler were among them. They live up the hill from Todd and Carolyn's home, near the southern gates of the mine.

On 16 February 2006, the day after he had recorded an 'enormous' shock, Phillip Batchler wrote to the West Tamar Council. 'The blasting is not only damaging the house but also my health and lifestyle,' he wrote. 'All of a sudden my house rocks and shudders, windows rattle and I jump with fright. I do not think it is fair that I should have to put up with this.' His diary of unexplained seismic activity went back to 26 October 2005, when it records 'largest blast, cracked bricks and mortar'. What he didn't know at the time was that the 915 tunnel directly above the 925-metre level had collapsed at precisely the time he registered the blast, 6.15 pm. No one had been injured or trapped, but mine management was so concerned that it closed sections of the mine for weeks and production slowed dramatically.

But that was nowhere near as violent as the jolt that went through the Batchler's house at 9.26 pm on Anzac evening. Judy Batchler was asleep one moment, wide awake the next. Phillip was sitting in the lounge-room and saw pictures bounce off the walls. This was no high-explosive blast, he thought. It was a seismic. An earthquake. A bit over three months previously, the mine's manager Matthew Gill had tacitly admitted that mining activity was causing mini-earthquakes. Gill wrote to Mick Wain, another resident who had been sending angry letters about the sudden earth movements, on 12 January 2006, acknowledging: 'A level of community concern has arisen in recent months surrounding blast vibration and mining-induced seismicity (mini-earthquakes) as a result of mining activity taking place beneath the town.'

Anxiety crept through Carolyn Russell. She pushed it down, climbed out of bed and sat in the lounge-room. The heads of stags Todd had stalked and shot peered sightless from the wall. Carolyn turned on the TV. Waited. A miner's wife.

Her eldest son, Trent, a sensitive, bookish boy aged 12, was awakened by the house shuddering, too. He worried about his Dad working in the mine. Worried about him because he was in the fire brigade, too. Trent had a phobia that his Dad wouldn't come home from fighting a fire.

He kept things to himself but Carolyn knew of his fears. Shared them, truth be known. She reassured the boy, told him everything was fine, go back to sleep. Dad would be there in the morning. But Trent lay awake. Heard everything.

The phone. It was Rex Johnson's wife, Brenda. A friend. The Johnsons had lived next door until they moved to Launceston. Carolyn worked as a clerical assistant for Rex, head of occupational health and safety up at the mine. 'Is Todd there?' Bev said. 'There's been an accident. A rock fall. They need him up there straight away.'

Carolyn's body went cold. Todd was on the mine's search and rescue team. Of course they'd phone him first, because he lived closest.

She knew within a breath that Todd was in trouble. Couldn't understand then or later how she knew.

Premonitions often visit those who live close to danger. Six months previously, Carolyn was driven from sleep by a nightmare. Something terrible had happened to Todd underground. She could never quite grasp exactly what the details were, but it hovered there in the night, a vulture snapping at her heart. She tried to drive away the terror of it, but it lingered. Carolyn never told Todd of the dream. She feared loading her trepidation upon him and she told herself that it was stupid. Nothing more than a delusion in the dark.

Yet she knew there was something that connected her with the otherworld. Years before, when she was just 17, her romance with Todd had cooled and she took up with another boy down the valley. One night she was seized with a powerful urge to call the boy and warn him of something terrible, but something with no name, no discernible form. She could not pinpoint the nature of her dread, but it was real enough. Her hand fluttered over the phone, but she never picked it up. How do you warn someone about something for which you have no words? The next day, the boy – a forestry worker – was killed when a tree fell on him.

The two memories collided as she sat in her lounge-room. Her dream about Todd had become real, she was sure of it, but the feeling that flowed from it did not mesh with the old, unnameable fear that had come to her the day before a boyfriend had died. This was quite different. There was no conscious effort to analyse the implications. Nevertheless, a conclusion rushed upon her as if it were a wind that contained knowledge. *Todd is suffering, but he is alive*. Alive. She would hold on to that belief.

Carolyn needed the comfort of another adult with her. She phoned her sister, but Melanie could not leave her children. Melanie contacted Todd's father Noel, and he walked around the corner and sat with his daughter-in-law, the night and the mystery of what may have occurred deep in the earth crushing them both. Nobby – hardly anyone called him Noel – could not bear the waiting. He had to seek information, but he could not leave Carolyn alone. He had worked underground, tending to the machinery down there, for4 years. Miners do not leave the women of their colleagues and their own families to face their fears alone when something dreadful has happened in the mine. Nobby summoned one of Carolyn's friends to sit with her while he set off to the minehead.

There was no one to sit with Mick Borrill's wife, Sandra. She was watching TV at home just down the street from the Russells' house when the walls banged and shook.

Sandra, a quiet woman in her mid 40s, met Mick in the NSW mining town of Broken Hill and they married 24 years ago. Together they have known only the mining life. Their only daughter, Jenna, is married to a Beaconsfield miner, Jamie Williams. Mick moved from the silver and lead mines of Broken Hill to gold mines in Bendigo and Stawell in Victoria before settling in Tasmania. He went underground at Beaconsfield when the mine was cutting its deepest level at just 480 metres, before the first gold bar had been poured.

When the lounge-room walls rippled, Sandra knew something serious had occurred underground. She stepped out the front door and looked up at the floodlit steel poppet a few hundred metres away. The whole town seemed quiet as a grave. Cold, clear, still. Not a car on the street. Nothing seemed to make sense.

Mick phoned within 20 minutes. 'There's been an accident,' he told Sandra. 'I'm all right. Don't worry.' And that was all. Mick had no time. He was in the 375 crib and he had to help Geard get the ambulance ready. Sandra was left with a guttering fire in the grate, her only task to try to get their little son William back to sleep. The boy had been awakened by the shock rolling up from beneath the earth. It would be a long, lonely night for Sandra. She could not bring herself to go back to bed. This would be the fate of the women of miners all over Beaconsfield that night. Worrying. Wondering. No sleep.

Up Weld Street past the Club Hotel where the miners drank and some of them had rooms, Garth Bonney and Robbie Sears, two of the most seasoned miners in town, were having a beer together after dinner in Bonney's apartment. When the earth shook, they knew it wasn't an explosive charge. They phoned the winder driver, Pete Goss, and he said 'I don't know what's happened, but it's bad.' The two men had a radio that linked up with the system underground, and they called up Cheesy. 'A rock fall,' he said. 'Yeah, it's bad all right.'

Bonney, 54, went down the Rosebery mine in 1972, a year ahead of Cheesy. He perceived instantly the tension in his old friend's voice. And he knew how hard it would be for a man who felt responsible for a tragedy. Bonney's own brother Ray had died seven years previously when a beam of timber fell on him in the Hercules mine at Williamsford, near Rosebery. Bonney, a rough, no-nonsense man, couldn't bear to stay on the west coast after that and moved to Beaconsfield working as an air-legger, climbing his way up to jumbo rigs. He and Robbie Sears knew they had to get down the mine to support Cheesy. He was down there alone. He needed men around him. When there's trouble, the senior miners stick together. No argument.

They put down their beers, drove to the mine, changed into work gear, stuck helmets and lamps on their heads and took the shaft to 375, hitched a ride on a ute and wound their way down to 925 metres.

Down there in the growling dark a little crowd gathered around Cheesy, pushing close to him so he understood he wasn't alone any more. Mick Borrill and Johnno Johnson, Robbie Sears and Garth Bonney.

Together, these men had more than a century of experience in the hard-rock underground. But they were afraid for their lives. They would have preferred to be anywhere but here. Appalled. Way down there, shattered rocks had spilled all over Todd's bogger, the walls and the roof were torn, mesh hung ripped where stone had plummeted through and the floor was strewn with debris. The ground, Mick Borrill would say later, was going off like you wouldn't believe. The walls and the roof snarled and cracked and split, blowing stone and spitting sand and dust.

Soon enough, Rex Johnson, who had raced from his home in Launceston when he got the call, came barrelling down the decline in the mine's ambulance with his mine rescue team. The Power Rangers, some of the miners called the rescue team – blokes who join up and get time off work for training.

The rescue team didn't even stop to consult Cheesman or those around him. Equipped with breathing masks and backpacks, air horns on their helmets to summon help in an emergency, the team charged into the 925 tunnel, down the access and to the crosscut. One of the men, Corey Verhey, remembers seeing the shoulders of the drive fretting, dumping dirt, and big cracks in the walls working their way clean back to the decline.

Corey, a friendly-faced local boy in his mid 20s with orthodontic bands on his teeth and a metal stud through an eyebrow, had never liked working in the 925.

'Yeah, I'd worked in that area so many times and it was horrible ground; everyone knew it,' he says. 'It was dangerous, no doubt about it. It was always making noises. And you wouldn't believe how much ground support had been put up. There was reinforcing mesh, metal straps, gooey bolts everywhere. These gooey bolts, they're 2.4 metres long and they've got two separate solutions of glue and when you push the bolt in, the chemicals release and hold them in tight. Each one of them should be able to hold 30 tonne of rock. Everywhere you looked there were bolts. We'd often asked how much ground support was too much.' Now he knew. All the ground support in the world hadn't saved the 925 and the men working within it.

The rescue team retreated from the tunnel to find Cheesman and his mates furious. The mine rescue team had a job to do, but to rush past the most experienced miners into God knew what danger . . . well, in the opinion of Cheesman's group, it was plain bloody stupidity. 'We're the senior miners in this place,' declared Mick Borrill, 'and we're standing out in the decline. You'd reckon we were standing out here for a reason, right?' Cheesman felt it showed a serious lack of respect. He was shift boss, he'd been down there for more than an hour and the rescue team hadn't so much as asked his advice. He didn't want anyone else putting themselves in avoidable danger.

The mine's underground manager, Pat Ball, a man in his late 30s with an unkempt beard and a world of responsibility on his shoulders, joined Cheesman. 'I've got to go back in for my own peace of mind,' Cheesy told Ball. Together they walked to the crosscut, turned right into the 925 drive, crept past Brant's parked ute and managed to climb over the first large pile of collapsed roof. Ahead there was nothing but another hillock of smashed rock blocking the tunnel. No sign of the telehandler.

Ball ordered the tunnel roped off.

Cheesman, Ball, Mick Borrill and a mine engineer named Jamie Karamatic were the last to leave the 925. A hopelessness settled on the little group. In this world, if someone needs a hand, you give him a hand. Without speaking, they wound their way back up the decline to the 700 crib room.

Cheesman gathered together the men of his night shift. Most of them were glassy-eyed, in shock. Cheesman knew instinctively there had to be symbolic act here; a bonding. He ordered all of his men to make their way to the 375 crib room and when they arrived, he told them, 'I want the whole crew to go up to the surface together.' Darren Geard agreed. 'We came down as one; we'll go up as one,' he declared. They trooped to the cage at the 375, rang the bells and Pete Goss wound them up the shaft. A unit. But every one of them carried the weight of the knowledge that three of their mates were missing.

CHAPTER 5

BRANT GOES TUNNELLING

In the darkness, Brant was beginning to despair. He had been digging for hours, ripping rocks from Todd's body. He had become obsessive about halting his work every now and then, flicking his cigarette lighter and checking that their cell was still being fed fresh air. The flame bent back and forth, indicating air was still wafting in, though barely, apparently flowing from the small void off to the side of the basket.

But the flickering light showed the void was filling with rock. There seemed hardly a square centimetre within the basket that was not crammed with stone, and Brant and Todd had taken to rolling rocks through the opening into that space beyond.

Most of Todd's upper body was freed. But he was still jammed on his left side, hard up against the basket's mesh. He could not feel his left leg. It was as if the limb was quite absent from his body. Paradoxically, he also felt pain down there where the leg ought to be. Pain, but no leg. He couldn't understand it.

Brant needed light. He couldn't keep his cigarette lighter flaming. It might run out of gas and anyway, the metal rim of it grew too hot to touch if he held it on for more than a few seconds. He had to find a better method if he was to gain any proper understanding of their predicament.

Brant abandoned Todd and went in search of his cap lamp. He slid around on his stomach, scrabbling behind him for the belt he had cut away from himself down in the rocks. The lamp's battery would be there somewhere and it would be connected to the lamp by its electrical cord. He found the cord and traced it to the doorway. In the confusion of the first moments, his helmet and lamp must have fallen out of the basket. And now he had covered them as he and Todd tossed stones out of their confinement. Painfully, hanging half-in, half-out of the basket, he began searching by touch. Flipping aside dirt and stone, pushing what seemed tonnes of rock away from the little doorway, creating a hole that kept frustrating him by collapsing back on itself, he was finally triumphant. He had his lamp and his helmet, too.

The clear light swept across a scene even more appalling than either Brant or Todd could have imagined. Stones hung so precariously from the tiny space above their bodies that it seemed certain they would be crushed any minute. Larry had laid their basket on the slope of the bund, the hydraulics of the telehandler holding its steel floor horizontal. But the weight of the rockfall had smashed the basket down and it sat now on an angle, the front higher than the back. Todd lay with his head to the rear of the basket, so his head lay lower than his legs.

And there was something else that neither man had perceived. Right in the centre of the basket reared a steel roof strap. 'Strap' is a poor word, for it suggests something flexible, supple. In fact, straps used in mines are solid lengths of steel 3 metres long and around 22.5 centimetres, or 9 inches, wide. They can be bent and shaped only by machines, and they have holes through which big bolts pin them to rock.

When the roof gave way in the 925 drive, one of these straps had been ripped from its bolts above and it had been driven at huge velocity, the tip of it first, directly into Todd and Brant's basket. It was as if a giant shovel-nosed spear had buried itself into the chaos.

Brant and Todd could only stare at the thing, awestruck. It had impaled itself in the scree right between the men. A centimetre or two here or there and it would have sliced one of them in half, clean as a hot knife through butter.

The men were at once horrified and elated. It seemed miraculous. Somehow, they had been chosen to survive.

The steel lance would prove a torture to them, for it dramatically reduced the already cramped space in which they hunkered; but the mere fact that they had been spared its impact gave them a surge of hope.

Brant's light revealed to him the makings of a plan. If they could only dig Todd out, they could haul rock back from the air void outside the basket and backfill the space currently occupied by the big man's body. They would fill the rear of the tilting basket with rock and attempt to build a roughly horizontal platform.

It was a tough, painful business, but both men were determined. A rock at a time. Brant was constantly required to redistribute stones as they piled at the doorway and beyond, while Todd picked rock from his own body and moved it as far away as possible.

About four hours after the roof had fallen in, Todd was free. It was, however, an awkward freedom. He had been contorted for all those hours. His left knee had been pushed through the mesh of the basket and his foot was twisted through the basket's little door on the left. The angle of his leg suggested it should have been broken, but he and Brant were able to ascertain that neither of them had broken a single bone. However, Todd's left leg wasn't simply numb from the weight and pressure of rock. There was no feeling in it at all and with the rock removed he experienced no pins and needles to suggest feeling might return. He pressed his fingers into the flesh of his thigh and it was as if he were prodding jelly. No reaction. His leg no longer belonged to his body. It was frightening, for he needed to move but could not. Yet within the inert mass was pain, though a pain that seemed to float all on its own, disembodied.

There was no doctor to explain what this meant. If there had been, the medico would have explained that Todd's leg wasn't the problem, but a symptom. The rockfall had ruptured a disc within his lower back and it had trapped and compressed the sciatic nerve. The sciatic is the longest nerve in the human body, and the largest, being about as round as a thumb at its largest point. It originates in the lower spine and travels from there through the buttocks and down the backs of the legs. The nerve and its branches supply both sensation and strength to the legs, but because of the spinal com-pression Todd had suffered, it was withholding both feeling and power from his left leg, and his right leg was tingling.

It presented both Todd and Brant with a serious problem. Todd was the bigger, physically stronger of the pair, but he was immobilised. Brant would have to help him while also coping with the difficulty of shifting rock and building a platform so that both of them could lie more or less horizontally.

They lay panting, sweating, exhausted, crunched uncomfortably in their miniature prison, for neither could stretch his body to its full length. What had happened? Perhaps, they thought initially, they had actually pulled the walls in upon themselves when they drew their cable net tight. Was that possible? Could it explain the massive quantity of rock that had roared down?

Small rocks and dirt continued to shower from the roof just above their heads and Brant decided he needed to take out at least some insurance. Carefully, carefully, he began levering some of the least stable stones out of the ceiling. It was nerve-wracking. What if just one of these stones was the key to all the tension holding together the mess above? The answer was obvious, he knew. They would be buried. Yet if a heavy rock suddenly became loose and crashed down, chances were that either he or Todd would get a broken leg or a crushed skull. There seemed no choice but to get on with it.

Todd could not stay where he was, utterly exposed. Anyway, Brant desperately needed to fill the space Todd occupied with the rock he was removing from the roof and all the mullock he and Todd had spilled into the void.

Together, with Brant levering and Todd dragging himself on his elbows, they manoeuvred Todd to the front of the basket where he could lie across its width, though there was no room for him to stretch his legs. Todd stood at 185.4 centimetres, or 6 feet 1 inch, so he was more than 40 centimetres – 1 foot 3 inches – too long for the space. Moving to this new, cramped position was a painful exercise for Todd because, as the two men would discover later, his back had been lashed by the rockfall. When they had settled a bit, the men checked each other for wounds. They were relieved to discover that neither had a major cut that might have left him bleeding to death. They both had welts and scratches and bruises, and every joint and bone ached, but they were remarkably healthy considering they had been overwhelmed by an underground mountain. Todd's back, though, looked as if a sadist had taken a stockwhip to him, and his weight pressed those wounds into the sharp rocks beneath him.

The new arrangement meant Todd's head and most of his chest lay beneath the small square of roof mesh that had fallen across the front right-hand corner of the basket, probably saving Brant's life in the first seconds. Todd's torso and legs, however, had no such protection. And Brant, lying squashed right alongside Todd, so close that one of them had to rest his arm on the other, was almost completely exposed to whatever might fall out of the roof. The mesh simply wasn't wide enough to protect him. His boots were gone, buried, and his socks offered no defence against the hard, splintered stone. He could not shift away from Todd's body. The vertical steel strap that had come so close to impaling one or other of the men pressed into him, unyielding.

Modern historians find themselves appalled by the living conditions endured by convicts transported from the British Isles to Australia, many of them to Tasmania. In the 1820s, the Surgeon Superintendent Peter Cunningham wrote the following dour description of the environment in convict holds:

> Two rows of sleeping-births, one above the other, extend on each side of the between-decks, each berth being six feet square, and calculated to hold four convicts, everyone thus possessing 18 inches of space to sleep in – and ample space too.

Make what you will of the idea that 18 inches constitutes ample sleeping space – to the modern ear, such an arrangement sounds like something approaching sanctioned torture – but Brant and Todd had no such luxury. The steel strap effectively cut the basket neatly in two at its widest, from footwall to the right and hanging wall to the left. It sat slightly less than halfway if measured from the rear of the cage, closest to the telehandler. It meant each man was left with about 38 centimetres, or 15 inches, on which to rest his shoulders. Two small men could not lie on their backs in such a space, but both Brant and Todd were broad and bulky. If one lay back, the other was forced to balance on his side, one shoulder pushing into rock beneath and the other brushing the ceiling, his arm resting across the other man's chest.

Brant's position had one advantage. His head was next to the opening in the right-hand side of the basket and, with a bit of effort, it meant he could slither out into the void alongside. The light revealed that out there water dripped slowly from a single point in the shattered roof. Both men were suffering from thirst, their throats coated with rock dust.

Brant had managed to retrieve both his and Todd's helmets, but Todd's water bottle had disappeared way beneath the rock. They had to capture some of that water. Brant reached out of the basket and placed his upturned helmet beneath the dribble.

Slowly, the water level in the helmet rose until there was enough for a mouthful each. Todd took a sip. 'Fuck!' He spat, revolted. Brant had been using his helmet for months – the miners replace them every two years – and the webbing inside had built up a stinking scum. The heat of working within a mine is so great that many of the men had a constant heat rash around the area of contact between their foreheads and the sweat bands on their helmets. Brant and Todd set to ripping the webbing from within their helmets and scrubbing them as best they could. Finally, they had a couple of passably clean containers with which to catch a little precious water. Once they had wet their lips, they settled on a plan to fill one helmet and drink from it while the other caught the drips. It was a slow process, but they felt they might have just enough water to get by.

Brant had also retrieved both his and Todd's lamp batteries from the belts they had slashed from their bodies. He'd found their oxy-boxes, too. They were hard plastic, but they had a curve in them to fit their hips. They would use them as pillows. The boxes were uncomfortable, but preferable to rocks. Brant discovered he had a large lump at the back of his head. Must have been whacked when the roof came down. He would have to lie with his head turned to the side, creating a crick in his neck.

The batteries were a consolation. Todd's lamp was smashed beyond repair, so he cut the cord free with pliers. His battery would become a spare. They stowed it in a corner of the basket and used the other to power Brant's lamp. It was possible to get 14 or 15 hours from one of these batteries with the lamp on full power, and much longer on low beam. Nevertheless, they decided they would use the light only when necessary, conserving as much power as possible. Lying in the dark was unnerving, but it was preferable to discovering they had no charge if they really needed light later on.

Later on. How long might that mean? It was the question that lurked within each man's mind, unspoken. Todd and Brant agreed – forced themselves to agree, really – that Larry must have escaped the rock fall. He would be out there, they told each other, raising the alarm and providing the information rescuers would need. Help would come.

Todd, unable to exert his physical strength, assumed the role of psychic comforter. He was, he told Brant, a member of the mine search and rescue team. He knew rescuers would be called by now and a plan would be underway. 'They'll get us out, mate,' he said. 'They will. That's what all the training is about.'

Silently, though, he was praying. Todd had never been a churchgoing man. Weddings, funerals. That was about it. His church was taking to the bush on a Sunday morning with a gun and his dogs. It was all beyond reach now. He began asking God to deliver him, get him out of this place. He had undergone confinement training with the search and rescue team, but nobody could expect to be confined in a chamber as tight as this. If he lifted his arms, he had to keep his elbows bent at 90 degrees to keep from banging into the rocks above and he could not squirm about because Brant was pinned up next to him.

In an attempt to lift their spirits, the two of them enumerated their blessings.

They were alive.

They had air.

They had a bit of water.

Only seconds before their world caved in, they were leaning out of the basket. Could have been cut in half. But it hadn't happened.

What about that steel strap? Missed them. No broken bones.

All that rock, sharp as razors, hadn't opened a vein or an artery.

And Larry had got out. He knew exactly where they were. So did Cheesy. He'd checked on them no more than two minutes before the whole bloody thing happened. They still had a light if they needed it. They simply had to wait. And survive.

They lay there, listening to their new, constricted world groan and crack and spit around them. There was another sound that slipped in behind all the more obvious noises. Was it an air vent flapping? Zzzzzzzzstttt! Zzzzzzzzzzstttt! On and on. It was weird, and played on their nerves. Brant flashed his light. No air vent, this. It was fine dirt fretting from above, swishing on to the rocks.

The two men entered a strange dream-world. Perhaps they slept. Neither could quite discern the frontier between consciousness and unconsciousness. They were lost in utter darkness, lost inside their dilemma. Exhausted. All that mad digging to get Todd out. Todd had a watch with an illuminated dial, but time had lost its meaning. Meaning had lost its meaning.

Brant snapped awake. Woozily, he had been picturing the layout of the mine. Of course, he thought. We were under the brow of the drive when it came down on us. Right ahead, no more than a few metres away, was the open stope, the yawning emptiness that led up to higher levels. If he could just reach that gallery, he could find a way out!

He would dig a tunnel. Clean through the loose fill that Todd had dumped to build the bund. The bund was all that stood between the basket and freedom. He could see it.

Brant shook Todd awake. Explained his plan. He needed Todd to stay awake.

Brant slithered out of the basket into the tiny space.

He could do nothing more than squat. Stuck his lamp on his head, dragged the battery with him. Hard broken rock all around. Brant began tearing at it, trying to open a gap to the west.

But his little space was too small to store much rock. He laid a bit of it back behind him, but it was still too much. The bund must be encased in fallen rock. He would have to burrow under it.

Brant scrabbled at dirt, inching into it. Rock fell into the hole he was digging, leaving a small gap above, and he knew this was the way to do it. The base supporting the entrance to his hole would be rock and he would roll over it and dig beyond. A cold madness came over him and he went at it.

Rock above and rock below, but he was making progress. He tossed dirt behind him and pushed it against the wall of the void with his stockinged feet, his hands in their work gloves scraping and scratching into the mullock. As he opened up a hole big enough to insert his head, a wave of exhaustion wrapped around him.

'Todd,' he called.

'Yeah, buddy?' came the reply.

'Can you give me 10 minutes? Wake me up in 10 minutes.'

And Brant zoned out, falling into blackness.

'Brant? Can you hear me, cock? Ten minutes.'

Brant floated out of his stupor. Gotta get this hole dug. 'Yeah, Todd. I'll give you a yell in 20.'

And he was back at it, ripping away at dirt with his hands. Little by little, his body disappeared into the earth. He was a wombat. He flung soil beneath his stomach, wiggled forward, pushed it behind him with his feet. Inch by inch.

'Todd, can you give me 10?' The muffled voice floated back to the basket.

'Yeah, mate, 10 for you.'

Black-out.

And so it went. Ten minutes of sleep, 20 of activity. Brant's knees burned, though he could not actually lift himself to a kneeling position. The hole was hardly higher and wider than his body stretched out. He writhed forward, developing a technique. Tear a little soil away, pitch it beneath him, wriggle it back, slip it beneath his knees, ram it back with his toes.

'Another 10, Todd.'

'Ten's up, cock.'

Thirst tormented Brant. He squirmed back up the hole, emerged in the void, gulped water from a helmet. Back into the tunnel.

Hours passed. Many hours. His work gloves wore away at the fingertips. The pain of hard dirt splitting skin was simply another insult to a body already screaming in protest. This was not soil that any gardener would recognise. It was large chunks of pulverised rock, heavy gravel, sharp and hard and unforgiving.

'I need 10, Todd, give us 10.' And nothingness.

Todd's voice, far away. 'Wake up! Ten's up. Gotta wake up, Brant.'

Brant knew he had been lying down here too long. Every muscle had seized. His joints were locked. Couldn't move. Todd had fallen asleep, let him drift on. He knew it. He forced his body to answer his determination. Had never felt pain like it. His knees shrieked, but he managed to plough on. Twenty minutes. Ten off.

Brant was barely aware of the transformation taking place in his tunnel. He had been sweating so hard his clothes had been wet for hours. But slowly he realised he was both wet and cold. Water was soaking through the rock. It was chilling him down. He began shivering, mildly at first. His muscles began tensing. Where had all this water come from? The cold seeped into him and he couldn't go on.

Brant forced himself to squirm back out of the hole, his muscles and joints complaining with every small movement.

By the time he got out, Brant's whole body was in spasm. He was freezing. Every surface of the rock was slick with water. The ground beneath his knees was streaming.

'Get in here quick,' Todd commanded. 'You're not going to like this, but you've gotta cuddle in to me.'

Todd was shivering, too. Wet. Brant pushed his body into the basket and he couldn't imagine how he accomplished it. He was convulsing, as if someone had stuck electrodes all over him and fed high voltage charges to his nerve endings.

The two men held each other, exchanging body warmth, and slowly the storm wracking their bodies passed.

They had begged for water and now there was too much. Their cell had sprung a leak and instead of a tantalising drip, drip, drip, water cascaded through the rock. Combined with the airflow, wherever it was coming from, the spring chilled their tiny world. Like a Coolgardie safe, used by Australians everywhere before the era of refrigeration. Water ran down the footwall and splashed from rocks above. There was no escape for Todd and Brant. The rock dust caking their faces and infiltrating their hair turned to mud. Their miners' clothes – Todd in his bib and brace, Brant in his overalls – were drenched.

Brant had to get back into his tunnel. Strike out for freedom. Todd had lent him the warmth of his body and he would keep the fire stoked by hard work. He slipped out of the basket and slid into the hole. He was deep into it now; couldn't be much further. There wouldn't be any more 20 minutes on, 10 minutes off, either. He would break out in a rush.

Brant burrowed remorselessly, hurling scree behind him. He was frantic. Couldn't rest; not now. He was through the bund, striking broken quartz. Go, go! The open stope had to be right ahead.

And then his fingers caught on wire. Steel mesh. He couldn't believe it. Burrowed up. Burrowed down. Mesh. Hard steel reinforcing mesh, down from the backs. Blocking his path. Brant almost wept.

He scrambled back up the tunnel. Must have taken him 24 hours to get this far. 'Todd!' he screamed. 'Gotta find bolt-cutters, a hacksaw, anything!'

The two miners dug through the mess of rock in their basket. They shifted what seemed to them tonnes of stone. And they found . . . nothing.

'Fuck, Todd,' said Brant and his voice sounded hollow even to him. 'I've tried to go east and I've dug as far as I can to the west. We're nothing but rats in a cage. Fuckin' rats in a cage.'

Brant was asthmatic. He dug his Ventolin inhaler from his pocket, stuck it into his mouth and sucked on it.

He had burrowed 5.5 metres. In the world, it was late Wednesday night or maybe early Thursday morning, 27 April.

CHAPTER 6

WISH UPON A STAR

Kaye Russell realised a storm was coming down upon her family the moment Beaconsfield's police sergeant Pat McMahon and Rex Johnson trooped in to her home. The men had their heads down, not wanting to look directly into her eyes.

'It's not good, Kaye,' McMahon said. 'It's not good.'

Neither man told her that her son Todd was trapped. They didn't have to.

Kaye Russell had been in the shower when the earth moved. Felt the shock, knew it was serious; the biggest she had experienced. Came out of the shower, saw her husband Nobby looking confused, consulting the time, shaking his head.

Noel's agitation infected her. He looked at the clock; said 'Oh, it's not crib time. I don't . . . yes, they start at six. No . . .'. He kept peering at the clock as if it was the key to a secret that evaded him. Looked at Kaye, circled the problem.

Nobby was aware from his years in the mine that blasting occurred at regular times, usually when the men were in the crib for midnight smoko, or as they finished their shift. This couldn't be normal blasting. It was too powerful, anyway. He had almost been thrown from his chair and the computer in the corner very nearly slid off its desk.

There had been phone calls since. The whole town seemed alight with them: alarmed townsfolk seeking reassurance and information. Kaye and Nobby had learned of the call to Carolyn, asking for Todd to come to the mine with the rescue team because there'd been an accident. Nobby had been over there comforting Carolyn; had organised a friend to sit with her while he tried to find out what was happening.

It was obvious to Kaye, now. Rex, head of the rescue team, had already been in the mine; had seen with his own eyes what had happened. A rock fall; men trapped. Now here he was with the police sergeant, keeping his eyes on the carpet.

Kaye ran from the house into the night, hysteria gripping her. She had to get out.

She knew, but she prayed, running. 'Don't let it be Todd. Please, God, don't let it be Todd. Let him be all right, please, please, please.' As she fled, she looked across the road, across Weld Street where the council had built a skate park for the town's kids, right alongside the new cenotaph. And for a fleeting moment she was transfixed by something that would stay with her for all the long days to come.

A star fell. Right between two trees in the park. A falling star. 'Oh, dear God, please,' she prayed. 'You wish upon a falling star. Please, dear God, let Todd be okay. Let him be all right down there.'

A few days later she was told by one of the miners that the 925-metre level was almost directly below the park. She still does not know whether it is true, but she would believe forever that the falling star was a sign from the heavens meant for her.

Kaye felt compelled to go to the home of her daughter Mandy who lived at the other end of Beaconsfield.

And there things became even weirder.

Mandy told her mother that Todd had come to her in a vision only moments before. Kaye would not forget that, either. 'Mandy told me "Mum, he's going to be all right. He's okay. I've seen him. I've seen them carrying him out on the stretcher. And he said to me, 'I'm not going down in that bastard of a place again'. If he comes out with little marks and that on his face, mum, I'm going to freak out."'

'Yes,' said Kaye later. 'Mandy told me she could see marks on his face where the rock had hit him. This is what she told me.'

The night was already becoming a blur for Carolyn. Rex Johnson brought her father Alan Bennett from the mine, sat her down and told her that three men were trapped underground. One of them was Todd. Johnson could offer nothing more. There had been a rock fall and men were trapped. It was all he knew. It was, anyway, simply confirmation of something Carolyn had felt in some secret place inside her heart hours before. She had already spilled tears, but as silently as she could because she did not want to alarm young Trent, knowing he was lying awake in his bed, full of fear. She had forced herself to hold things together until she had solid information.

But she had phoned her sister Vicki in Port Sorell, avoiding the necessity of calling her mother Jill. She knew her mother would react with too much emotion, and with her own nerves stretched like violin strings she couldn't face the prospect of it. Not on the phone. Now Vicki and their mother were hurtling through the night, over dark hills and darker valleys to Beaconsfield.

Alan Bennett was almost certainly the only man in the mine that night who did not hear or feel the earthquake. He was manhandling a truck with 25 tonnes of ore in its tray up the decline, about 605 metres down. Encased within his cabin, the windows up and the roar of the truck's big motor blotting out all exterior sound, the first Al Bennett knew that something might be wrong was the sound of Cheesy calling for Larry on the radio. What really got his attention, though, was when Cheesy began calling for Todd. Why would he be calling for Todd? And why wasn't Todd answering? And then Cheesy began cursing the dust and telling every man to get up to the crib and ordering the truck drivers to park up anywhere they could find.

Bennett's world began to tilt. He caught a ride up to the crib where men who had seen the devastation within the 925 drive told him there didn't seem to be much hope for Todd, Brant and Larry.

When Alan Bennett emerged into the fresh night air of Beaconsfield, no man carried more weight on his shoulders than he.

He was leaving his son-in-law Todd down there and it tore at him. Seemed altogether wrong. An abandonment. But he had to get to Carolyn and try to support her, reassure her. He had always had a special

FOR THE PEOPLE OF THE TAMAR VALLEY.
AND ALL THOSE WHO REFUSE TO YIELD.

OUT
CREW 1
CREW

Previous page: The opening to the tunnel that was drilled 14.5 metres towards Brant and Todd by the raise bore. **This page:** The safety tag board at the Beaconsfield gold mine. The right-hand side of the board holds the identification tags of miners who are underground. When a miner surfaces, he moves his tag to the 'Out – Safe' side of the board.

Left: A biker studies messages left on the gate at the Beaconsfield mine. **Above:** Miners contemplate the difficult rescue.

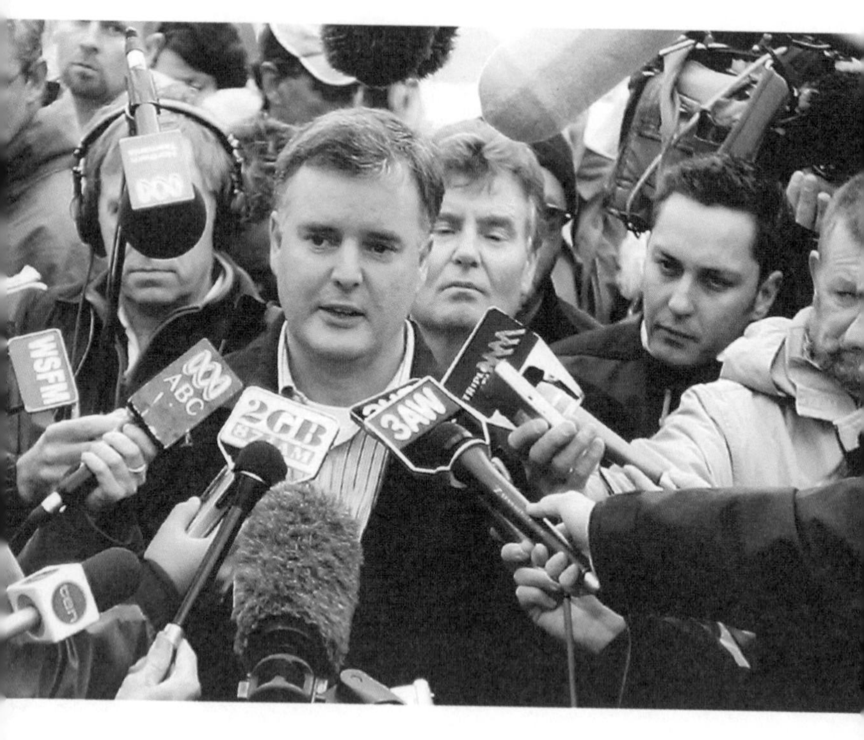
WSFM
ABC
2GB
3AW

This page: Richard Carleton, second from right, prepares to ask the last question of his life as mine manager Matthew Gill faces the media, 7 May 2006. **Next page:** Robbie Sears, air-legger and jumbo operator, emerges during attempts to rescue the trapped miners.

Clockwise from top left: Two local children place a goodwill message on the gates of the Beaconsfield mine. A woman kneels in prayer, oblivious to the surrounding media frenzy. A basket left by out-of-town well-wishers, containing bottles of beer and nuts. Beaconsfield mine workers Greg White (left), an underground fitter, and Peter Brennan, a diesel operator.

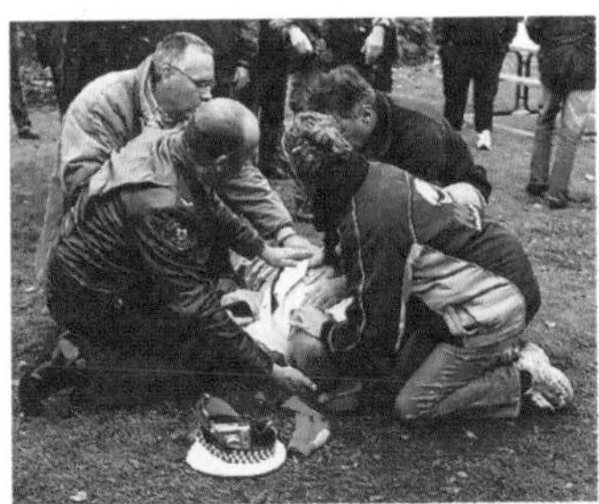

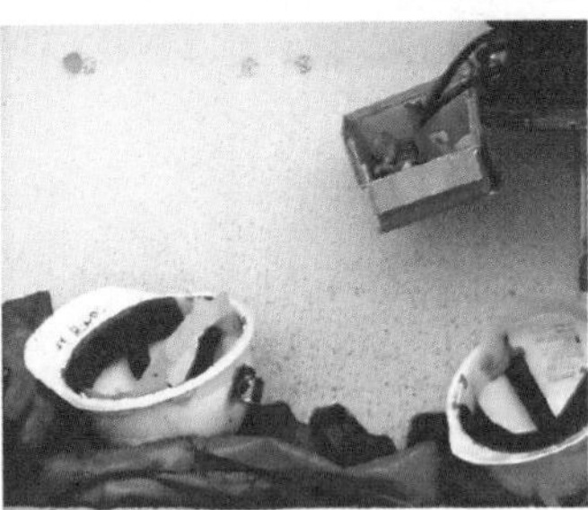

Clockwise from top left: The sign of a mine. Bystanders rushed to help 60 Minutes journalist Richard Carleton after he collapsed during a media conference outside the mine. Mine workers' safety equipment. Mine maintenance worker Rodger Gates grinds a metal tube constructed, but never used, to line the rescue tunnel. **Next page:** The Beaconsfield poppet, bathed in floodlight, towers above historic mine buildings.

Left: Worshippers sing hymns of hope at Beaconsfield's Uniting Church. **Above:** Sign scrawled outside the Uniting Church in Weld Street, Beaconsfield.

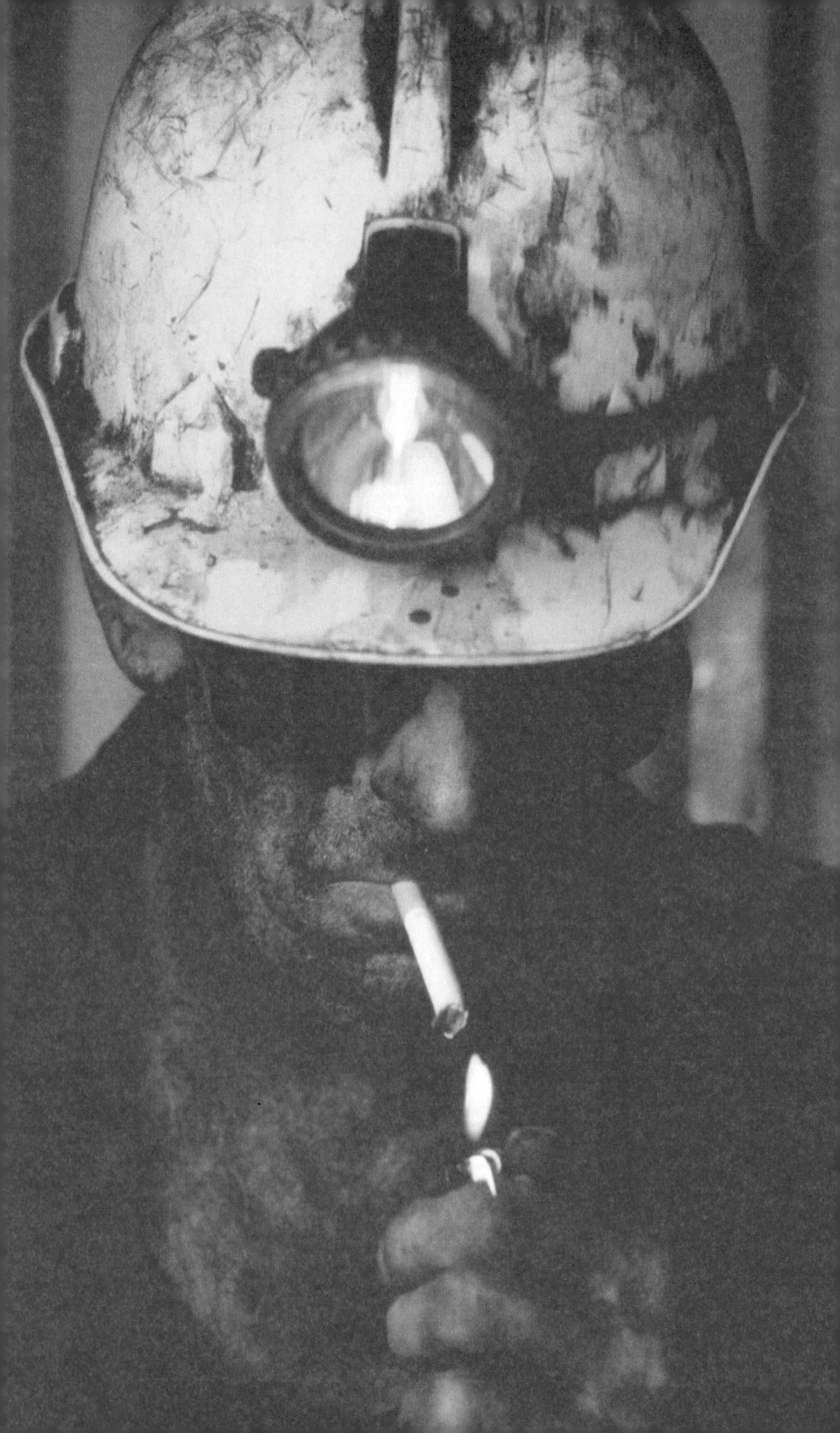

bond with his daughter. He was cracking up but he couldn't allow himself to do it. Had to be strong.

Carolyn turned out to be the strong one. She met her father at the door to her home. She seemed so calm, it was eerie. 'Dad,' she said, 'he's still alive. I know.'

Al Bennett wanted to believe it too, but he knew what the men at the mine were saying. He wouldn't tell Carolyn.

'Well,' he said, 'You know what Todd's like. If there's a way, he'll get out.'

Bennett's wife Jill had already arrived from Port Sorell and she was frantic with worry, weeping.

Here, then, was a man who in the space of hardly more than an hour had gone from driving a truck on another routine night at work to trying to soothe a wife nearing hysteria and supporting a daughter who seemed to have entered a plane beyond a reality she might not be able to confront – all the while entrusted with the secret knowledge that his son-in-law was probably dead. This was going to be a long night, the worst night in Alan Bennett's life.

Kaye Russell could not contain herself. She had to keep moving. Almost out of her mind, she walked to Carolyn's house and the two of them agreed the most likely place they might discover real information was at the offices of the West Tamar Council, right across the road from the minehead. Together, they hurried up Weld Street, the cold of the night barely registering, turned left up West Street and found a confused little crowd already gathering outside the red-brick council chambers.

Kaye's younger son Stephen and her daughter Lisa were there, and the nightshift crew, wall-eyed out of the depths, milled about. The council had finished drafting its disaster plan only days before, and council officials, police and a team of psychological counsellors called in from Launceston were arriving. Every man who had been down the mine that night would receive counselling, reliving their ghastly moments, just talking, talking, before they went home. There would be sleepless nights ahead, they were told, and feelings of guilt because they could not help their mates. It was normal.

A big policeman from across the Tamar River at George Town, Inspector Paul Reynolds, offered no false hope. He told the Russells the circumstances of the rock fall made optimism a difficult path. Kaye was aghast.

My God, that's my son down there, she thought.

Darren Geard, a slight nervy man with gingery hair, was struck hard by the sight of the Russells searching for reassurance that simply wasn't available.

He stumbled across the road and sat on the steps of a small house by the mine and cried for 20 minutes. The night's events tumbled through his head. He thought, *Shit, you know, looking at Carolyn, that could be my wife Pru.*

Mick Borrill had the wives of the missing miners on his mind, too. He wanted to make sure that miners – recognisable faces – would break the news to the families. Rex Johnson, he knew, was the man to tell Carolyn Russell. But Borrill had also been told that police would be dispatched to contact Brant's wife Rachel and Larry Knight's partner Jacqui.

'It can't happen,' he protested. 'You've got to get blokes from the mine who know the wives. I mean, this is going to be a terrible shock to these women, and they need someone they know.' Borrill had met Jacqui at a

Christmas function in Launceston and had found her to be a nice woman. A female police officer offered to drive him in to Launceston to get her and the two little kids. But he was told it was all sorted out and not to worry, one of the miners would go.

Borrill later discovered that two police officers, no familiar faces at all, were dispatched to rouse Jacqui in Launceston, and he was appalled. It was callous. Cruel.

Borrill and a policewoman set off to the Webb home in Beauty Point. Rachel was in a deep sleep. They pounded at the door and tapped on windows for more than 10 minutes.

Rachel was confused and frightened when she heard the commotion at her door. She was alone. Her twin children, Zac and Zoey, aged 18, were away partying in Launceston.

Rachel had never lacked courage. She had run a little farm alone out in Tasmania's lonely mountain country for a year when Brant had first gone mining in Beaconsfield. A few months previously, however, someone had stolen Brant's motorcycle from the back shed right here in Beauty Point. Rachel had been no wilting violet then. Shortly after the break-in she was driving in Beauty Point and saw the motorcycle with a young man aboard skid out of a side street. She gave chase towards Beaconsfield, yelling over her mobile phone for Brant to call the cops. She kept right on the tail of the bike as it jumped concrete street dividers, ran stop signs and eventually left the road, ploughing across open parkland. She lost her quarry only when the boy dropped the bike and took off on foot through trees and disappeared. Still, a thief had been in her home. It shook Rachel up. Brant hoisted security cameras along the side of the house and strung lights that stayed on all night after that.

And here were people banging on her door and tapping on the windows and shouting in the night. It was 12.30 am. She hunkered down beneath the blankets. Mick Borrill eventually roused her by calling the house on his mobile phone. The police officer went in while Rachel dressed. Borrill felt Rachel wasn't comprehending when he told her there had been a bad accident at the mine and that Brant was involved.

Rachel, however, seized the meaning of everything she was told.

She realised straight away that she had to have control, to think rationally, get as much information as she could. Decipher the facts. Don't panic. Not yet. For Brant. For her.

'How much air have they got?' she demanded of Mick.

'Heaps,' he said. 'They've got airflow.' Not knowing at all.

'What happened?' Rachel asked.

'It's pretty big; a big seismic activity,' said Mick.

Rachel wanted to know why Brant was down so deep in the mine. She thought he was working above ground.

Mick explained that Cheesy had asked Brant to help out on this job. At 925 metres.

Rachel was shocked. So deep. She and Brant had discussed all the danger that went with the seismic activity that seemed to be becoming more frequent. He'd agreed he wouldn't go deep down any more.

When Rachel and Mick arrived at the council chambers, tea and coffee had already been set up outside for the miners and members of the families who had hurried through the night: the beginnings of a disaster plan.

Rachel looked across the road, up at the big frame where the winder sat unmoving. Everything was so still. They'd shut down the mine. No noise. There was a haze of dust. Right up around the frame, hanging there in the light. A strong smell. The smell of soil. The scent of the earth had been pushed up with dust from all that way beneath the ground.

She understood. This really was a disaster. The evidence of it boiled into the air up here. She could smell the earth that was trapping her husband.

Soon, those around Rachel began urging her to call her children, Zac and Zoey.

She knew they were suggesting that Brant was dead; that she had better prepare herself and her twins. But they had nothing to show her and she would not believe Brant was dead. No, she wouldn't prepare herself for that.

A single thought: *He's down there, trapped. How are they going to get him out?* She told Zac and Zoey to stay in Launceston. She didn't want them driving through the night on a lonely road to . . . what?

Later, Rachel sat in a room of the council chambers aware only of inactivity. No rescue was being organised. Her parents, Michael and Julie Kelly, sat with her. They had raced from their graceful old federation home above the Tamar River at Legana, half an hour from Beaconsfield near Launceston. Now they watched desolation settle on her. They could hardly bear her anguish, but they had no way of helping her.

Larry Knight's partner Jacqui was there, too. Jacqui was terrified. She clung to Mick Borrill. Hung on to him for an hour until Larry's mother Pearl and her partner Harry Banks arrived.

The burly George Town police officer Paul Reynolds tried to explain to the families the gravity of the matter. 'It's so big; a bad cave-in. It's grim.' Rachel felt he was really saying that Brant and Todd and Larry were gone.

How can you think that? she wondered. Rachel put her head on the table and wouldn't look at the policeman. *If that's his opinion,* she thought, *everyone thinks it and they won't be rushing*. Time was fleeing. *If Brant's under rock, they've got to hurry*. Why weren't they hurrying?

Down the street, Carolyn's house was filling with family. Todd's sister Lisa, Todd's brother Stephen, Todd's parents Noel and Kaye. Carolyn's parents Alan, still in shock from his experience underground, and Jill, frenzied and panicked. Vicki brought her two small children and tucked them into bed alongside Carolyn's youngest, Liam and Maddison.

Noel and Kaye and their family eventually drifted away to their own homes. Carolyn, recognising she would need strength, sought sleep. She and Vicki stretched out on the couch and their parents nodded off on easy chairs. By dawn, none of them felt they had managed more than half an hour's sleep.

More than 2,000 kilometres north, at Beenleigh on the Queensland Gold Coast, Lauren Kielmann was in bed when the phone rang at 7 am on Wednesday, 26 April. It was Jacqui, the woman her father had been living with in Launceston for the past five years. Lauren had never got along well with Jacqui. Why would she be calling?

For most of Lauren's life, her dad Larry Knight had flown her regularly from Queensland to Tasmania for holidays. But Lauren hadn't made the journey or seen her father for the past three years.

There was urgency in the Tasmanian woman's voice.

'Your Dad's been in an accident at the mine,' Jacqui said. 'Turn on the TV.'

And there on the screen was a reporter telling of a rock fall in the mine at Beaconsfield. A mini-earthquake had brought down a tunnel. Three men were missing. Lauren was enveloped in shock. Of all the mines in the world, of all the miners in the world, it had to be Beaconsfield and her father.

In a whirl, Lauren pulled out her biggest suitcase and began throwing clothes in it. Later, she would have no idea why she packed bikinis and evening frocks. There were phone calls, a hurried farewell to her boyfriend Jason, a rush to the airport. It was as if she were in a trance. Her grandfather – her mother's father, Reginald Toms – had died on Easter Sunday, only 10 days previously. Lauren was still grieving for him. Her world was collapsing around her.

Lauren is 20 and had never known Larry Knight as a traditional father figure. He and her mother, Carolyn, married in 1984. Larry was already a miner, and the couple lived for a while in the little tin mining town of Waratah in the Tasmanian west coast wilderness. Lauren was born a couple of years later, but the marriage ended when she was just two. Her mother remarried, to Peter Kielmann, a diesel mechanic who these days travels Australia and the world training road-paving crews, and he became the man who really raised Lauren. The Kielmann family moved to Queensland when Lauren was still a little girl aged maybe five or six.

She calls Peter Kielmann 'Dad' and she took his surname as her own. He was always the father who attended special days at her school, was there for her graduation, sat with her through illnesses, took her to the beach. He and Lauren's mother have another daughter, Jessi, now 17, but there was never any suggestion of difference between the girls. They were sisters; Kielmanns.

Lauren considered herself fortunate. She had two fathers. Called them both 'Dad'.

Larry was the father she visited on school holidays. He had green-grey eyes, the same as hers. They were both left-handed. Larry the Tasmanian Dad was exotic to Lauren. He loved walking in the forest and trawling around graveyards, peering at old gravestones, piecing together the past. Often he took Lauren to the Beaconsfield cemetery, where his grandparents were buried. He was forever collecting: strange-shaped bottles, rocks, number plates, old motorcycle parts. He was infatuated with motorcycles. Larry had a shed full of motorbikes, wore a bikers' goatee and rode a big Harley-Davidson. He never joined a motorcycle club, never wore bikers' colours, but he had plenty of mates in bike clubs: Devil's Henchmen, Satan's Riders, God's Squad. When Lauren, still a little girl, came to Launceston to stay with Larry, his mate, a big biker named Barrel, read bedtime stories to her.

Larry for the most part of Lauren's life was a voice on the end of a phone. He often called for a chat. Often too he would natter for half an hour or more to Lauren's mother, Carolyn. The long-dead marriage couldn't kill off the friendship. Larry valued connections with his past and had a loyalty about him. About six years ago during his two-month odyssey around Australia, Larry and his mate Justin 'Stevo' Stevenson, Jacqui's brother, set up house on the Gold Coast not far from Lauren's home. They stayed for months, and Larry and his daughter spent good times together. She thought of him sometimes as a best friend rather than a regular father; a bloke in whom she could confide. A few years ago, she was picked up in a Gold Coast car park by the police for drinking while underaged. She couldn't bring herself to tell her mother. Instead, she phoned Larry. He sent her $200 to pay the fine.

Three years ago, when Lauren was in Year 12, she sat down and wrote her father a long letter for his birthday. It told him that she had often felt keenly his absence from the special days of her life but that she treasured the periods they had spent together as she grew. She was proud to be his daughter and had come to understand the reality that though they were physically apart, they were connected by a bond. She joked in the letter that he had taught her it was okay sometimes to forget to brush her teeth and to stay up long past her normal bedtime. Larry phoned her after he received his birthday gift and told her he would keep it forever. It would be their secret – he would conceal it from all others. And he confided to her its hiding place: in the winding cavity behind a big old mahogany clock on his mantelpiece. Their hearts would reside there as the years stretched by. But no air tickets came in the mail and they had not physically seen each other again.

Lauren sat numb in her economy seat as the airliner soared south. Complicated memories and emotions crowded in on her. Perhaps Larry would be released from the mine by the time she reached Tasmania. Surely she would see him again.

She was required to change planes in Melbourne. As she settled into her new seat, bound for Launceston, a passenger with dark hair, a circular beard and black sunglasses plonked himself down beside her. He looked at the pretty young woman, her head down and blond hair falling across her face, and used the words he always used to break the ice on planes. 'Business or holiday?' he asked.

Lauren needed to speak to somebody, anyone, and it came out in a rush: she was travelling to Beaconsfield where her father was trapped in a gold mine.

The man beside her was flabbergasted. He was a miner. Worked these days in the big uranium enterprise at Roxby Downs in South Australia. He had a few days off and was heading home to Deloraine in Tasmania. His name was Kym Ronin.

'Who's your dad?' he asked. Her response knocked the breath clean out of him. Ronin had worked years before at Que River near Rosebery in Tasmania's west, mining lead, zinc, copper and gold. One of his workmates was Larry Knight. Ronin had kept in loose touch with Larry over the years, but hadn't seen him for ages. Wasn't even aware he was working at Beaconsfield.

But he remembered clearly Larry's pride at fathering a baby girl named Lauren. He had held the child in his own arms. Almost 20 years ago. And here she was sitting next to him on a plane, a grown woman, despairing. Ronin tried to comfort the girl. Larry, he said, was a cool, calm bloke. He'd know what to do in an emergency. But Ronin knew the dangers, how easily and quickly a life could get snuffed out underground. It wasn't so long ago a miner had been killed at Roxby Downs, blown up by explosives. He vowed to go to Beaconsfield.

CHAPTER 7

HAS HE GOT AIR?

Rachel had to talk to someone who knew everything there was to know about mines. At four o'clock in the morning, sitting dazed in the council chambers, she picked up a phone and dialled Kerry Butler's number. 'Brant's trapped in the mine,' she said, and he could hear the fear in her voice. 'There are three of them down there. Trapped.'

Butler is one of Brant Webb's closest mates. At 50, he is more than that. A father figure. He lured Brant into the underground in the first place.

Butler remembered the moment he recognised that Brant had it in him to venture down the mineshaft. It was six, maybe seven years ago. Out on the ocean.

'I met Brant through another bloke we both knew, and when he found out I had a boat, it was like a magnet,' Butler says. 'It's an 8-metre Hobson, an ex-crayfishing boat from King Island. Got a 6-cylinder Volvo motor in it. I like my fishing, but I reckon Brant knows more about fishing than I ever knew.

'He was living down on his farm at Western Creek those days and when I said we ought to go fishing for stripy trumpeter out of Bicheno, over on the Tasmanian east coast, he jumped at it.

'There was Brant, me, my son Kyle – he's 21 now, but he was just a kid then – and another bloke called Mudguts. Mudguts's real name is Merv Cross. He lives at Bicheno, runs a barge at an oyster farm at Coles Bay and he's a beer drinker from hell. Knows all about the fishing over there, though.

'So anyway, we trailered the boat over to Bicheno on the back of a transporter. I used to keep it at a different port every year to try all the different sorts of fishing around the state.

'We went out to the shelf, about 10 miles out. The land was just a speck on the horizon, and it's a bit of a funny feeling out there, knowing that if you get into trouble – well, you're a long way from anything.

'We started setting drop lines in more than 40 metres of water and pretty soon we pulled a couple of big stripies. We threw the heads and the guts over the side and it wasn't long before we had a shark circling around.

'He was a monster, a mako, almost as long as the boat. The hair stood up on the back of your neck just to look at him.'

The mako is a creature of fearsome beauty, one of the fastest and most aggressive fishes of prey. It is of that species of shark known as mackerel, and its close relative is the white pointer. It is not unusual to hear fishermen speak of a mako as a blue pointer, and big game hunters of the sea tell of seeing makos jump 6 metres clear of the water. They have been known to ram boats and if you happened to be strong enough to pull one aboard a boat, you had better step carefully because it would casually snap off your leg with a bite from its teeth, long and curved like scimitars.

The finest description of such a beast is in Ernest Hemingway's *The Old Man and the Sea*:

> He was a very big Mako shark, built to swim as fast as the fastest fish in the sea and everything about him was beautiful except his jaws. His back was as blue as a sword fish's and his belly was silver and his hide was smooth and handsome. He was built as a swordfish except for his huge jaws which were tight shut now as he swam fast, just under the surface with his high dorsal fin knifing through the water without wavering. Inside the closed double lip of his jaws all of his eight rows of teeth were slanted inwards. They were not the ordinary pyramid-shaped teeth of most sharks. They were shaped like a man's fingers when they are crisped like claws. They were nearly as long as the fingers of the old man and they had razor-sharp cutting edges on both sides. This was a fish built to feed on all the fishes in the sea, that were so fast and strong and well armed that they had no other enemy.

This then was the vision that transfixed Kerry Butler and his fishing mates as they lazed off the continental shelf almost out of sight of Tasmania's eastern coast.

'Well, we were concentrating on the shark and we drifted over one of the lines – we had them hanging from buoys – and we got the propeller all wrapped up in a buoy rope,' Butler recalls.

'And there we were all the way out there and we weren't going to be able to go anywhere and I looked at my son in horror. I thought what in the bloody hell are we going to be able to do now?

'And the next thing, no discussion at all, Brant's got his tee-shirt off, grabbed a knife and he's slipped over the side into the water!

'There he is over the back, chopping at the rope around the propeller and all we're thinking is oh shit, he's in there with this bloody great shark. We couldn't believe it.

'Then he's up back over the side, the job's done. I looked at Mudguts and my young bloke and they looked at me and Brant's laughing away, no worries at all.

'He was either mad or he had a backbone or both, this bloke. He got a bit of respect from me that day, I can tell you. Yeah, he had a backbone.

'All I could think to say was, "Have you ever thought of working underground, Brant?"'

Butler had been a miner since he was a boy. In 1974 he went underground in Western Australia near the old gold town of Coolgardie. He and his brother David became specialists in the esoteric art of air-legging, lumping hand-operated drills in the most confined of spaces. Air-leggers are the royalty of underground miners and Kerry's proud to tell anyone that his brother David has won more air-legging competitions in Australia over the last 10 years than any other miner.

Kerry Butler figured after a few years of living from pay to pay and spilling rocks onto his head that there was a better way of making money out of mining than working for someone else. He went into business, establishing a contracting company called Brereton Mining.

At his peak, he was employing 70 miners at the Renison Bell mine between the Tasmanian west coast towns of Zeehan and Rosebery.

When the Beaconsfield shaft reopened in 1999, Brereton Mining provided the miners. Recruited them from all over the place. Todd Russell was one of them. A local. A big, strong fellow is always useful in a mine.

But Brant was special to Butler. A mate and a bloke crazy enough to jump in the sea with a mako shark and chop a rope from a fouled propeller.

Butler knew well that not everyone could abide mining. He'd seen strong men who seemed unafraid of anything brought low by simply entering the cage for the journey down the shaft. Claustrophobia grabbed them and spun their heads. The black tunnels below could get them pleading to be removed. He was in the habit of taking any potential recruits down into the earth to observe their reaction. Any negative response and he'd have them out of there. He did not judge them poorly. The environment was simply too confronting for some people.

But Brant proved to be fascinated by the world below Beaconsfield. He was not perturbed by the dark, the heat or the noise. Quite the reverse. He was transported by the machinery crawling around down there in the gloom. He was, he said, 'roped, just hooked' by the experience. He loved the raw power of the boggers charging into shattered ore on the stopes, the howl of their motors cannoning off the walls. And the heat? Why, he had spent his youth in north Queensland. It was welcome compared with Tasmania's cold winds. Butler put Brant to work operating one of those boggers, loading dirt, and watched him as he moved through the mine's food chain over the years, learning the ins and outs of most of the tasks.

But now Brant was lost somewhere in the deep. And Rachel, her voice pleading for reassurance, was on the phone at four o'clock in the morning, telling Kerry Butler – the man who had persuaded his young mate on the ocean there was a future underground – that her man was locked away from the sky.

'Has he got air?' Butler asked. It was the only thing he could think to say. The sort of thing a miner had to know. If there was air, there might be a chance. Without knowing it, he was throwing a lifeline to Rachel. Mick Borrill had already told her the boys had ample air, though he had no way of knowing it, and she had no way of knowing that Borrill was making it up.

'I'll be there tomorrow,' Butler said.

Rachel asked her parents to drive her home. She needed to anchor herself within familiar surroundings, to sit in the snug TV lounge that Brant had wired up with sound systems and the TV linked to the security cameras. She needed to think; to connect with her husband.

Rachel could not stay within sight of the poppet head in the night and could no longer bear to breathe in the scent of collapsed earth wafting out of the shaft, dust settling. The gold mine management had declared the whole place too dangerous, and every miner had been ordered out of the underground. Brant, Todd and Larry were left down there, beyond assistance. The sense of silent lonely tunnels beneath her feet made Rachel dizzy. She felt about to crumble at the thought that no one was rushing to Brant's aid.

Once she was home and her parents had gone, though, panic threatened to engulf her. Threats without name trod the pre-dawn. Rachel needed a friend.

Vinnie Tunks had been sitting by the phone at his home in Beaconsfield for more than an hour. He knew Rachel would call. The close mates' network had been running hard in the night. A friend, Greg Crowden, had already been in touch.

Crowden, a young miner of two years' experience, a remote bogger operator, had received a visit from Corey Verhey from the mine rescue team. Verhey, fresh out of the mine after witnessing the devastation in the 925 tunnel with the rest of the rescue team, banged on the door at Crowden's place up on the hill above Beaconsfield around 3 am. Woke him up. 'Sit back down, mate,' Corey told him, shaky. 'I've got something really bad to tell you. Three blokes are dead in the mine and one of them is Brant.'

Crowden could hardly process the news. 'It really spun me out,' he recalls. He had to contact Vinnie.

But when Greg Crowden phoned, Vinnie Tunks refused to sanction the idea that Brant's life could be over. He sat there after his first conversation with Crowden, filtered it through his mind and called back. 'I'm not having it, Greg,' he told Crowden. 'I won't accept it. Brant's not dead, that's all there is to it.'

Vinnie had a specialty. He was a welder. For three or four years he'd been contracted to the mine, welding machinery and equipment that got banged up among the hard rock. Prided himself in over-engineering the gear he tended because he knew the punishment a mine could hand out.

He'd never been impressed by the baskets used to hoist men on the booms of telehandlers. They didn't seem strong enough to him. Flimsy. So he'd taken pains to make them tougher. Vinnie had replaced the steel posts in the corners and sides of the baskets with sturdier pillars. The baskets had gates on hinges at the front and they seemed superfluous. So he welded them up, lending greater strength to the whole apparatus.

If Brant and Todd had been in the basket when the tunnel fell in on them, he figured, they would have a chance. It could take a big hit without collapsing. He was sure of it.

Vinnie at 25 was a decade younger than Brant and Rachel. It didn't seem to matter and they had become firm friends. Afternoons around at Brant and Rachel's place were long parties that went on into the night, and age was no barrier to anyone. Kerry Butler was heading towards 50; Tony Lyall, the doctor, was in his mid-50s; Greg Crowden was 34; his girlfriend Jodie Curran was younger. Vinnie Tunk's girlfriend Kirsty was still in her teens.

When they could all get together, the blokes poured big glasses of Bundaberg rum or bourbon and cola, Brant headed to his bar and mixed up cocktails, steaks and pork chops were tossed on the barbecue and Rachel fried chips and steamed vegetables in her kitchen. Friends appeared from nowhere, the music system was cranked up. Foo Fighters, matchbox twenty, Nickelback; guitar riffs, jokes and tall stories ricocheted across the table on the enclosed back porch. Once the sun was gone, the porch glowed blue and green and pink from multi-coloured lights Brant and Rachel had strung up. There were more soft-tinted lights across the lawn beneath a gazebo Brant had built, and in the gazebo was a big hot tub steaming away. Pretty soon the party would move to the tub. Just about everyone who visited Brant and Rachel knew to bring their swimming costumes, but there were always spares around the house for those who forgot. More drinks were poured and there was another stereo on the spa's deck. The lights changed colour to the beat and the steam shrouded them when the nights were cold.

Brant and Rachel seemed like family to Vinnie. They all had a touch of scallywag about them, loved joking around, and on warm days they ripped up the water out on the Tamar in Brant's ski boat.

Vinnie and Brant both took pleasure in motors, motorbikes,fast cars. Brant had an oversized motor fitted to the ski boat, 115 horsepower, and Vinnie designed and built a stainless steel frame to take the strain of it. He'd fashioned ski poles for the boat, and he and Brant spent hours in Vinnie's workshop in Beaconsfield, mucking about with tools and machinery and designs.

Vinnie was transported by the pursuit of speed. Raced motorcycles. Rachel worried about him. His last crash on his Honda CR250 had fractured his skull. Rachel and Vinnie often sat and talked for hours about . . . everything and nothing. They shared a passion: both of them hero-worshipped Brant.

No, Brant couldn't be dead, Vinnie thought. He sat waiting for the call he knew would come from Rachel. No way he could sleep; not with his best friend in danger.

Vinnie had the receiver in his hand before the first shrill of the phone was through. 'Hello,' said Rachel, and it was hardly more than a whisper.

'Hello,' said Vinnie. 'I'm on my way.' It was all either of them needed to say.

He was at Rachel's house within five minutes. Rachel clung to the boy.

'He's going to be all right, you know,' Vinnie said.

'I know,' Rachel replied. 'I can feel him.'

They sat together in the small lounge-room, barely speaking, pictures on the TV moving with the sound turned off as dawn spilled in.

'I think I'm going to need you, Vinnie,' Rachel said.

'I'm not going anywhere,' Vinnie declared. She looked at him. A sweet boy. A wispy goatee, like so many men around here. Five rings in his ears, a silver stud through an eyebrow, another in his tongue and when he stripped to shorts for parties in the tub, his nipples were pierced, too. A Beaconsfield boy seeking identity. His eyes always looked steadily at you. Dependable. A quiet strength in there. Vinnie was about to set up his own steel fabrication and welding company. Going to make something of himself. Now, though, he was going to look after his friends.

He took himself out into the living-room and stretched out on the couch. He wasn't going to leave until all this dreadful business was over. Rachel needed her private space. He would be the gatekeeper.

A few hours later, Rachel roused herself. She felt the need to go to the mine, remove all Brant's belongings from that place and bring them home. Vinnie drove her to Beaconsfield, went in to the mine's above-ground offices and cleaned out Brant's locker. Overalls, a few pullovers, the clothes he had worn from home the day before. Someone handed over Brant's crib bag, a canvas satchel with reflective strips sewn onto it. Vinnie found Brant's car keys and Rachel insisted on driving her husband's black Commodore home. Brant might be trapped deep in the mine, but she didn't want anything left that could connect him to the place. He didn't belong here. Not any more. When he came home, his mining days would be over.

Rachel dreaded what she might feel when she sat in Brant's car. His favourite peaked cap with the Bundaberg logo on it sat in the passenger's seat and she touched it. She would never be able to explain it but she felt soothed. There was an absence of loneliness.

She drove through Beaconsfield and stopped at the service station. Filled Brant's car with fuel. Felt impelled to do it. She wanted everything to be ready for her man when he returned.

When she pulled up in the driveway at home in Beauty Point, her parents were there. Her father Michael approached, expecting to find his daughter distressed, maybe out of her mind. To his astonishment, she seemed perfectly serene.

'It's okay, Dad,' she said. 'Everything's going to be fine. I have this strong feeling that Brant wants me to know that everything is going to turn out right.'

Kerry Butler was as good as his word, too, and travelled in from his home at Ulverstone, about an hour away. But before he visited Rachel he caught up with Cheesy, Geardie and Garth Bonney. He wanted their versions of what had occurred underground. When he had listened to their straightforward accounts, Butler came to a single conclusion. Brant, Todd and Larry were all gone. Beyond help. Couldn't have survived what their fellow miners, who knew the underground better than anyone, had seen with their own eyes.

'I knew the percentages were zilch,' Butler says. 'I've been in mines all my life and I could visualise what went down.'

He resolved, though, that he would be no prophet of doom. Not publicly, and not to Rachel. A TV news camera caught him outside the mine and he said that if the men had air and water they had a chance.

When he reached Rachel at her home in Beauty Point, he found her strangely calm. 'Brant's still alive,' she declared. There was a fierceness to her conviction.

CHAPTER 8

WATER TORTURE

The frustration was almost too much to swallow. That mesh blocking the end of the tunnel drained Brant's will. So close! He was sure he had been within a body length of escape. He'd give 10 years of his life for bolt-cutters.

Todd felt it, too. He couldn't allow Brant to lie there in the dark, his spirit sapped. They needed a new plan. Needed to keep busy.

If there was to be no escape and they were forced to loll on the rock, waiting for rescue, their most pressing tasks were to stay alive and to get their minds off the devastation entrapping them. Todd had the small square of mesh protecting his head and chest from falling rock, but it was not wide enough. Most of Brant's body and half his head and chest were unprotected, no matter how hard he squashed up against Todd's body. The mesh gave the men an idea.

A bundle of short cab straps hung from the wire of their cage. The straps, made of strong webbing, were each about 25 centimetres long, with steel hooks at both ends. A plan began to emerge. If Brant could fashion the straps into a criss-cross netting, he could string the arrangement from the steel pillars of the basket and grant himself some protection from stones falling from above. It wouldn't be as satisfactory as steel mesh because the webbing straps would 'give' and slip aside to allow smaller rocks to skid through. Still, the net might hold a very large rock, and prevent it from crushing Brant.

Besides, the business of stringing the straps together, working out the most suitable pattern and settling on precisely where the net could be anchored passed the time. The slow passage of minutes turning into hours sapped a man's resolve. Half an hour seemed an epoch. A full hour was unthinkable. Todd, still shattered and in shock from his time spent crushed beneath the fall, slipped regularly into the mercy of sleep. Brant worked away with the intricacies of his net. There were not enough straps to provide protection for anything more than his head and chest, but the contraption gave him some peace. The work also kept his body active. His muscles jerked with cold, and his knees and back ached.

Brant needed a smoke. Todd was a reformed smoker. Hadn't had a cigarette for nine months. He was sickened by the idea of cigarette smoke hanging in the limited amount of air in the tiny chamber. 'Ah fuck, cock. Just give it up. Filthy habit,' he told Brant.

No chance. Brant was addicted and the whole rotten circumstance of his incarceration tore at his nerves. He needed that nicotine. Had a plastic cigarette case almost full burning a hole in his pocket. He waited until Todd drifted into sleep, stuck his head out into the void and lit up. Smoke curled up into rock, hanging like a fog. Brant puffed, calming himself, but he stubbed the cigarette out, half-smoked, and stuck the butt back in his case. There were few worldly pleasures down here, and he would conserve everything.

Todd woke up, sniffed the air. 'You've been smoking, you fucking prick,' he accused.

'No, I haven't,' Brant replied, guilty as a schoolkid.

'Bullshit,' said Todd.

'Yeah, all right, I have. So what?'

The men were falling fast into a relationship not unlike that of many old married couples. Nagging, yet knowing there was nothing for it but to tolerate the other, ride out the small annoyances of their captivity. They could squabble, but what would it gain either of them? They needed each other, and they couldn't go anywhere.

Neither man spoke of it, but each recognised a hideous truth: if he had been trapped down here alone, his sanity would have evaporated.

Brant and Todd agreed that they could not both sleep at the same time. One or the other must always be listening for any sound of rescue, and they could not afford to miss the warning signs if the earth were to shift again.

It meant, of course, great loneliness and discomfort for the one nominated to stay awake as the other floated into unconsciousness. Dread lurked in the darkness, clawing away at hope.

Lying there, shivering with cold, cursing the water that flowed and spattered and gurgled all around, hearing the occasional rock falling and rattling into the scree, aware of the breath of the other man right beside your ear; there was torment in all of it.

Brant and Todd began to understand the meaning of water torture. The rhythmic *drip, drip, splash* drilled into their brains. There was no relief. It built into a maddening symphony, hallucinogenic, dragging the mind on disconcerting excursions into unreality.

Neither of the men could stretch his body to its full length. The width of the basket could not accommodate them. Their legs were always bent. Their heads, resting on tough plastic oxy-boxes, pushed hard against rigid mesh and unforgiving upright steel pillars and their feet strained against the opposite side of the cage. Brant's feet and ankles, unprotected by boots, banged against stone every time he tried to shift to a more comfortable position.

There was, too, the distasteful business of urination. Lacking food, they slurped water. When the bladder of one of them could no longer hold out, he had to roll himself away from the other and piss as carefully as he could into the rock.

Neither wished to spray the other, and neither wanted to urinate on his own clothes or into his bed of rock, even if it was already soaked with water. Grit worked its way into their eyes, filth built up on their clothes and on every exposed part of their bodies, but they couldn't abide the final indignity of lying in their own waste.

It was a complicated act in the dark, disturbing both men every time it took place. Their bodies were crushed together and any movement compromised the minuscule resting space of the other. They grumbled and swore at each other as they thrashed about attempting to deal with this most basic of nature's requirements.

Todd's bulk infuriated Brant. The steel strap felt like a knife at his side and he could get no relief because Todd's body pressed into his other side. 'Move over, you big bastard,' he hissed often. But Todd could not move – he was squashed between the mesh wall at the front of the basket and Brant's body. Even when both men heaved themselves on to their sides, the edge of the steel strap dug into Brant's back or into his stomach, depending on which way he lay.

There was only one possible escape. Through the imagination.

Paradoxically, it proved the most painful exercise of all.

During their waking moments, Todd asked Brant if he had children. The fact that he didn't know spoke of the gulf between these men's lives. In time, Brant's exposition on the divisions between them would become famous: 'Nah, him and I had nothing in common. He doesn't like fishin', he likes shootin'. I like watching animals run around, he likes 'em on his wall. He's a Ford man, I'm a Holden man. I'm rugby league, he's AFL. I like rock music, he likes country and western. So I'm goin', fuck, you know, we've got nothin' in common.'

They did have something familiar, though, and Todd's question about children had touched a spark to gunpowder.

Brant would put it this way later: 'And there we are and he says, "You got kids?" "Yeah." "Oh, we've got somethin' in common. You got a missus?"'

And suddenly the two of them were crying together, wailing, in Brant's telling of it: 'Oh, bugger me dead, the kids . . . the missus.

'And then we realised we can't talk about that. So the only thing we had together we can't talk about.'

In fact, they *would* talk about their families. Endlessly. But in the hours after that first painful broaching of the subject, they lapsed into private dreaming.

Brant and Todd both knew they could die any minute. Their wives and their children would be forced to survive without them. The thought of it and the knowledge that they were powerless to do anything about it drove them further into despondency. There was guilt, too. Todd and Brant were strong, healthy and still young. Todd was 34, Brant 37. They felt impotent, as if they were letting down their families.

Todd already knew what that felt like. Years ago, maybe a decade ago, he and Carolyn had separated. Todd blamed himself. In a town the size of Beaconsfield, where everyone knows the business of everyone else, it had been a public failure, humiliating for both him and Carolyn. But they had patched over the wounds, got back together, forged on.

He was a plain country boy, elevated by his physical prowess to the status of alpha male, yet riven deep down by the fear that perhaps he just wasn't *good enough*. There was no shortage of people around town who thought Todd was arrogant – it was a word even his own mother used about him – but those few who got close to him suspected his bombastic attitude was overcompensation for the sort of uncertainty that resides in the hearts of many men, particularly those who have expectation thrust upon them.

Years ago, scouts for the big Australian Rules football teams, Collingwood and St Kilda in particular, had spotted

Todd on the football fields of the Tamar Valley. The opportunities laid out before him – money, fame, glory – came to nothing because he relied too heavily on his natural talent. He couldn't bring himself to train hard enough and go through the pain required to hone his body into the sort of machine that the top clubs demanded. Couldn't be bothered, really. Eventually the scouts lost interest, though Todd was the stand-out athlete in the local leagues and had represented his state.

It seemed a re-run of his school days. He coasted and never finished high school. Todd's closest mates knew he accused himself of letting his academic chances drift through his hands. He was condemned to the fate of so many young men in the bush, working unsatisfactory jobs that lacked security. He got a job in a factory across the river manufacturing magnesium wheels, but when there was a downturn, he found himself redundant.

Jobs were scarce in Tasmania in those days and scarcer still around Beaconsfield for a young man without a trade certificate. Todd had a young family and commitments, so for years he crawled out of bed early and drove the 40 kilometres to Launceston to drive a waste truck. It put bread on the table.

When the gold mine reopened, he was determined not to miss the opportunity it held. He used contacts around town to get himself on the recruitment list. A job underground paid well and was secure. His workplace would be a dawdle from his own home. He would work with his father down there, and his father-in-law, too. It gave him a sense of achievement.

A hard-rock gold miner. In Beaconsfield, it was a badge of pride.

Todd had a nice house and a loyal wife he had known for most of his life who worked at the mine, tolerated his volatile outbursts, took care of the kids and, hell, loved him. Understood him, probably better than he understood himself. Three kids. The quiet, intelligent Trent, a bit of a mystery to Todd. Beautiful little Maddison, unformed yet, life ahead of her. And Liam, always kicking a football, just like Todd. A kennel of hunting dogs, a house dog – an enthusiastic labrador called Harley – and forests all around for shooting expeditions. Life had worked out all right.

Till now. Trapped and helpless, Todd felt all those emotions that might overwhelm a man delivered the news that he has cancer: anger, sadness and the sense that all the certainties of life have suddenly fragmented.

Brant was in anguish at the thought that Rachel would be crazy with anxiety. She'd always worn her heart on her sleeve. Called herself 'an emotional Cancerian'. Brant and Rachel, a little blonde girl with a wide smile and a cheeky attitude, had connected instantly when they met at school in Bowen, north Queensland, and had been together ever since. Nobody who knew the couple ever talked about them in the singular. It was always Brant 'n' Rachel; Rach 'n' Brant.

They were hardly more than kids themselves – Rachel almost 18, Brant 19 – when they became parents to twins, Zachary and Zoey. They courted for a year at Bowen High School. Rachel was still in school, studying for Year 12, when she discovered she was pregnant. Brant was by then away in Cairns. He'd just sat his trawler skipper's certificate when Rach called him and told him he was going to be a father.

Here was another link for Todd and Brant to explore – they had both married childhood sweethearts.

Brant, too, had known times when he wasn't sure how he was going to buy a carton of milk for the house. The road for Brant and Rachel had presented plenty of hills and a lot of valleys. After three years on trawlers, hauling prawns out of the sea all around Queensland's northern waters clear into Torres Strait, he had stepped back on land to become a proper father, working any job that presented itself. At a service station, in car parts in a motor dealership, driving tractors on a farm. Never quite knew exactly what he wanted to do.

And then the search for a new life, a long caravan journey down the east coast of Australia with Rachel and the twins, across to Tasmania. He'd never realised how beautiful the island state could be. Bought a little farm at the foot of the Great Western Tiers, grew hydroponic lettuces. Brant remembered Rachel seeing snow for the first time, running out the front door, kicking up a white storm, laughing with the joy and the beauty of it. It had snowed one year on Christmas Day. A white Christmas. Zac and Zoey growing up in the country, animals all around. Rachel took in stray animals and the farm filled with sheep, pigs, turkeys, cats, dogs, cattle. There were a couple of Shetland ponies for the kids.

And then Woolworths demanded they quadruple their lettuce output – otherwise they would lose their business. It was impossible. They already grew 12,000 fancy lettuces. No contract.

The chance to go mining couldn't be ignored. A solid, steady income. Half the year off to go sailing and fishing. Leaving the farm had been a wrench. But Brant and Rachel had decided it made sense for the whole family. If Zac and Zoey were going to have a chance at a decent education and jobs with a future, they needed to be closer to a population centre. In Tasmania, a state of less than 500,000 people, that meant either Launceston or Hobart. Beauty Point was only 50 kilometres from Launceston.

It wasn't worth it. Not now. Rach was up there worrying. Brant concentrated on her. Trying to tell her he was okay, fighting to get out. Through 925 metres of hard rock.

As Brant and Todd fought their fear and wrestled depression, Brant's brother Shaun flew from Brisbane where he worked as a cook. Shaun, seven years younger than Brant, was stuck for hours at Melbourne Airport waiting for a connection to Launceston. He sat hunched over a notebook, trying to pin his scattered thoughts to paper.

> I wonder how long it's going to take. How big will the passageway be? Is there no complications? Is any of them unconscious? Is bro' moving around? How much time do they have? So many elements, such a big hurdle . . . He knew the risk but that I guess is what gave him the thrill. I mean, they would have some emergency training . . . how would they get food and water; do they have their lunch or is it in the crib room? All I can imagine is that they are in a warm dark damp environment having to conserve their light.
>
> This totally sucks but it would suck more for big bro'. News in the departure lounge – they're using boggers; this could take some time. I don't

know how long they could last. The reporter said no news is bad news. This better not be a colossal fuck-up. It will destroy a lot of people if he doesn't make it. I feel so lost. I can't imagine how everyone else feels. I hope he made it to safety. Where would they go? Under a digger? No safety points and little hope. They have to get out; after all he's so lucky in bad situations it often makes me sick. Well I hope on this occasion this is the case – I hope I'm sick to the core.

Brant, you make it out! I know you have what it takes. I just hope it wasn't over before it started.

I love you, bro'.

'You can't leave me here by myself. Get through it. Just live through this and I will do anything you want. Just name it.'

CHAPTER 9

STRANGERS IN THE STREETS

■ ■ ■

News editors around Australia awoke on Wednesday morning, switched their radios to the ABC's AM program and knew right away they had to get reporters on planes.

The host of AM, Tony Eastley, began the report with a simple enough introduction.

'Most people wouldn't have felt the minor earth tremor that brushed the town of Beaconsfield in Tasmania last night, but the tremor was just enough to cause an underground rock fall at the town's gold mine. Nearly 1 kilometre underground, three miners were immediately cut off from the surface.'

Those few words had the makings of a riveting story, a story with all the elements needed to hold readers, listeners and viewers in thrall. An earthquake. A gold mine. Men trapped. One kilometre from the surface. Some little place in Tasmania.

News editors listened harder. Eastley spoke to Melissa Lewarn from the ABC's Launceston office, one of the first reporters to reach Beaconsfield.

> **EASTLEY**: Melissa, has there been any contact with the men since the rock fall occurred?
>
> **LEWARN**: As I'm aware, no, at this stage there hasn't been . . . you know, the family and residents and the mine have grave concerns about the wellbeing of these workers because of that.
>
> **EASTLEY**: So the local officials are saying what – that a rescue mission is possible, but it's not being undertaken yet?
>
> **LEWARN**: Well, at the moment they've got the mine rescue teams there trying to coordinate this search and that's all we've really been told at the moment.
>
> **EASTLEY**: Is oxygen still getting to the affected area, do you think?
>
> **LEWARN**: I'm not aware of that. Not sure.

The story that was unfolding here could fill columns of newspaper space and prime segments on the TV news.

Beaconsfield couldn't know it, but it was about to be invaded.

Larry Knight's daughter Lauren was boarding a plane out of Coolangatta, Brant Webb's mother Christa Jeffery was hurrying to leave her home on the Atherton Tableland and his father John Webb was making arrangements to rush south from his home in Agnes Water, a small seaside town north of Bundaberg.

Many of the reporters being dispatched from Melbourne, Sydney, Canberra, Hobart and points between and beyond had to consult maps. Beaconsfield, Tasmania? Didn't ring a lot of bells. Launceston – the second biggest city in the state, with a population of around 100,000 – had the nearest airport.

Just hire a car and drive north-west, reporters were advised. Follow the West Tamar Valley Highway. Forty or 50 kilometres. Can't miss it.

It was true. You couldn't miss Beaconsfield. The mine's poppet saw to it. The big steel A-frame rears into view the moment you drive out of forest around Middle Arm Creek south of the town. Without it, Beaconsfield would be just another little town that the traveller would forget within minutes of driving through it.

It turned out to be not much more than a long main street boasting the Red Ruby Chinese restaurant, Karenz Beauty and Nailz, Kramer's newsagency, a post office with a couple of small supermarkets (an IGA and a Foodworks), the Tamar Valley Wholefoods and Coffee Shop, a butchery called Tamar's Goldfield Meats, Pete's Hardware, Manion's Jubilee Bakery (established 1887), Manion's Motor Garage, Tasmanian Gemstones. The handsome old Alicia Hall (established 1899), once a picture theatre, was now an antiques and collectables business. Crusty's Pizza, Savoir's Hair Studio (ladies and gents) and down the way a bit, the Pot of Gold Take-Away.

And yes, three pubs. The Exchange and the Club ($12 steak night Thursdays, all you can eat servery) on the left and, way to the north, the Ophir, named in the Bible as a legendary place of stupendous wealth that supplied King Solomon with cargoes of gold, silver, sandalwood, precious stones, ivory, peacocks and apes. The Ophir's swimming pool is filled in now, but there was a time hired strippers leapt about out there while the local boys spilled their beer. A big night these days was when the fishing club held a meeting there, and the pub was now up for sale.

There were three churches, too. The Uniting Church in the centre of town and, further up the street, the Anglican and the Catholic churches.

Perhaps to remind parishioners that God resides underground, too, St Francis Xavier Catholic Church has a miners' memorial out the front: a rough, welded sculpture with impressions of a mine's tripod, a windlass and miners' tents, all bound together by a cross in the centre.

If the reporters streaming down the highway expected to find themselves in a bucolic landscape with fine vineyards spilling to the wide waters of the Tamar River they were mistaken.

Beaconsfield is unique among the towns in the valley – most of it has no view of the river, though the Tamar's closest arm is no more than 3 kilometres away. Swampland sits between. In the evenings, a chorus of frogs reminds the citizens that water is nearby, but to reach the nearest of the splendid vineyards for which the Tamar has become famous, you needed to take a lonely road out of town and wind your way through bushland.

The township was not built for the pleasures of the river. It struggled out of the ground to serve a single purpose: the mining of gold.

The headframe of the town's gold mine sat there at the foot of Cabbage Tree Hill just up West Street from the centre of town, and that's where the journalists headed, pulling up in a sprawl around a little car park right beside the mine's chain-link fence. They were no more than 30 steps from the poppet, the cage at the shaft's head sitting immobile.

It seemed, briefly, that they had ringside seats to a drama. But it didn't take long for those assembling to understand that they may as well have travelled to the other side of the moon. Whatever spectacle they had come to witness was taking place 925 metres below their feet, in a place they could scarcely imagine.

The mine manager, Matthew Gill, a boyish-faced man forced to grapple with disaster, ventured out to speak with the media contingent. All he could say was all he knew. A large seismic event had caused a rock fall within the mine and three men were unaccounted for. These three men were working at the 925-metre level in the vicinity of the rock fall, 'and we hold grave fears for their safety'. Mine rescue personnel had undertaken searches, the Department of Workplace Safety had been briefed and had officials on site, and a recovery plan was underway to attempt to re-establish access to the area affected. 'But under the circumstances this will take some time,' Gill said. A support centre had been established at the council chambers and a hotline had been set up.

Gill was speaking to a script. Twelve months previously the trainee coordinator with Mines Rescue NSW, Peter Hatswell, had run an incident management course at the Beaconsfield mine. The training included tips on how to handle the media if there was a big accident. Gill called in a public relations consultant, Mike Lester of CPR Communications and Public Relations in Hobart, and a Sydney-based crisis manager, Anthony McClellan, of AMC Media. Both these men were experienced media hands – Lester was once a state political reporter and had handled media relations for the former Tasmanian Premier, the late Jim Bacon. McClellan had worked for the ABC's *This Day*

Tonight, Nine's *A Current Affair* and *60 Minutes*, and Channel Seven's *Witness*. He had also brokered two of the biggest interview deals in Australian television history: with Lindy Chamberlain when she was released from jail, and with Stuart Diver after he survived the Thredbo landslide.

Neither Lester nor McClellan, however, could forecast just how intense the media's interest would be in the rock fall at the Beaconsfield mine, or how long the story might last. McClellan began fielding phone calls from Sydney while Lester drove to Beaconsfield.

McClellan's speciality was keeping the media at bay. Reporters became frustrated early when he told them any information would be forwarded by press release. Lester set himself up in the mine's control room and settled on a system of writing press releases and sending Matthew Gill out for daily press conferences.

Neither of these approaches could hope to sate the gathering media's demands for information. Radio and TV required 'actuality' – real voices and moving pictures. Newspapers and magazines wanted details with which to fill long empty columns. All the reporters had editors shouting down phones demanding more, *more*.

But in the first hours the mine and its hired guns had nothing more to give for the very simple reason that they knew nothing beyond the stark details: three men were trapped. And Gill and his colleagues were working desperately behind the scenes to find out more and to organise a rescue.

The mayor of West Tamar Shire, Barry Easther, a man with the mournful visage of an undertaker, also spoke to the media. He told Channel 9 it was 'a devastating time in the local community'.

'We all live on hope, but it's a bad rock fall. Thankfully the other miners who were underground at the time have come to the surface safely. We have to brace ourselves as a community and pull together.'

The news reports that shot around the nation focused on the emotive words. 'Grave fears', 'devastating', 'brace ourselves'. Here, it seemed clear, was a tragedy in the making.

Around the corner in the main street, someone had scrawled a message and tacked it up outside the Uniting Church. 'Prayer for Our Miners,' it said. The stories rolling off the wire services and zinging into newsrooms spoke of a small town praying, the outlook grim.

Soon, mine workers made it clear they wanted no intrusion even on the cluttered spaces around the minehead above ground. They strung up large sheets of green plastic along the wire fence and around the entry to the shaft. The shire council closed the Grubb Shaft museum next door, claiming publicly that the decision was out of respect for the missing miners. In fact, the museum granted a clear view of the working mine's surface and its shaft head, and those in charge wanted no journalists or camera crews using it as a platform.

It was a lock-out; the beginning of a stand-off that would last far longer than anyone might have guessed.

Frustrated, reporters set off to approach the families of the missing men. It was an error of judgment that would set much of the town against the media.

The families of Todd Russell, Brant Webb and Larry Knight were barely holding themselves together. They were confused, shocked and suffering the early stages of grief. They also had no experience of reporters.

When a small group of journalists turned up at the home of Noel and Kaye Russell, dozens of family members and townsfolk were gathered there.

Noel Russell was already at his wits' end. In the first hours after word had flashed around the country that three men were trapped in the Beaconsfield gold mine, reporters across the nation had hit the phones in an attempt to glean information.

The names of the three men had not been released, so journalists did what they always do. They went to the phone directory and scanned for names of businesses containing the word Beaconsfield. It was easy now the White Pages were on the Internet.

The Beaconsfield Garage was the only business listed with an after-hours number and a mobile phone service. And the Beaconsfield Garage was owned by Noel Russell. The Russells' home phone – the after-hours number – and Nobby's mobile rang incessantly.

Neither Nobby nor Kaye dared to ignore the phone. It could be news from the mine concerning their son Todd. But every time they answered, it was another reporter from Melbourne or Sydney or God only knew where asking if they knew what had happened up at the mine. Nobby, a friendly man of generous soul, had tried to be polite, but his patience and his nerves had worn thin.

Thus, when reporters came to the front door, they were told to piss off. Neither Nobby nor Kaye had to do it. Their son Stephen, other family members and their friends took care of the unpleasant business.

The door at Rachel Webb's home was also shut firmly in the face of reporters. Vinnie Tunks had vowed he would be the gatekeeper and he made sure Rachel wasn't pestered.

Luke McIlveen of Sydney's *Daily Telegraph* was the first reporter from the mainland to arrive. With little action to observe around the mine and the families making it clear they didn't want to be interviewed, he and a photographer from the Melbourne *Herald Sun*, John Hargist, figured they might pick up some intelligence at the Club Hotel, where many of the miners drank.

McIlveen felt he was in some kind of bad western movie as he stepped through the hotel's front door. If there had been a pair of swinging doors, they would have creaked. Inside, sturdy, goateed miners hunkered over the bar. As one, they swung their heads to observe the arrival of obvious outsiders. The silence was profound. McIlveen bought a round of rum and Cokes, but the gesture cut little ice. These were men at a kind of wake, still in disbelief at the events of the previous night. McIlveen eventually managed to draw Gavan Cheesman and Darren Geard away from their mates and tried to engage them in conversation in the hotel's dining room. Cheesy, however, was beyond rational discussion. The rum and the memories of a night when he had forced himself to hold his nerve against catastrophe had done their work. Geard told McIlveen that he had to back away, and Cheesman was led off by friends. 'Cheesy stuck by his men and if it wasn't for him, there would probably be a lot more down there,' Geard explained.

The message couldn't have been clearer. No miner would impart information from the underground to nosy reporters from the outside world. In the hours and days that followed, that message passed around, and it became law.

There was a disconnect here that would never be broached.

The people of Beaconsfield are as friendly as the citizens of any small town – and as shy and suspicious of outsiders, too.

Journalists chose from the start to use that old cliché about country towns – close-knit – to describe the community as if it were a singular entity, not possessing the layers of more sophisticated places, but it sold Beaconsfield short.

* * *

A history as turbulent as that of Beaconsfield – boom town a century ago, settling into resigned contraction for 80 years, struggling by on the growth and slow death of an export apple industry and then required to spark into new life with the reopening of the mine – made it a place more complicated than most.

Beaconsfield's population had changed substantially. The latest gold rush brought new workers and their families to town. No longer could nearly all the residents trace their families back to a time when horses drew carriages along a tramway to a wharf down on the river.

It wasn't just the mine that brought new faces to Beaconsfield. As house prices on the mainland rose during the late 1990s and surged with the speed of a tsunami in the first years of the 21st century, Tasmania suddenly grew attractive. Retirees could sell their homes in Sydney or Melbourne for a small fortune and move to Tasmania with money to spare. After the 11 September terrorist attacks on New York and Washington in 2001, Tasmania's natural charms also threw a spell on many people searching for a bolthole remote from a chaotic and disturbing world.

There was no stampede across Bass Strait, but in a state as small and sparsely populated as Tasmania, a state that had rolled along to a placid rhythm for generations, it was possible to discern change even in Beaconsfield.

It was still small enough for everyone to speak of Launceston as if it were the big smoke – you never went to Launceston for the day, you 'went to town'. But it was no longer quite the back blocks, either, even if it remained working class and almost exclusively Anglo-Celtic.

John and Penny Farrar's coffee shop wouldn't have been out of place in a trendy suburb in a mainland city. It served decent coffee and excellent quiches, pies, tarts and gluten-free rolls, and the shelves were crammed with olives and chutneys and all manner of wholefoods. The Farrars were outsiders, refugees from the mainland in search of a gentler pace of life, but they were embraced readily by the locals. Why, they'd put a Turkish prayer mat and a water bowl on the footpath outside so that dog-owners could allow their dogs to rest and rehydrate.

Still, Jim and Miriam O'Toole found themselves a bit nonplussed these days to discover there were people on the street they just didn't know. Jim and Miriam, both aged 92, were the oldest married couple in Beaconsfield. They were born the year the old mine closed and all the boys went off to the Great War. Been married 74 years. They could remember when Cabbage Tree Hill was a sea of cinders from the old boilers that ran the pumps and there were open shafts all over town. The Bonanza and the Phoenix and the Florence Nightingale and the Ophir and the Lefroy and, oh, a lot of shafts that didn't even have names. There was a big hill of sand from the mine battery that extended two or three miles down the valley when Jim was a boy. Everyone these days said the big mine had closed because they couldn't pump enough water out of it, but Jim remembered the old blokes saying that wasn't the reason at all. It was because of all the ghosts on the payroll; 70 or 80 fictitious names that got paid every week. All that money disappearing, just like the payroll manager when bells started ringing about his scam.

Jim had never been attracted by the idea of mining. He was a sawmiller for 40 years. The only time he'd ever been down a mine was years ago, when about five fellows including Eric Reece – who later became the Tasmanian Premier – got the idea they might be able to hit pay dirt below Beaconsfield. Jim brought in the timber for shoring up the shaft and these fellows invited him to go down. He stood on a platform about the size of a beer barrel and they lowered him down to 120 feet. Couldn't stand it. Got them to take him out and he'd never wanted to go underground again.

Miriam had been the engine of the Beaconsfield hospital auxiliary ever since she'd joined it when she was 21. Remembered when she and the girls of the town mended and darned everything at the hospital, even the towels when they frayed. She got the very last British Empire Medal, for meritorious service, before Gough Whitlam ditched the old British medals and brought in Australian awards. No one ever came to her house without getting a cup of tea and one of her fruit rolls or a plate of scones. Workmen who ran drilling rigs around town, searching for new veins, checking the strata, got hot plates of soup from her kitchen every morning.

Apples. They were what kept Beaconsfield going once mining died out. Miriam could close her eyes and see fields of apple orchards and she could name all the popular and fancy varieties. Granny Smith, Jonathan, Sturmers, Ladies in the Snow, Cox's Orange. Jim recalled the steamships down at Beauty Point wharves loading half a million crates of apples for export, year in, year out.

The apple orchards were gone now. All grapes. And most of those miners up there at the Hart Shaft were newcomers too.

Yes, Beaconsfield had changed and there were strangers in the streets.

Up next to the mine, there was a full-blown alien incursion. By Thursday, the car park outside the mine gates was jammed with hire cars and TV outside broadcast vans. Reporters, photographers, video camera crews and technicians were everywhere.

CHAPTER 10

BROKEN ON THE ROCK

Daniel Piscioneri remains haunted by the moment he found Larry Knight's body. It keeps him awake nights and when he drifts into sleep, it inhabits his dreams.

It was 7.22 on Thursday morning, 27 April. Piscioneri had been at work hardly more than an hour, and his task was to deal with the stockpile of shattered rock being removed from the 925-metre tunnel.

The mine's managers and the Tasmanian Inspector of Mines, Fred Sears, had judged the tunnel too dangerous for miners to try to dig through the collapse in an attempt to reach the three men caught in there. It would have to be done by remote control.

Remote bogging is a technique used regularly underground to remove ore once a large stope has been blasted, leaving a cavernous area littered with broken rock and smashed quartz. Such an area is too hazardous for men to enter, even in machines. Rock falling from high in the black hollow of the cavern could mean instant disaster.

In such circumstances, heavy front-end loaders fitted with remote-control guidance systems are put to work. These loaders, known as boggers, are all brawn. Low-slung to creep through tunnels, their massive motors and counterweights hang out the back. Up front they are equipped with scoops called buckets capable of lifting tonnes of ore. Everything about a bogger is menacing, as if it were a monster from the Jurassic, an impression intensified by the dark environment in which the loaders crawl, bellowing.

When a miner drives a bogger, he sits sideways because the machine is forever juddering forward and then snarling into reverse. But when a bogger is remotely controlled, its operator stands sweating in a hole in the tunnel wall drilled for the purpose, the great power of the motor churning waves of heat into the confined space. The operator needs the safety of such a hole, called a cuddy, because the radio guidance system he wields, rather like a muscled-up PlayStation, is not foolproof. The signal bouncing from hard surfaces can distort, and it is not unknown for a bogger to roar out of control, smashing into walls.

It is difficult to imagine a more perilous position than to find yourself in a narrow tunnel with a crazed bogger. You would be better locked in a feedbox with a stallion gone wild. At such a time, the operator squeezes himself back into his cuddy, works frantically at the controls on the remote apparatus slung over his shoulders and hanging off his belly and prays for the radio signal to bring the machine to heel.

But the 925 tunnel presented many more difficulties than any normal remote bogging operation could manage. Even if there had been a cuddy carved in a suitable position within the tunnel – and there was not – no man could risk his life in such unstable surroundings. The roof and the walls, already fractured, could collapse at any moment.

In the wake of the Anzac night cave-in, Beaconsfield mine management had been swamped with offers of rescue experts and specialist mine-rescue gear from all over Australia. The Henty gold mine in western Tasmania between Rosebery and Queenstown used a system called tele-remote bogging, and its equipment seemed the best available for the task of clearing rubble from the 925 tunnel.

It would not only enable a machine to bog out the worst of the collapsed rock, but it would allow operators to 'see' what they were doing at a safe distance from the operation. It involved mounting cameras both fore and aft on a loader – two at the front, two at the back. Powerful lights were also attached to illuminate the tunnel.

Fibre-optic cables connected the video cameras on the machine to a TV screen and an operating panel out in the main decline, far from the hazardous workface. For extra safety, a large concrete block was brought down the decline to shelter the operators if anything went seriously wrong.

The task of this video-equipped machine was to clear a path down the collapsed tunnel towards the telehandler that Larry Knight had been using to hoist Todd Russell and Brant Webb. It was a brutal mission that had to be handled as sensitively as possible. The last thing anyone in the mine wanted was to cause any further damage, and there still remained the wild chance that one or all three men down there could be alive. Everyone involved knew also that the colossal machine could come across bodies.

As the riderless loader scooped smashed rock, it reversed back down the tunnel, performed a pirouette at the crosscut and rumbled down the access towards the decline, dumping its 5-tonne bucket-load into a growing stockpile near the intersection of the decline and the access. Fred Sears and Pat Ball had ordered that every bucket of rock must be inspected carefully. It was tough work, because this was no ordinary heap of fine mullock. There were huge slabs of rock that had peeled from the walls, boulders of all sizes and numerous steel bolts that had ripped from the roof interspersed with coarse dirt and splintered quartz.

Load by load, though, the machine cleared the first of the large collapsed areas in the 925. Then it was confronted by the light four-wheel-drive vehicle Brant had parked in the tunnel. The bogger operators simply guided the big machine's bucket beneath the utility, hoisted it and dragged it out.

Ahead was the next pile of debris, which had crashed in over the telehandler. In all, it spread perhaps 20 metres along the drive and was stacked almost 5 metres high.

Daniel Piscioneri's assignment was to deal with the stockpile built by the tele-remote operation.

At just 26 years of age, another of those Beaconsfield district boys who wore a goatee, he was built strong, a footballer. His is a big, old family from the Tamar with links to many other families that could trace their roots back to the early days of settlement, and he was already a skilled miner.

Mounted on the biggest bogger in the mine, an Elphinstone 1600 capable of scooping 12 tonnes at a time in its bucket, he was to push the stockpile into a manageable heap, preventing it spilling out of the access into the decline; and as it grew, he was to dig into it and transfer it, load by load, to a dump in a tunnel deeper in the mine, at 940 metres.

As he drove his bucket into the pile, intent on pushing rock further up the heap to make space for a new load from the remote machine, he realised there was something alien hanging from the loader's blade.

Horrified, he flicked levers, trying to dislodge the object. Blue overalls, gumboots. Hanging limp, a rag doll. Instinctively, as if recoiling from something too confronting to bear, Daniel threw the loader in reverse and switched it off, its bawling motor dying away. The boy leapt from the cabin and his legs gave way. Couldn't hold on to reality. Shouted at the remote operators. Lay there in the dirt. Someone came to him and held his head and pushed a cup of water to his lips.

'I was 98 per cent sure it was Larry,' Daniel said later. 'I was in a bit of a daze.'

Daniel Piscioneri had never seen a dead body before.

Pat Ball and Fred Sears had left only minutes before, heading to the surface for breakfast. Radios squawked, men came running. Ball and Sears hurtled back down the decline.

All the cameras, all the monitoring of floodlit pictures beamed back to the screen in the decline, all the inspections of the bucket-loads being brought out of the tunnel – all of it had failed. And now a body lay there on the broken rocks.

Larry Knight's body had been scooped out from beneath the rockfall in the 925 tunnel and dumped in the stockpile and no one had noticed. If Daniel had not been ordered to scrape the pile into manageable order before he hauled away tonnes of smashed rock to dump it into another tunnel with hundreds of other tonnes of waste, the body might never have been found. It would simply have been buried in the dark.

'It was a small miracle, really,' Daniel says now.

Pat Ball laid down the law. No one there could leave the mine, and no one could enter. A coroner would have to be called to inspect the scene. Forensic specialists from the Tasmania Police Force would have to investigate. Difficult arrangements had to be made.

Underground mining, like all the old, hard crafts, has built its own traditions. Call them superstitions. Cornish fishermen through the ages wouldn't take a man out on their boats if he could swim. Perhaps it came from the belief that a man who could swim wouldn't take the proper care to keep a boat floating. Underground miners won't touch the dead body of one of their workmates; not if they can help it. Perhaps it is that complicated concept of respect for the dead. Or perhaps it is because the very act of touching a man who has fallen prey to the danger that hovers in the back of the mind of every man who ventures into the underworld is too much of a disturbance to the spirit, as if it could transfer – in some mysterious way – misfortune to the living.

Whatever it was, every man down there on Thursday morning knew that others, men from another mine who would understand these arcane matters, would be required to deal with Larry Knight's body. And so it turned out.

The mine rescue team from the Mt Lyell copper mine in west Tasmania was brought down to act as the 'neutral' outfit. But two of the Beaconsfield shift bosses, Dale Burgess and Steve Homan, oversaw the operation. Tradition was served – the outsiders tended to the gruesome details, but two of Larry's colleagues never left their mate's side.

Kym Ronin – Larry's old workmate, who'd found out about the trouble his old friend was in from Lauren on the flight to Launceston – stood outside the mine on the day Larry's body was found. He hoped against hope it would not be Larry, but when the name of the man found dead finally swept Beaconsfield, he, like the whole Knight family, could hope no more.

The discovery of Larry's remains, though, drove a new resolve into the rescue. The miners in the decline recognised that now they had found Larry, they were close to Brant and Todd. They couldn't stop now. The bogging operation had to continue. Five more bucket-loads. They would send the tele-remote down the tunnel five more times and try to bore through the scree. If they could reach the telehandler, they might find the two other missing men. But every load that came out had to be inspected with the greatest of care.

Over the next hours, the operation proceeded at a snail's pace. Dale Burgess and Steve Homan and a team of mine rescue workers equipped with torches slowly picked through the stockpile and all the contents of each bucket. By hand. Four hundred tonnes of rock. Searching for something they did not wish to find.

Todd and Brant heard the bogger crawling and grunting up and down the 925 drive. Larry, they decided, had found his way out and had called in the cavalry.

Good old Larry. He would have explained to everyone out there exactly what had happened. Told of how Brant and Todd were in the basket, resting up on the bund. It gave both men a sense of relief, knowing that Larry could direct things from his certain knowledge of how it all was.

Todd still couldn't feel or move his left leg, but he could exude hope; lend a bit of buoyancy to Brant's wavering spirit. After five years in the mine rescue team, Todd knew exactly what was happening, he told Brant. The blokes out there had to take their time, do everything just right. The fact that it all seemed to be so slow was reason for confidence, not despair. All he and Brant had to do was have patience. The rescuers were coming. You could hear them. Getting closer.

Yet Todd had his own fears. He knew anything could go wrong at any moment. He simply had to try to suppress his dread and summon the strength to keep the apprehension out of his voice.

Brant had the physical ability to dig a tunnel and pull stones out of the roof, but Todd, lacking movement, would have to dig down into his soul to find the calm that might save both of them. He couldn't afford to let Brant lose control. Panic could kill either of them as easily as another rock fall.

Brant, though, was having difficulty holding his mind together, let alone finding confidence. The water spraying from the rocks had chilled both men to the core and their biggest struggle remained the fight against creeping hypothermia. They had to hug each other's bodies constantly just to steal a bit of radiated warmth from the other. It meant rolling on to their sides, spooning, one wrapping his arms around the other. And then, painfully, reversing the process.

The only escape was sleep, and Brant was jealous of Todd's ability to slip away into unconsciousness. He lay there in the utter dark, his imagination running riot, feeling loose rocks above his head waiting to crash and smash his legs, leaving him writhing in agony. The gushing water refused to let up its maddening song. Its sound overran the moan of the bogger out there in the drive and Brant worried that if someone called, he wouldn't hear them.

Even when Brant succumbed to sleep, he seemed to hover in a place for which there was no name. He flitted in and out of dreams, Rachel and the twins, Zac and Zoey, inhabiting his mind. When he awoke, he was not sure whether he had returned, because there was no border between the blackness of sleep and the crushing darkness of his incarceration.

And then, some time during the long hours after Brant had emerged from his tunnel to nowhere, the earth convulsed.

He and Todd felt the shock of it beneath their bodies and heard it ripping along the walls. Another seismic. The power of the ground shaking itself free of stress jolted them into alarmed consciousness. The first wave of seismic energy returned, undulating in the opposite direction. Their whole world banged and shook. Small rocks spilled from the roof, pitter-pattering on the stone within the basket. Fine dirt dribbled through the mesh, spattering their faces. The two men drew their feet as far as possible up towards their bodies, grabbing their knees, trying to make themselves tiny.

They lay shaking, waiting for . . . what?

'We're going to get fuckin' buried in here, Todd,' Brant yelled. Todd heard the panic in Brant's voice, but couldn't do anything about it.

Before Todd could get hold of his own racing heart, Brant had slid out of the cage, out into the pouring water, screaming that he was going to find a way out.

He was intent in getting back into his tunnel and ripping his way through the mesh at the end of it with his bare hands.

But Brant almost wept when he flipped on his lamp. The tunnel had collapsed! The opening was now no wider than the span of his hand and he could see that inside there was nothing but dirt. Any hope that the hole in the ground might have held no longer existed.

The sight of it sobered Brant. Calmed him right down. He could have been down there when the tremor hit.

He could feel how it would have been. Trapped. Choking. The life squeezed out of him. But he'd been driven out by the cold, the wet and exhaustion. Had been lying there with Todd when the seismic ripped through. Hadn't been crushed by rock. He wasn't meant to die. Might be a bastard of a place, but the basket suddenly seemed to offer comfort. He wormed his way back through the little door, and he and Todd lay and listened as the bogger returned mumbling down the drive.

Time requires occurrence if it is to have any meaning. One needs a measure by which to gauge its passage.

If you remove the shift of light, day turning to night and night yielding to day, the rhythm of meals, of work and play, the mind melts into a state of suspension.

This is the state into which Brant and Todd sank. Todd consulted the illuminated dial of his watch from time to time, desperate to keep track at least of each 12-hour period so he could calculate the passing of day and night. But the space between those consultations and calculations curved and twisted in the darkness, floating beyond any conventional significance.

Brant had a muesli bar in his pocket. It was the only food in their cramped world. It gained a connotation as important as time.

When should the men consider nibbling a little sustenance? Not yet, they agreed. Not yet.

Tuesday night – the period of freeing Todd's body from the rocks that covered him – had come and gone. Wednesday, daytime, the era of the beginning of Brant's tunnel, had gone. Wednesday night, when the torture of water and cold had started and the tunnel had lost its promise – that had passed, too. Thursday morning, the earth tremor, the loss of the tunnel. Vanished. But still Brant's muesli bar rested in its wrapper. Not yet. Not yet. Now, though, the men were drained of energy. Maybe just a nibble. Brant unwrapped the small bar, broke it in two and gave half to Todd. They each gnawed a sliver from their treats and stuffed the remainder into their pockets.

They dozed.

Clang!

Brant and Todd snapped awake. Knew exactly what they had heard. Didn't need to discuss it.

The bogger's bucket had hit the rear of the telehandler. The clatter of metal on metal had travelled clear through the telehandler, vibrating down the boom arm and shivering the steel pillars of the basket.

A single short, sharp tap. No more than 6 metres away.

'Todd,' said Brant. 'If they try to move the telehandler, we're fucked. Everything will come down on us.'

'I just hope to Christ they don't put a chain on the back and try to pull the fuckin' thing out,' Todd agreed.

Suddenly, the bogger's motor died away.

Brant grabbed his pliers, hammering on the bars of the basket, and both men began screaming. 'We're here, we're here! Can you hear us? We're here!'

No response. The gurgle of water on rock seemed overwhelming.

Brant's frantic pounding on the basket caused rocks to pelt down into the basket. 'You better quit that or we'll be bloody dead,' Todd advised.

Brant scrabbled around and found a steel plate normally used to anchor bolts into the roof. He set up a new din, beating his pliers on the steel plate, willing the noise to penetrate the tumbled rock separating Todd and him from their rescuers.

They stopped, ears straining for any sign they had been heard. And resumed, hollering until their throats hurt.

Silence. Minutes stretched, elastic with hope and fear.

Listening. Banging. Yelling. Todd almost hoarse.

Suddenly, every prayer was answered.

Beeeeep!

A single long blast on the bogger's horn. Ten seconds later, the two men heard the big motor churn back to life and the machine rumbled away.

They were saved! Todd and Brant slapped hands together, hugged, babbled their relief.

'They've found us. They're comin' to get us,' they sang. A sort of hysteria filled the minuscule cavern and it seemed to the men they were no longer as cramped as before.

'Don't care what you say, Todd, I'm havin' a cigarette,' laughed Brant.

'Better give me one too,' Todd told him. 'Fuck it, I'm takin' up smokin' again.'

And together they rested on the rock, puffing happily.

Wouldn't be long now. All those blokes out there know we're in here and they'll just rip through and get us, the two men agreed.

They could not know there was no driver at the controls of the bogger. Could not know that the men operating the machine were way out in the decline, beyond hearing range, simply watching a TV screen. Were unaware that the operators had agreed only to take five remaining buckets of shattered rock out of the tunnel, that the task was completed and the only reason the big machine had stopped was to allow the operators to take a good long look at the rear of the telehandler. The operators could see only that the machine was under so much collapsed earth that it would be futile to continue – each time they tried to clear the area behind the telehandler, dirt reeled down.

There was something else that Todd and Brant did not recognise. Under the strict rules enforced during the search, the operators had to give a blast on the bogger's horn before they could start and move the machine. Just to be safe.

Every one of the assumptions made by Todd and Brant was false. As false as the hopes that flooded their minds and gladdened their hearts.

The bogger would not return.

Fred Sears and Pat Ball would order the 925 drive roped off. No more men or machines were to enter. It was non-negotiable.

A new method had to be nutted out in an attempt to discover what might have happened to Todd Russell and Brant Webb.

The men out in the mine and on the surface looked at each other and shook their heads. Larry Knight was dead. Young Daniel Piscioneri was all shook up. Talking to counsellors upstairs. Matter of time, really. Two more bodies down there. Somewhere.

CHAPTER 11

A MESSAGE FROM BEYOND

Corey Verhey felt as if a bolt of lightning had passed clean through his being. Larry Knight's body had been found, and something spooky had been creeping around in Corey's mind.

Almost exactly a year previously, on Friday, 22 April 2005, Corey had allowed his sister to talk him into a consultation with a psychic.

Psychic conventions are big business in country Australia.The slow death of formal religion and the emptying of traditional churches have left a spiritual gap. Part of it is being filled increasingly by smooth-talking preachers with a talent for summoning up the sort of charismatic experience that wouldn't be out of place in a tent show in the dirt-poor counties of the southern states of the US. Whole families in bush towns pour into bare halls on Sunday mornings to speak in tongues, to clap along with pop gospel, get born again and generally rejuvenate their spirits.

Alongside the Christian revival has come renewed interest in the old crafts of communing with the spirit world. Mediums, channellers, astrologers and prestidigitators claiming knowledge of the paranormal ply their techniques from shopfronts, school fetes, the Internet, magazines and their own homes. Psychic conventions are held all over the country every few weeks. Tap a country town and belief in magic flits from doorways everywhere.

In April 2005, the old central Victorian gold rush city of Bendigo was alive with palm readers, clairvoyants, tarot readers and spirit guides, some of them from the United States. They crowded in to set up their stalls at the Bendigo Psychic Expo at the Golden Dragon Museum and Convention Centre.

Corey had never had much time for those claiming supernatural powers.

'I'd always been a sceptic because I think they play mind games with you,' he says.

Still, when he travelled to Bendigo to visit his sister and she insisted he ought to give a psychic a chance to read his future, he thought he'd play along. Couldn't do any harm. No skin off his nose.

The palm reader, a Bendigo woman named Mary Dean, seemed to know more than she ought about his past, what drove him, the fears and the strengths he hid away in his heart.

Mary Dean, 53, has been a professional psychic for 30 years. Her specialities are palm and tarot readings and 'psychic ability'. She believes the 'lousy life' that enveloped her youth – violence in the household, her mother walking out when she was eight, marriage at 16, her baby dying when she was just 17 – gave her the edge that allowed her to tune in to the hearts, the very souls, of others.

She predicted that Corey Verhey would leave Tasmania and his life would take a big upswing on the mainland, working in Bendigo. Corey was planning to move to the mainland. To Bendigo. Part of his reason for coming to town was to apply for a job at the new gold mine burrowing its way into rich quartz beneath the city. He'd dropped in to the mine's office to make the application only an hour before. And here was a palm reader saying he was going to move to Bendigo and his life would improve. How could this woman know?

Corey had paid for a package that included a tape-recording of the reading.

As Mary Dean wended her way through her exposition, she suddenly paused.

'Now,' she said, her voice changing, slowing down. 'You are going to be responsible for two people being alive. Whether you physically save their lives or talk them out of killing themselves, I don't know.

'But there will be two people alive because of you.'

Corey took the tape recording with him. He hadn't made the move to Bendigo, it was true. Not yet. Instead, he had spent long months building himself a fine stone house on a bush block about 6 kilometres outside Beaconsfield, and he was still working underground in the Beaconsfield gold mine.

But he had been unable to forget the prediction that he would save the lives of two people, and every now and then he would slip the tape into his stereo at home and replay it.

Now here he was, deep in the Beaconsfield mine, helping search for three men lost in a rock fall. And Larry Knight's body had been found.

Corey had believed ever since he saw the chaos in the 925 tunnel on Anzac night that all three men must have been crushed.

But suddenly, he was convinced the palm reader had laid it all out for him. One of the men was gone, but that left Brant Webb and Todd Russell still missing. They must be alive. He was a member of the mine rescue team, he was part of a huge effort to search for the miners. All of it fitted. 'You are going to be responsible for two people being alive.' It seemed to Corey that destiny was touching him on the shoulder.

Corey would drive his fellow miners to distraction over the next few days. He was the only man down there convinced that Brant and Todd would be found alive. It was only a matter of time. He told everyone, and his colleagues wearied of it. Miners might be superstitious, but there were limits. Some palm reader a year ago couldn't understand the conditions Todd and Brant faced. Ridiculous. Corey began keeping his thoughts to himself.

* * *

Gavan Cheesman's view was diametrically opposed to that of Corey Verhey. Cheesman and all the other men who had been with him underground on Anzac night were banned from re-entering the mine. Management, Rex Johnson, Pat Ball, counsellors and a psychologist, Bev Ernst of Launceston, all believed the men of the night shift were too traumatised and too emotionally involved to take part in the search and rescue.

It left Cheesy with time on his hands, the events surrounding the rock fall rewinding in his mind. He couldn't sleep and the weight of responsibility was becoming a burden almost too heavy to carry. He had to confront the facts and he believed the families of the three missing men needed to do so, too.

Soon after word hurtled around Beaconsfield that a body had been found, Cheesy could no longer contain himself. He drove around to Kaye and Noel Russell's house and told them there was little hope their son could have survived the rock fall. He explained exactly what he had seen within the 925 level on Anzac night. He felt it was better they know stark facts than live with counterfeit hope. It was cruel, he knew, but he believed it would be crueller still if they were allowed to drift on, dreaming of the happy ending he did not believe was possible.

Then Cheesy screwed up his courage and went around the corner to see Todd's wife Carolyn.

She realised what he was about to tell her the moment he walked into her kitchen.

'Carolyn,' he said. 'I want you to look me in the eyes because I want to tell you the truth.'

Carolyn kept her eyes averted. 'I won't look at you, Cheesy,' she said. 'I won't listen to this.' Gavan tried again. 'Carolyn, I was in there that night. You should know what I saw.'

But Carolyn refused to listen. Todd was alive. She was not going to give up on him, no matter what anyone said. Not even Cheesy, a man she respected and liked.

Within a day of the discovery of Larry's body, the team of mine managers, rescue personnel and advisers in the mine's control room on the surface had reached a tough decision. They would have to blow a tunnel through to the area within the 925 drive where they assumed Brant and Todd must be.

CHAPTER 12

IN THE DEEPEST DARK

Expectation fires the heart. Hopes and dreams are lesser pleasures, for they come sprinkled with apprehension; the potential to turn sour. An expectation is chunkier, invested with promise. Reservations confirmed for a holiday; the contract specifying a pay rise next year; a schoolgirl in receipt of a date for her first formal social occasion. These are pacts justifying the luxury of reverie. Consolations from the future.

Sir Isaac Newton, however, might have been thinking of expectation when he drew up his third law of motion. For every action, there is an equal and opposite reaction. For every trust there is the prospect of a broken heart.

Where were the rescuers?

The euphoria that had swept Todd and Brant at the sound of the loader's horn had slunk away. Time crept on.

‘No, she’s right,’ Todd kept telling Brant. ‘They’re just checking every contingency. When they’ve got it right, they’ll be here. That’s how rescue works.’

Nobody came. As Thursday rolled into Friday morning, Brant’s despondency deepened. His nerves jangled. He couldn’t sleep.

Most of his cigarettes were gone. He and Todd had smoked with abandon. Yeah, a celebration. Of what, he wondered now.

Their single muesli bar was just about gone, too. A nibble here, a nibble there. Brant’s half had shrunk till it was not much more than a stub. Todd had broken his in two, stuck one piece in his pocket and gnawed away at the other until it was gone. Now, the piece he had stuck in his pocket had disappeared. Fallen out while he slept, most likely, down into his rock bed. He would never find it again.

The water they drank was so heavily mineralised, it tasted gritty. Their stomachs growled.

Hours ago, no, days ago – how long had they been down here? – they had decided it was no longer acceptable simply to urinate on the rocks beside them. They needed only one helmet to collect all the water they needed, so had employed the other helmet as a pisspot. They tossed the contents away down the back of the basket, hoping this small nod to sanitation might protect them from infection.

They had done it hard for so long. Then those blokes out there with the bogger had just about reached them, gave the signal, the toot on the horn and then . . . nothing. They should be out by now. Talk about dashed expectation!

The rocks beneath their backs were a misery. Both men were developing pressure sores and kept shifting, a little at a time, searching for relief. Cramps shot through their legs; their backs ached, quivering with cold. The only way they could give their legs any respite from the spasms that ran through their muscles was to push on the mesh, move their feet upwards, little step by little step, and rest them on the top bar of the basket. There was a tiny space up there, just a few centimetres. Newton's third law was relentless, though. When Brant and Todd elevated their legs, the sharp rocks dug harder into their buttocks and their backs, worrying at the sores developing in the soft tissue.

Todd lay quiet for long periods and Brant believed he was sleeping. Lucky bugger. But Todd was praying. He prayed silently almost every hour. Not formal prayers with the rhyme and rhythm of childhood, but free-form pleas for deliverance. He prayed that he would see Carolyn and the kids again, and offered a treaty. If God could get him out of this place, he would be a more attentive husband and father. He would spend more time with his children and put aside his own selfish requirements. Watch the kids grow up, teach them a bit about life.

Todd had another weight on his mind. He was trained in mine rescue; had trained for years. With ropes and oxygen and all sorts of special equipment. He'd also undergone confinement training. The first lesson was to remain calm. The second was to help calm your mates. Reassure them. Keep panic at bay. Brant was not trained in any of it, and Todd felt a responsibility to him. Brant's asthma worried him. Panic, claustrophobia, the very state of feeling imprisoned could send a man over the edge.

It would be exceedingly dangerous if it brought on an asthma attack. There were times when Todd had to fight down his own horror at his predicament. He couldn't move. He was buggered if he was going to have to deal with a man struggling to breathe. And so, even though Todd often didn't quite believe what he was saying, he spun calming stories about how the men out there were organising a safe and careful rescue.

Brant opened his cigarette box. Needed a steadier. There was not a single smoke left. He and Todd had smoked the lot. There had been eight left when the bogger had tapped the telehandler. Here was a new form of panic for Brant. Not a simple gratification remained in this prison. He swore, the fear of the nicotine addict eating at him. He had full packets in his crib bag. No way to get at them. The thought of it amplified his craving, filling his head with frustration and loathing.

Brant had promised Rachel months ago that he would no longer work deep in the mine. The seismic events and rock falls that started in October had spooked her. Him too. The chance to work in the backfill plant above ground had seemed perfect. Needed to go underground only to the crib, potter around with the service crew. Stay safe. He had never been in the 925 drive. Neither had Larry. But when Cheesy needed them to lend a hand, build a simple wall . . . well, it was just a routine job. Finish it before crib time and spend the rest of the night up there in the backfill silo, checking dials and watching a bit of TV. A doddle. But now Rachel would be up there, torn apart, unable to understand why he had broken his promise and headed into the deep. It ripped at him.

Todd and Brant occasionally heard in the distance the

hum of machinery, the movement of vehicles and the whine of drills. It was all indistinct, mixed with the incessant babble of water in their cavern.

It was a rescue underway, Todd declared. Men were rehabilitating the tunnel, meshing the walls, bolting the roof. Making it safe for their saviours to proceed.

And then their world exploded. *Boom boom boom boom boom!* Staccato detonations, each less than a thought apart, going on – it seemed – forever. Brant and Todd had no time to think as rocks cannoned out of the darkness, pounding on the stones within their basket. Instinctively, the men shrank as far as they could under the little segment of mesh sheltering Todd's head, trying to make themselves disappear. They reached for their knees and squeezed their legs towards their chests. The earth below and around them heaved. Concussion in waves engulfed them. Their ears felt ready to burst. They were deaf.

Silence. Shaking. Breathing. Dust.

Blasting hard rock is a brutal business. It requires big machines, a couple of hundred kilograms of high explosive and a great deal of faith. When the mines safety officers, the Tasmanian Inspector of Mines, the most experienced drill men and the rescue team decided any attempt to reach Todd Russell and Brant Webb through the 925 tunnel was too perilous, a new plan had to be drawn up.

Hours of furious discussion took place in the control room on the surface. Plans were hatched and trashed, charts were studied and diagrams scribbled on white-boards as the mine's senior management team frantically sought alternatives.

They reached the toughest conclusion. They would have to blast a new drive towards the area the men were last seen.

The mine's surveyor, Simon Arthur, carries in his head a mental picture of every cubic centimetre of the ground beneath Beaconsfield. He also has graphs and computer models of the whole confusing layout of access tunnels, drives, vertical rises, air shafts, stopes and all the rest of the subterranean riddle. His knowledge and his ability to read the earth would prove critical in every phase of the operation to come. First, he had to plot as precisely as possible the whereabouts of Todd and Brant. There would be no point in blasting a tunnel that did not point in their direction.

The decline, that winding artery to the bottom of the mine, was at a particular point roughly parallel with the drive at 925 metres where the men were last seen standing in the basket at the front of the telehandler.

However, because the decline was precisely as its name implied, it fell away from the access to the 925 drive at its gradient of 1 metre in every six. At the point at which it was parallel to the drive where the men might be, it was therefore close to 5 metres lower.

The tele-remote bogger operators had found the back of the telehandler within the drive. The telehandler was 4.8 metres from rear to jib, but its boom arm was telescopic. It could be extended by anything from about 1 metre to 3 or 4 metres in front of the machine. And hanging off the front of the boom was a basket about 1.5 metres long. No one knew if the basket was hoisted high towards the roof, or had been smashed to the floor, or simply hovered at some point between.

These loose facts added up to a significant challenge for Simon Arthur. He was required to calculate all the known variables and then throw in a guess.

What he did know was that 36 metres of solid rock stood between the decline and the drive where the men were presumed to be.

He settled on a plan to blow a new tunnel 4.5 metres high by 4.5 metres wide sloping upwards towards the area he calculated the men would most likely be found.

It would be laborious. Before any blasting could begin, the decline had to be reinforced to offer reasonable safety to the men who would do the job. Mesh and numerous heavy steel straps had to be pinned across the roof, and extra rock bolts installed.

Matthew Gill, like the rest of his critical management team, was suffering stress, sleeplessness and the nagging doubt that what was proposed could end in greater disaster. He also had half the nation's media pressing for information on what was going on and why the whole thing was taking so long.

At 8.30 am on Friday he issued a press release that revealed his inner turmoil.

'Work on the new tunnel is progressing. We have to drive a tunnel 36 metres long and about 4.5 metres high and wide,' his statement began.

'Just because you can't see much going on up here doesn't mean that nothing is happening.

'Safety is paramount. The biggest issue is seismicity and we are therefore planning for worst-case stress scenario. Before we fire the first blast we have to support the opening in the decline with upgraded ground support – putting in rock bolts and straps.

'The first lot of blast holes have already been drilled in preparation. Overnight we had a team of miners down in the mine, four, plus supervisors. That team has put in 14 rows of bolts and straps. Further strapping and bolting is still required. A new shift went down at 6 am to continue this work.

'We are all working as hard and as quickly as we can so that everyone knows as soon as possible, but we cannot rush this. We cannot risk more lives.'

Most of the journalists camped outside the mine had little idea of what was meant by strapping and bolting, and they could hardly conceive of the scene as that 'first lot of blast holes' were drilled.

A twin-boom jumbo drilling rig was driven into position in front of the rock face that would be blasted, and an operator stood on its platform, carefully aiming the big drilling arms at the rock.

A pattern was stencilled on the face, marking out more than 40 targets. The jumbo operator guided the hydraulic booms of his rig – each independent of the other, jerking about like the claws of some creature from a space fantasy movie – to these targets. The pneumatic drills on the end of the booms sank into the rock, hammering and rotating, water gushing from each to clear the holes of debris as the bits dug deeper. Each hole would be 3.5 metres deep.

The machine screamed, requiring every man in the vicinity to push plugs into his ears or risk deafness. Again and again the drills scorched their way into the rock until the entire face was a Swiss cheese, though the holes followed a symmetrical design suggesting diamonds and squares interlinked.

The men of the charge-up crew took over. They rammed into each hole a long, sausage-shaped plug of light, plastic explosive 32 millimetres wide and 200 millimetres long. A detonator was driven into each of these explosive plugs, attached to a lead trailing out of the hole. Next came a tractor carrying a large steel kettle containing an explosive called ANFO – an ammonium nitrate/fuel oil mixture. ANFO resembles nothing so much as the small balls that form the filling of a bean bag, except that the balls are ammonium nitrate – the same substance widely used as a fertiliser – steeped in diesel. The balls were blown by high-pressure air from the kettle into each of the dozens of drill holes, filling them. More than 2 kilograms went into each hole.

The modern world learned the power of just such a mixture when a disgruntled young man named Timothy McVeigh set a fuse to 5,000 pounds (2,268 kilograms) of the stuff outside the Murrah Federal Building in Oklahoma City on 19 April 1995. The explosion pulverised most of the northern face of the nine-storey building and 168 people died.

In 1947 a ship named the SS Grandcamp containing 2,300 tonnes of ammonium nitrate blew up in the port of Texas City in the Gulf of Mexico. The catastrophe is documented graphically in Michael Richardson's book A Time Bomb for Global Trade: Maritime-Related Terrorism in an Age of Weapons of Mass Destruction.

> Not long after 9 am, barely an hour after the smoke was first spotted, the ship disintegrated in a massive explosion that was heard as far as 150 miles away.
>
> A huge mushroom-shaped cloud billowed more than 2,000 feet into the sky. The rising shockwave knocked two light planes that were

flying overhead out of the sky. Steel shards scythed through workers along the docks and a crowd of curious onlookers who had gathered at the head of the pier where the *Grandcamp* was moored. Many were killed instantly: the ship's crew, bystanders and almost the entire volunteer firefighter corps of the town. At the nearby Monsanto Chemical Company plant, 145 of the 450 shift workers on duty died. A 15-foot tidal wave thrown up by the explosion swept a large steel barge several hundred feet inland, carrying dead and injured people back into the blast zone as the water receded.

The miners at Beaconsfield were using less than a tenth of the amount of ammonium nitrate that Timothy McVeigh employed, and around one ten-thousandth of that carried on the unfortunate ship in the port of Texas City. But they knew it was not a force to be trifled with.

The men cleared the decline, retreating to the crib room where the electrician stood ready to touch a charge to a firing line that runs the length of the decline.

The detonators within the plastic explosive that would set off the massive release of energy were timed to fire a few milliseconds apart.

As the first blew, opening a hole, the next found space into which to propel its surrounding stone. On and on, a chain reaction smashing and pulverising a wall of rock compressed deep in the earth by the burden of millions of years. Four and a half metres square and 3.5 metres deep.

Left piled on the floor of the new hole and thrown out across the decline was nothing but waste sprawled beneath grey, smoking dust.

This, then, was the rippling shock that pulsated upwards through more than 30 metres of solid rock to Todd and Brant huddled in their hole.

They lay panting, blood pounding in their ears. Touched their limbs, their bodies. Nothing broken. Switched on the lamp. No wounds. Dust everywhere.

Slowly, their hearing returned.

'They're gonna kill us,' Brant breathed. 'They're gonna kill us because they think we're already dead.

'We're fucked, Todd. They've given up on us. They're comin' to get bodies. And that's what they'll find, because they'll kill us.'

Brant was edging towards hysteria.

'No, mate,' Todd said. 'It's always a rescue. The only time it turns into a retrieval is when they know there's no hope.'

'Pig's arse, Todd. They wouldn't be firin' if they thought we were alive.'

Brant's voice came in gasps. Todd could tell he was veering towards an asthma attack.

'I'm tellin' you, cock, I know about rescue and this is a rescue,' he said. Firm. He didn't quite believe it himself, but he had to talk Brant down.

Brant wouldn't be swayed. He was yelling, desperate, twisting this way and that. The terror was on him.

'Listen,' Todd bawled. 'If you don't settle down . . .'. He thought of the worst punishment he could inflict on a man. 'If you don't settle down, I'll kiss you right on the mouth and I'll put me tongue down your fuckin' throat!'

Brant very nearly choked at the absurdity of the threat. He began to laugh and it came out almost as a sob. He giggled and guffawed and reached for his Ventolin inhaler and sucked on it, spluttering, tears running into the dirt around his eyes. Suddenly both of the men were laughing and roaring.

Hell, they had survived. Again. Another confirmation that nothing could destroy them.

But they knew this could be the last time. The odds were stacking up against them.

Brant still had a pen in his pocket.

Sober now, his breathing back to a manageable state, he pulled out his pen and his empty plastic cigarette case and asked Todd to hold the light for him.

Attached to the cigarette case was an old sticker, worn shiny white.

He wrote on the sticker. Tiny words.

'Fired 28th Friday at 12.30 pm. Waiting for next firing. No injuries by two. Thought of you the whole time, lots of love Rach.'

It didn't seem enough. Had to squeeze some more words in.

'Love you all Rach Zac Zoey.'

Brant lay there chewing his pen. Todd held the light, saying nothing.

'Will look after you all from above. Love, Brant.'

There. He had said it. If he were to die, the message would be found, passed on to Rachel and Zac and Zoey. He loved them. He'd thought of them ceaselessly. And he would never be far away. He would look after them from beyond, from above.

Neither Todd nor Brant could speak. They could hardly breathe.

'Better give us the pen, cock,' Todd said eventually. 'You'll have to hold the light this time.'

Todd had no paper, no sticker. He wrote his letter of love and farewell on his bare arm. Added the time and date of the blast. They'd find that, the buggers.

There was a new intimacy between the men. They had shared much through the long hours and days in the darkness. But this was different.

They talked of their families. Could finally speak of the fear that they might not live to care for their wives and children.

They settled on a pact.

If Brant survived and Todd did not, Brant promised that Todd's family would live under his protection. Anything that Carolyn and the three children might need, he would provide. Stuff for school, trips to the football, attendance at concerts or graduation days. He would be there.

Todd made the same promise to Brant. If he were to get out of here and Brant did not make it, Rachel, Zac and Zoey could rely on him forever. No question. No qualifications.

They pledged also to carry messages. Todd would sit down with Rachel and tell her that Brant loved her, always had, and that he'd fought to stay alive for her and the twins. Brant would do precisely the same thing for Todd, relaying to Carolyn the conversations he had had with Todd about his feelings for his family and all the effort he'd taken to survive.

Todd had never met Rachel. Brant did not know Carolyn. But there it was.

The two men shook hands on it. A deal. Sealed. They lay on the stone. Breathed.

CHAPTER 13

THE CRUSH ZONE

■ ■ ■

Todd and Brant knew the drilling and blasting crews weren't about to quit. They knew too that they would probably die in the next explosion or the one after that.

But they weren't about to give up without a battle.

Todd figured it might be possible to gauge when the next blast would occur. They would have to strain their ears, try to block the water's song and listen hard for the sound of machines and drills. There was a rhythm to the process; a sequence that never changed.

Once the dust had settled in half an hour or so, a bogger would muck out the waste rock that had been blown from the face and load it onto trucks. A crew would scale loose rocks from the walls and the backs – the roof – of the new tunnel using the booms of the jumbo and hand-held scaling bars. Then mesh, bolts and arches of steel straps would be drilled and pinned to the walls and the roof.

Eventually, the rock face would be stencilled and the jumbo would drill new holes. Plastic explosive would be rammed down each hole and the 3.5 tonne machine carrying its kettle of ANFO would rumble in to the new drive.

Finally, the charge-up crew would leave, heading to the crib. When that happened, Todd and Brant would have to be ready.

They had earplugs in their pockets. All miners carried them. The noise from jumbos and air-leg drills could not be endured without them. They'd ram the plugs into their ears when it was time. They practised bracing their bodies, dragging their legs around and up, clamping their arms around their knees, tensing every muscle. Turning themselves into defensive balls.

Brant checked his net of cab straps, tightening the web.

Falling rocks were going to be the most obvious danger.

Todd took a deep breath.

'You know anything about crush zone injury?' he asked Brant.

It was a subject that freaked out miners everywhere, because mine cave-ins are among the leading causes of the most serious manifestation of crush injury: crush syndrome. And crush syndrome is likely to kill if it is not handled correctly.

Simply because a part of the body has been crushed does not necessarily mean that crush syndrome will result. Normally, massive pressure on a large muscle mass such as a leg is required, and the longer that pressure is applied the more likely it is that the injury will evolve into crush syndrome.

The blackest irony is that the patient's life is most at risk when the pressure is relieved. Muscle that has been severely damaged by enormous pressure releases its contents into the circulation on being freed, often giving rise to acute renal failure.

The subject had been playing on Todd's mind ever since he was crushed almost to death in the first moments of the 925 rock fall. He had listened to lectures about crush injury during mine rescue training. And the cascade of rock that had accompanied the latest mighty blast had concentrated both his and Brant's minds.

If the roof came down again, either one of the men could find himself crushed with no prospect of release. All those toxins building up in a smashed leg.

'Listen, cock,' Todd said. 'We might have to do something that you're not going to like.'

He laid out a hideous plan. Both of them still had their Stanley knives. The unused, razor-sharp ends of the blades were still tucked away in the handles.

If it came to it and one of them got his leg trapped beneath rock below and a heavy compressing rock from above and they couldn't free the limb quickly, they'd have to attempt amputation. It was that or die down here.

They had their webbing belts. They could apply tourniquets.

A tourniquet would be almost as dangerous as the original injury because it too, left long enough, would cause crush syndrome. Leave a tourniquet in place for 6 hours and the treatment is . . . amputation.

And how might they hack through the large bones of the leg with Stanley knives? Neither knew. They could imagine the stupendous screaming agony, though. They recalled the story of an American rock climber who amputated his own arm with a pocket knife because he couldn't free himself from a boulder that had trapped him. He had used a tourniquet to stop himself bleeding to death after the operation, and he survived. (The mountaineer Aron Ralston, 27, cut off his arm below the elbow after becoming wedged in a desert canyon in Utah in May, 2003.)

Anyway, Todd and Brant told themselves, what choice did they have? There was no doctor. No medical assistance of any kind in their little cell.

An amputation by Stanley knife would probably befatal. Both men knew it. But they agreed. They would fight for the merest hope of life until they had no more fight in them.

Ceremonially, they withdrew their Stanley knives and in the light of their lamp, switched the blades around, sharp ends to the fore.

And waited.

Corey Verhey was out there, offsiding to jumbo operator Shane Smith. A roster had been organised, and the jumbo operators would rotate through the shifts. Johnno Johnson, Dennis Newson, Glenn Whiteaker. Corey watched the men hurrying through their tasks, worry etched into their faces. Few of them believed Todd and Brant were alive. Each man in the decline understood, though, that if the two lost men had managed to survive, they were putting them in peril. The concussion from the blast would travel through the rock. The only thing the men could do was to concentrate on their work, do it as carefully as possible. Hope. Corey was locked in his belief that both men were alive and he had to save them. But he was swept up in a course of action that seemed to him the reverse of rescue. He kept his thoughts to himself.

It took around 12 hours before the second firing was ready to go.

Todd's plan to listen out for the various stages of the process paid off. Neither man slept. They detected the sound of the drills and picked the moment when the charge-up machine brought the ANFO kettle to the drive. But it was the absence of noise that gave them their strongest clue. It must mean the last of the work was done and the crew had taken off up the decline to the crib.

'This is it, Brant,' said Todd.

The two men had drained their helmets, swilling out the cap used for urine.

They jammed the helmets on their heads. Stripped of webbing, the helmets sat loose, uncomfortable. When Brant squashed back in the basket, the rim of his hardhat banged painfully against his nose.

Brant and Todd braced themselves, burrowing as hard as possible against each other, pushing their bodies beneath the mesh. Rocks dug agonisingly into spines and hips taking all of the weight of their bodies and their curled legs. Minutes ticked by. They were freezing, the shakes exacerbating the sores on their backs. Cramped. Pain in every tensed muscle. They couldn't let go of their knees, couldn't move at all, for they could not know when the electrician would touch off the explosives. Long minutes ticked by. The men could not breathe properly; feared taking deep breaths lest the coming shock waves burst their lungs, but worried they shouldn't exhale fully in case they found themselves winded. They drew in little puffs of air, growing faint. Willing the blasting to begin. Afraid that when it did, they would be gone, or worse.

Boom boom boom boom boom! They rode the percussion, screaming inside their heads. The whole basket shook and stone and loose dirt pelted down. Felt worse than a car accident.

It was over. No injuries. Unbelievable.

The two men grasped hands, slapped palms.

Todd checked his watch, grabbed Brant's pen. The lamp showed that all the water splashing down had worn his message to Carolyn and the children from his arm. Only one thing for it. Todd scraped away dirt caking his overalls and wrote the time and date of the first and second blasts on his pants leg. Gotta keep track. Leave evidence of how long he and Brant had endured.

The two men had been without food apart from some bites of a muesli bar for four days. Their energy was spent but they felt no hunger.

They were, Todd knew, in survival mode, when the body closes down its unnecessary functions and runs on stored energy. It would call on adrenaline when it was needed for fight or flight. Weight was stripping off the men. Their clothes hung limp on them. It was an odd consolation. It gave them an extra centimetre or two in their poky compartment.

■ ■ ■

In the hours before that first blast, Todd Russell's dad Noel decided he'd had enough of journalists phoning the house and photographers hanging about outside. He felt hemmed in and put upon and it outraged his sense of small-town propriety.

Paul Howes, the national vice-president of the Australian Workers Union, had become a confidante since he'd flown in from Melbourne soon after news of the Beaconsfield rock fall had shot around the country.

Howes, a chubby-faced young man in a union bomber jacket, had taken it upon himself to shuttle between the Russell, Webb and Knight families, trying to offer comfort, bringing scarce information and arranging beds for the growing number of family members and friends flying in from all points of the compass.

He had tried also to become a siphon for information between miners and journalists. He had burst into tears during a press briefing when he attempted to describe the devastating impact the hours of waiting had wrought upon the families. 'I've never in my life had to do a harder job than talk to those poor people,' he said, pleading with reporters and photographers to back off and give the anxious families space and respect.

In conversation with Nobby, he'd hit on an idea. If Nobby would come out and face the press and the cameras, make a short statement, he felt it would reduce the pressure. He'd make sure of it.

Nobby and Kaye Russell shunted the idea back and forth. The prospect was terrifying. Here was a family that had never imagined in its wildest dreams it would have anything to do with the media, let alone national TV channels, radio stations and newspapers. And now, just about felled by grief and worry, Noel Russell, the proprietor of the Beaconsfield Garage, was being asked to tell the world how he felt.

Well, he'd do it for Todd, he decided.

Kaye ran to the Uniting Church. She had to talk to somebody outside the family. Frances Seen was the church's community minister. Was brought up in Beaconsfield.

Her father-in-law had worked up on the old water race in the hills. She'd understand. All Kaye's fortitude just flew away as she stepped into the church and into Frances Seen's arms. She spoke in ragged sentences: 'God, what if Todd isn't alive? We'll have to help look after those kids. Todd won't be there to take Liam to the football – we'll have to be there with him every time and we will, we will. And Noel's going to go up to the mine and talk to all those media people . . .'. Frances Seen helped Kaye to the front of the church and they sat in a pew, holding each other, candles flickering on the altar.

Nobby couldn't do this on his own. He'd need his son Stephen with him, and his son-in-law Tim Scott, Lisa's husband.

Paul Howes called the media together in a park across West Street from the mine. He wanted guarantees, or there would be no press conference with Noel Russell. The deal was non-negotiable. Noel would read a short statement. There would be no questions. If Noel broke down at any stage, all cameras would be switched off and he'd be given time to compose himself. He was a proud man who deserved respect. When it was over, no one was to chase him. And there'd be no harassing of the family beyond that.

It was the sort of ultimatum that no professional public relations consultant would dare lay before a pack of hungry journalists. No questions? Cameras switched off at the moment raw emotion took over?

Yet many of the reporters in Beaconsfield were already questioning their own conduct. In the absence of a story that could be discerned, some of them had taken to buttonholing anyone who walked on the main street.

Most of these innocent souls knew no more and often a lot less than the media, which, after all, had been receiving press releases and updates from mine management, the mayor and the union. And this was a town in shock. It was frustrating and uncomfortable for all concerned, and the less hard-bitten within the media pack felt intrusive.

Howes's deal was accepted.

Noel Russell, Stephen and Tim Scott walked uncertainly across the park and stood in front of a picnic table, a forest of cameras trained upon them. Noel's big body was bowed and he held a lit cigarette in one hand.

'Okay,' said Howes. 'Noel will read his statement and then he'll go. No questions. Are we right?'

Noel dragged on his cigarette and focused on a sheet of paper. His hand shook so violently he had trouble reading his own handwritten words. His son and son-in-law stood either side, their arms supporting him.

'Todd is a loving husband, father, son . . . and mate,' he said, his voice not much more than a quaver, reporters leaning forward to catch his words.

'He would have been the first person to arrive to help in any rescue.'

'On behalf of our family, we wish to thank everyone for their support and especially our thanks go out to all those who have been and are still working in the rescue attempt to bring Todd and Brant home.

'The love and support that we have received has been so overwhelming and we thank you all from the bottom of our hearts. We request that our family's privacy be respected at this difficult time.'

And then Noel shuffled away with the two boys, Stephen outraged when a photographer ran across the road to get a picture of the family climbing into their car. 'You've been fuckin' told!' Stephen shouted. 'Fuck off now.'

Paul Howes had brought a picture of Todd, Carolyn and their three children. It was taken in a studio, framed, Todd standing at the back, the patriarch, his goatee carefully trimmed. The picture lay on the picnic table while cameras captured the image. None of the journalists knew it, but it was the first and only family portrait taken of Todd Russell and his family. He'd never made the time. Always away hunting. He'd robbed his family of a father's attention.

The thought of all that time lost harried Todd.

At the precise moment his own father was standing up there in the park, speaking of his love for a son he didn't believe he would see alive again, 12.30 pm on Friday, Todd Russell was 925 metres below, borrowing Brant's pen to write a message of love for the family he didn't believe he would see again, either.

As Noel Russell drove away, the media caravan was already moving on.

A new star was about to be born.

Bill Shorten had arrived.

Shorten was the national secretary of the Australian Workers Union. A tousle-haired 39-year-old, he had just won preselection for an Australian Labor Party seat in the Federal Parliament and enthusiasts were speaking of him as a future Labor Prime Minister.

He had been on a union delegation trip to study Canada's industrial relations system when he heard of the Beaconsfield disaster. Had just alighted from a plane in Ottawa when he received a phone call from Paul Howes. 'There's been a catastrophe at the Beaconsfield mine,'

Howes told him. 'Three men missing.' Three members of the union, indeed.

Shorten got himself on a plane to Chicago, Los Angeles and home to Melbourne, keeping himself informed of developments at every stop. He was on a quick stopover in Los Angeles when he learned that Larry Knight's body had been found. Three and a half hours after landing in Melbourne, he was on a plane to Launceston, and soon he arrived at Beaconsfield.

Cynics in political circles and the media saw Shorten's rush to Beaconsfield as opportunistic. Here was a man on a political trajectory stepping into the sort of limelight that would give him a national profile.

Shorten had a response to that. Wherever union members faced disaster, the AWU had a policy of standing at their side. The union had been with its members after an explosion killed two men at Esso's Longford gas plant in Gippsland, Victoria, in September 1998. Union officials had also rushed to the Santos gas plant in Moomba, South Australia, when an explosion and fire occurred on New Year's Day, 2004.

'Every time our members are in trouble, we send officials,' Shorten said. 'You have to move quickly. You need to know what is happening so you can get on top of things – to use an unfortunate metaphor, when the funeral is over, the blame game starts. I don't want our people, who are the lowest down the food chain where big business is involved, left copping the blame.'

The union, however, represented less than half the 130 workers at the mine. A lot of these weren't up to date with their financial membership, either. There had been at Beaconsfield a long history of quarrels between the AWU and the mine management, and it was only within the last few years that the union had managed to get a presence there, persuading miners they would be better off under collective bargaining than contracting. There was still a pay differential between those who had joined the union, working under awards, and those opting to stay on contract. Shorten claimed the mine was so bloody-minded it paid contractors more than employees, and those individuals who chose Australian Workplace Agreements got 3 per cent more than those who opted to remain on union-negotiated Enterprise Bargaining Agreements.

On top of all this was the union movement's campaign against the Howard Government's new industrial relations system, which was weighted towards union-busting individual agreements between employees and employers. Shorten was involved in more than a mere display of solidarity with missing members in a gold mine and he was acutely aware that his presence would be scrutinised by sceptics and enthusiasts alike.

He spoke briefly to journalists after Nobby Russell departed, declaring that what he had learned meant circumstances were grim, but that no one was about to give up hope. Before he said anything more, he wanted to meet the miners of his union.

Within 24 hours, Shorten had transformed himself into an unofficial spokesman for the rescue effort. He was able to bring news on Saturday morning that the crews underground had blasted twice, opening a drive 7 metres long.

The process, he said, was a catch-22. The men wanted to get to their mates as quickly as possible, but safety was paramount. Meanwhile, the families were suffering frustration and helplessness.

'People don't like that their lives are on hold and that they don't know where their men are,' he said.

As to whether the Beaconsfield gold mine was finished: 'The future of the mine is secondary to the fate of the trapped miners.'

Shorten had a talent for the quotable quote. He declared he did not want to venture into any political argument, but when he was asked whether he believed the Prime Minister or his representatives ought to be in Beaconsfield, he couldn't resist.

'The carrier pigeons have gone out, but nothing has been heard from the Howard Government,' he said.

Shorten, in a few hours, had wrested control of the public relations surrounding the Beaconsfield mine disaster and rescue effort by the simplest of means. The men of the union, many of whom were working underground, would speak to him and keep him abreast of developments when they finished their long shifts.

And Matthew Gill, exhausted from running a complex operation in the mine's operations room, was content to brief Shorten. It took a bit of the weight off Gill's increasingly heavy load of responsibilities. Press releases would continue to be issued and Gill would still appear daily before the media. But Shorten could translate it all into reassuring sound bites for the cameras and the microphones and the media could hardly get enough of him. He had his own media assistant, Ainslie Gowan, alongside and a team of AWU officials, including the Tasmanian secretary Ian Wakefield, a former hard-rock miner himself who understood the esoterica of what was going on.

CHAPTER 14

THE COOL KID IN GRADE 12

Heavy clouds rolled in from the ocean as the week dragged by, trapping Beaconsfield in grey gloom. As the district digested the bitter news that Larry Knight's body had been found, those clouds grew darker. There seemed no way out of the oppression. Colin Smee tended his flags, hoisting them each morning to half-mast, stepping out in the cold wind in short pants while everyone else hunkered down in sweaters and drew their coat collars tight.

Evenings settled early and the pubs drew only a few customers staring silently into beer glasses.

Saturday, hallelujah, brought sunshine.

The Tamar Cats, Todd Russell's old football team, were to play down at the Beauty Point oval. Up against St Pat's from Launceston.

Football is the social glue along the Tamar Valley. Aussie Rules. A few of the journalists in town decided to join the parade to Beauty Point. If anything was happening in the mine, it didn't feel like it on the surface. Shifts of rescue workers, exhausted, came and went, invisible behind the green plastic wall strung between the shaft head and the media circus. Above, the windlass whirred.

There is a comforting timelessness about country footy on a Saturday.

Ken Pinner, the president of the Tamar Cats Football Club, sat at a small wooden booth at the gates to the ground, extracting the entry price of $7 as supporters rolled in.

Pinner, a wiry little bloke with dicky knees, had wrestled with a big decision. A lot of the Cats players wanted to wear black armbands for the match. It's a tradition – the armbands are brought out when a club official, a former player or members of families attached to the club pass away.

Pinner wouldn't have it. A few days before, he'd shared a drink with a journalist at the Club Hotel. He lives at the pub, helping out the proprietor Chris Rundle, his nephew. Pinner – everyone calls him Pins – enjoys a glass of wine or two on a warm day or a cold day or any day in between. He spent decades as a travelling salesman and no stranger who wanders through the door of the Club is likely to be short of a yarning companion if Pins is around.

When he fell into conversation with the journalist, sitting out the front of the hotel puffing on a cigarette because smoking is banned in enclosed places right across Tasmania, Pins was pretty sure Todd and Brant and Larry were all beyond help. He'd been in bed on Anzac evening when Beaconsfield shook, and the power of it almost tossed him to the floor. Downstairs in the bar, bottles and glasses rattled and swayed on the shelves. Pins had soaked up the wisdom of the miners who drank at the Club and there seemed no doubt. Nobody could have survived in the 925.

But here was this journalist telling him about how he had been at Thredbo in the days after the earth had slid in the winter of 1997, burying whole ski lodges in mud and rocks and debris. How just about everybody in the ski village had given up hope of finding anyone alive until 55 hours after the disaster, when rescuers heard the faint cries of Stuart Diver, buried beneath three great slabs of concrete, half drowned and freezing. How it took another 10 hours to get Diver out. Alive.

'It's not over until it's over,' the journalist had told Pins. It had got him enthused. You've got to hold out hope, he decided.

So when the boys from the footy team came to Pins and asked about wearing black armbands for Todd – and Brant, too, because he was a Beauty Point boy even if his preferred game was rugby league – he told them it would be wrong. 'Remember Stuart Diver,' he said. 'Nobody's dead until there is a body.' He was the president and he won the argument.

Cars encircled the footy ground, nosed up to the fence. When the players ran out onto the field, car horns tooted; when someone kicked a goal, the horns blared.

Over by the clubhouse, girls in a little booth boiled up saveloys and served them with bread and tomato sauce. Beer flowed at the bar. Kids kicked footballs among the cars and old blokes sat along the fence, each voicing a running commentary to himself because no one else was listening. When a St Pat's player stuck an elbow into the face of a Cat, they roared and shook their fists, and they cheered when the Cat dragged himself to his feet and started throwing punches.

Inside the clubrooms hung pictures of the glory days. And there was Todd Russell with his team and on the opposite wall, pride of place, a photograph of him as not much more than a boy, clean-shaven and looking the camera in the eye. 'Tasmanian Amateur Representative 1991–92', the caption declared.

Todd hadn't played with the Cats for three seasons, but he was remembered as a gun full-forward, and he'd picked up a few best and fairest awards during his career. He had played for clubs all up and down the Tamar Valley: the Cats, Hillwood, Campbell Town, more than 300 senior-level matches. Every club he had played with had won a premiership with him at full-forward. There is not much money in country football, but Todd had always copped a decent match fee. He had recently signed to play full-forward with Bridgenorth Football Club, the Parrots, but had never taken the field – an injury to his foot was playing up, and he was waiting on an operation.

The game at Beauty Point seesawed and the sun shone, players ploughing through a load of sand dumped in the middle of the oval over its cricket pitch. The Cats' latest full-forward, an 18-year-old boy mountain named Quinton Tahiri, rose above himself and kicked 11 goals, sweeping his team to narrow victory. Tahiri's father, improbably, was playing, too. This was country football at its most delicious.

The long, shining autumn afternoon seemed far away from the troubles at the mine along the river and up the road, and a lot of the crowd streamed away to a large brick hotel perched on the river bank. The Riviera. A log fire blazed and drinkers stood three deep at the bar. Proprietor Marshall Brien was in the midst of a rush season bigger than any summer holiday tourist influx. He had packed journalists, union officials and friends of the Webb family into his rooms, and still the phone rang. His kitchen was under strain, the dining room filled. You need a big appetite to cope with the size of the meals served up and down the Tamar Valley, but at the Riviera the kitchen's slogan seemed to be that too much is barely enough. A specialty of the house was the 'paddock and pen' – an immense steak and an equally large chicken fillet crowned with prawns and cheese sauce.

Among Marshall's guests was a small man with a weather-beaten face, a Roman nose and a grin that would melt a heart. John Webb, Brant's dad. Webb and his partner Val Rodiger, an attractive self-contained woman, had arrived from Queensland a few days before and were already among the most popular people in the pub.

John's long-time mate, a fellow from Port Macquarie in NSW named Dave McIlveen but known as Cyclone because he was said to have left a trail of damage wherever he went in his younger years, stood by the open fire regaling locals with fishing tales. Webb had plenty of those, too. He'd made a fortune years ago on trawlers in north Queensland. Made it and lost it. Lost everything, really, after he fell for another woman and divorced his wife Christa, Brant's mother. Brant was a happy-go-lucky young man skippering trawlers himself by then. He and Rachel and their baby twins lived in a wing of John and Christa's huge house at Bowen. They had to watch the marriage fall apart, the family home sold. John eventually lost his last boat as the maintenance bills stacked too high to reach.

Brant shared his mother's pain as she set about rebuilding a life in ruins. Christa later met and married a former miner, Bob Jeffery. A fitter at the Kidston gold mine, 280 kilometres north-west of Townsville, Jeffery received serious back injuries when a truck tyre fell on him. He and Christa worked hotels for friends and eventually leased a hotel in Herberton, in far north Queensland. But Christa's new happiness ended when Jeffery died of cancer about four years ago. She forged on, met a new partner, Don Parson, though she kept Bob Jeffery's surname. Don Parson, who had lost his own wife to cancer a year before Bob Jeffery died, is a builder and a skilled cabinet-maker. He and Christa settled down together at Kairi on the Atherton Tableland above Cairns.

The old wounds between Christa Jeffery and John Webb had healed over the years, and they talked occasionally on the phone. But they were no longer close and here they were in Beauty Point, their son Brant in peril. Occasionally, they put aside the fraught past and sat down for dinner at the Riviera, new partners at their sides. Other guests at the hotel looked on in confusion, not quite sure who was who.

Don, Christa and her sister Corinna Mitchell, of Bundaberg, moved in to the Beauty Point Hotel, an appealing, modern establishment sitting above a marina on the Tamar River. The hotel has been rebuilt since it burnt down years ago. Todd Russell was on one of the fire crews fighting the fire and fell through the roof as it burned away beneath him. Townsfolk still remember it.

He threw out his big arms and stopped his fall before he crashed into the flames beneath, dragged himself out, grabbed a fire hose and kept pouring water on the conflagration.

The various strands of the Webb family chose to give Rachel a bit of space. She sat in her lounge at home, trying to hold herself together, a stream of friends filling the house but hardly on her radar.

She was trying to commune with Brant. She believed their partnership was so tight, so designed by destiny, that their souls were tuned to a wavelength that could transcend everything. And yes, penetrate the very earth.

Rachel carried in her head a picture of the moment she first saw Brant. It was a hot January day on a beach in Bowen. Rachel was the new kid in town and rode her bike to the beach to look out across the sea. Her family was a bit nomadic. She was born in Canberra in July 1970 while her parents were on holiday from their home in Victoria. When she was 12 the Kelly family moved to Townsville, her mother seeking sunshine and her father a new opportunity selling cars.

Now they had all shifted again, to Bowen, where Rachel's father wanted to set up his own car dealership. Rachel had an older brother, Jason, and an older sister, Natalie. In Townsville, her mother volunteered for nursing duties at an orphanage and she fell in love with two Aboriginal babies, Mona and Lee. She fostered both of them and the family expanded.

Now Rachel was about to start a new life at a new school, Bowen High.

She saw in the distance a jogger on the sand. Rachel was attracted to the powerful style of his running. As he approached, she decided he was handsome. But he kept running and she rode away.

A couple of weeks later she saw the same young man at her new school. He stood beneath a tree with friends, laughing and telling some story, his hands waving in the air. He was Brant Webb. The cool kid in Grade 12. Rachel was in Grade 11. The next day, he walked towards her on the way to his class, smiled, said 'Good morning, Rachel' and kept walking. *What does that mean?* she asked herself. *How does he know my name?* Everything about him was perfect – the cut of his hair, the scent of him. A few days later, one of Brant's friends passed a message to Rachel. Would she go with Brant to a mate's 18th birthday? On that first date she said to Brant, 'I don't kiss a boy unless we're going out.' 'Well,' he said, 'are we going out?' And that was it. Brant and Rachel. Right through the school year.

Brant graduated at the end of the year and went off to Cairns to study for his trawler boat skipper's certificate. He invited Rachel to visit him during her school holidays. She was planning to attend radio and television school in Brisbane after she completed Grade 12; wanted to be a producer. But in the first weeks of school, she phoned Brant in Cairns.

'Guess what,' she said. 'I'm pregnant.' Brant was about to sail. He was at sea for five months. When he returned, he and Rachel went to Mackay for an ultrasound test. The result bowled them over. Rachel was having twins. Brant came home from the sea to attend the birth of the children on 20 October 1987. Rachel was 17, Brant was 19. He moved to Bowen to live with Rachel and the babies, picking up a trawler out of the port, a week at a stretch. One day, sitting at the kitchen table, Brant looked at Rachel and said, 'So are you going to marry me?' They picked out an engagement ring, three big sapphires. Brant was savvy and didn't have much money. He talked the jeweller into a 50 per cent discount.

Rachel was a natural mother and she came to believe it had been her destiny to have her twins, Zachary and Zoey, so early in her life. It meant her grandfather, once a miner himself at Mt Lyell on Tasmania's west coast, got to see great-grandchildren. Family had always meant much to Rachel.

She was a Kelly, descended from hard doers, rebels and fighters. Her great-great-grandfather dug for gold at Ballarat and took up a gun at the Eureka Stockade in 1854. His son, Michael Kelly, was a boy at the time and ran buckets of water into the stockade for the miners, knowing the troopers wouldn't shoot a child. Michael Kelly went on to support the leader of the Eureka revolutionaries, Peter Lalor, as he took up politics in Victoria.

Michael Kelly's passion for tough causes ended up getting him blinded. Hired thugs threw lime into his eyes as he marched on Victoria's Parliament House in support of striking shearers.

Rachel's family believed it was entirely possible they were related to Ned Kelly, the bushranger. They had come from the same Irish county, Tipperary, as Red Kelly, Ned's father. They had never bothered to track through the genealogy, but when Rachel's father Michael and her mother Julie finally left Queensland and settled in Tasmania, they set up a business manufacturing salad dressings and relishes. They called it Red Kelly's. On Rachel and Brant's back porch stood a replica set of Ned Kelly's steel armour.

A rock fall in a mine couldn't take a Kelly girl's man, she resolved. They'd been through so much together. Couldn't stop now, with the twins right on the cusp of their transition from childhood to adulthood.

The house swirled with people. Food was cooked and brought in by neighbours and strangers. Zac and his girlfriend Kimberley, Zoey and her boyfriend Richard tended to Rachel, brought her food and sat holding her hands. Zoey worked at Dr Tony Lyall's surgery and Lyall swept in and out, keeping an anxious eye on his friend and patient. Rachel's sister Natalie came from her home in the Tasmanian village of Perth and brought her 9-year-old son Jack. For the first few nights, Natalie and Jack slept with Rachel in her bed. 'The greatest gift Natalie could bring was her boy, her comfort, and she gave that comfort to me,' was how Rachel put it later. An old school friend from Bowen, Kym Price, came and shared Rachel's bed, too. Natalie put the story around that Rachel had to be left alone because she was heavily sedated. It was not true – Rachel wanted her mind clear to process every piece of information that came her way – though it stopped Gavan Cheesman from attempting to visit on his mission to persuade the families that Brant, Todd and Larry could not have survived. Natalie's story was, however, unnecessary. Vinnie Tunks roamed about making sure that Rachel wasn't disturbed when she wanted to be left alone. He was perfectly direct. 'Sorry,' he said, shaking his head, even to family members.

Rachel kept a talisman on her lap. The day after Brant was trapped, his new driving licence arrived in the mail. Rachel wouldn't let it out of her sight. It had Brant's photo engraved on it. It had been taken only the week before. His last photo. She believed it was a sign.

Rachel prayed for air for her man. She prayed for water. And in that half-world before she slept, she felt she was alone with Brant; could talk to him. She believed utterly that she could transport messages of strength to him. One night she concentrated so hard that she was convinced his voice came to her. 'I love you, Rach.' It was him. No one could persuade her otherwise.

The tiniest sign gathered immense significance. One night Val Rodiger, John Webb's partner, wanted to mix herself a cocktail at Brant's prized bar in the corridor. Rachel turned on the light and it flickered. Over Brant's bar.

Every evening Rex Johnson or his offsider Craig Large arrived to tell Rachel of the day's efforts in the mine. They trooped mud into her house. She had never felt so happy to have mud on her carpet.

It came from deep in the earth, down near Brant somewhere, proof that men were trying to rescue him.

Left: Brant and Rachel on their wedding day, 10 December 1988. **Above:** The family in 1995: Brant, Rachel, Zac and Zoey.

Clockwise from top left: John and Christa, Brant's father and mother, with his brother Shaun. Rachel and Brant (aged 17). Brant on a knee board, 2005. Brant, his father, John, and their catch, 1986. **Right:** Brant, Rachel and Zoey at Montes Reef Resort, 1990.

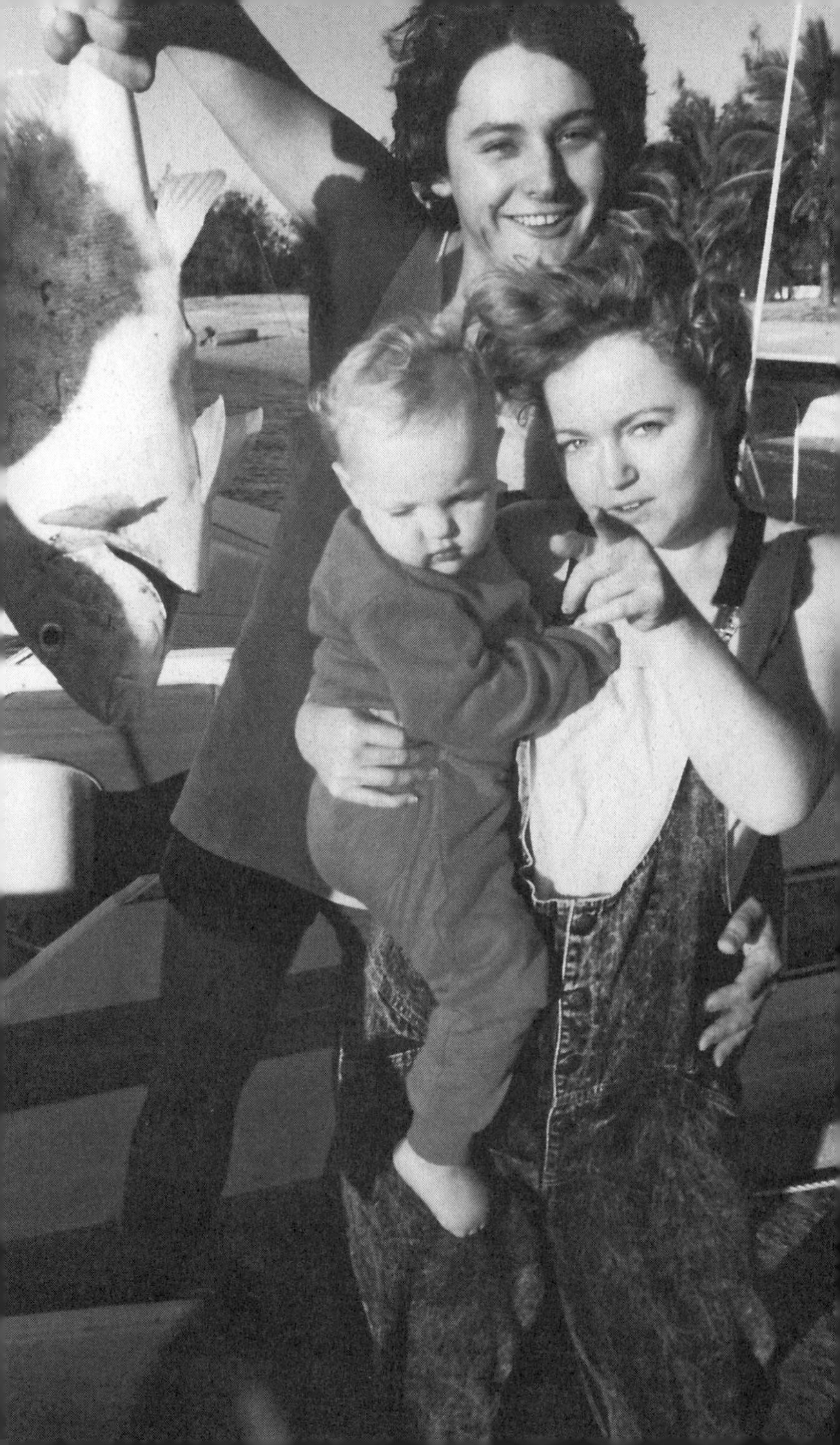

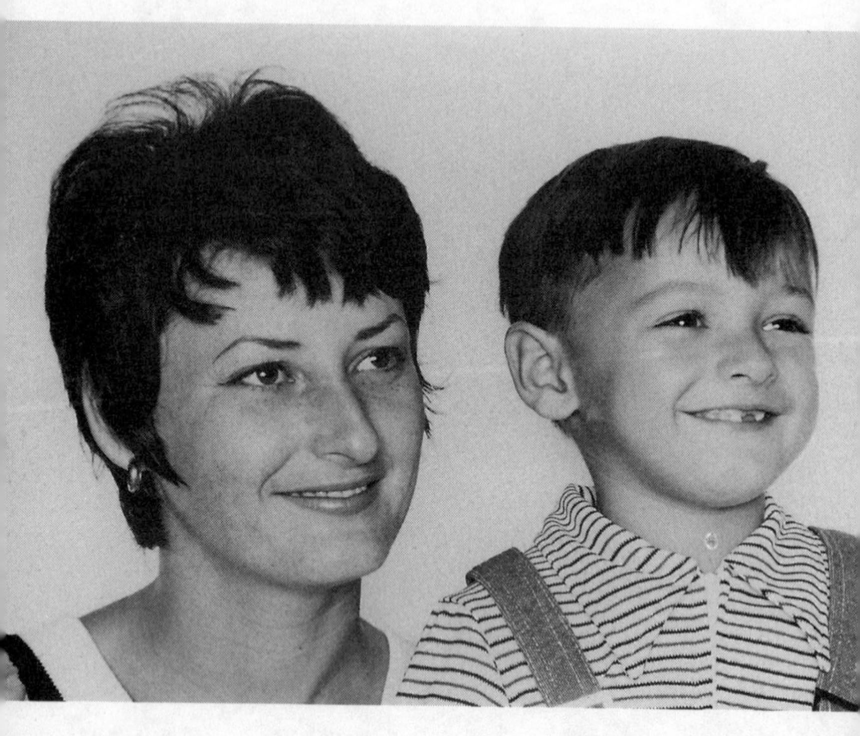

Above: Brant aged about 5 years with his mother, Christa.

Above: (from left) Zachary Webb, Her Excellency Mrs Marlena Jeffery, His Excellency the Governor-General Michael Jeffery, Rachel Webb, Brant Webb and Zoey Webb.
Next page: Beaconsfield mine site, April 2006.

Above: Carolyn and Todd Russell (back) with their children Trent and Maddison (middle) and Liam (front), 2005. **Right:** Todd with his father, Noel, at the junior football grand final, 1984.

BMU

Clockwise from top left: Todd (right) as a young child with his brother, Stephen. Todd on his fifth birthday. Todd as team captain with coach Max Pearce, 2000. Todd and Carolyn at St Columba Falls near St Helens, Tasmania. **Left:** Todd, aged 19, Tasmanian representative in Perth, WA.

Above: Todd and Carolyn at their first dinner together.

Above: Todd's family at his brother Stephen's wedding, 1999.

Above: Todd with Hillwood football club.
Right: Todd and Carolyn on their wedding day, 2 October 1993.

CHAPTER 15

VOICES FROM THE DEAD

■ ■ ■

Sunday, 30 April. Afternoon.

It seemed impossible to Brant and Todd that they were still alive. They had endured six firings now. Todd knew it because he had carefully noted the time and the date on his overalls, so heavily encrusted in filth showering from the roof and turning to mud with all the water that he had to scrub away at it before he could write anything. Each series of blasts had become louder and more violent than the one before. Getting closer. Their nerves were gone.

The crew out there was drilling again and the drills seemed to be about to scythe through the wall.

Todd and Brant were beyond exhaustion. Something past 100 hours had floated by since they stood in the basket to finish off a wire wall. An hour, though, was bereft of meaning: it could be a minute or a week or a year.

Brant had slipped into a deep funk. He was a shadow of the comedian Todd knew from the crib. He was giving up, disappearing into himself to escape the sound of the drills and what it meant. Todd had to rouse him. Somehow. He needed to revive Brant's spirit so Brant could keep Todd going. Couldn't have one without the other.

'Hey Brant. You know any of Alan Jackson's songs?'

'Nuh. Never heard of him.'

Todd was astounded. Never heard of Alan Jackson? Brant was having a lend of him. Hell, everyone had heard of Alan Jackson. Best country singer in the world. A superstar! Wore a righteous white cowboy hat and a moustache. Wrote that song about the terrorist attack when those mad bastards hijacked jets and flew them into the World Trade Center in New York.

Where were you when the world stopped turning
that September day
Out in the yard with your wife and children
Working on some stage in LA.

Brant must have heard that song.

'Never heard of it,' mumbled Brant.

Unbelievable. Todd loved those lush steel guitar licks, the voice, that chugging country rhythm. All those good lyrics that got him deep down.

Carolyn teased him about it a bit. Only a few weeks ago she'd joked that she'd play an Alan Jackson song at Todd's funeral. And truth be told, he'd be happy with it, except he didn't want a funeral anytime soon. He knew the song, too. 'Farewell Party,' it was called. Sad words.

When the last breath of life is gone from my body
And my lips are as cold as the sea

When my friends gather around for my farewell party
Won't you pretend you love me?

Shit. Can't think like that.

'What about Lee Kernaghan? He's pretty good.'

'Todd, I don't like country *or* western.'

It offended Todd. Here he was trying to cheer up old Brant, get him into some sort of shape, and he was insulting his taste in music.

'Well, what do you like?'

'Rock music. Foo Fighters.'

Foo Fighters? What was that?

Those blokes out there would be organising another firing soon.

'C'mon, Brant. Let's sing something.'

'What're we gonna bloody sing? Do you know any Midnight Oil songs?'

Todd didn't know any Midnight Oil songs, no.

He began singing a country song called 'Ghosts on the Highway.' Spun Brant right out.

'You know any Kenny Rogers?' Todd asked.

That got Brant's attention. Of course he knew a bit of Kenny Rogers. Anyone who'd ever been to a bar had heard Kenny Rogers. Todd led Brant into it: 'The Gambler.'

On a warm summer's evenin' on a train bound for nowhere,
I met up with the gambler; we were both too tired to sleep.
So we took turns a-starin' out the window at the darkness
'Til boredom overtook us, and he began to speak.

Brant began getting his sense of humour back at that. It all seemed perfectly absurd lying there waiting to be killed and singing a song like this. Both too tired to sleep. Yeah. Right.

When they got to the chorus, the men bawled it out.

You got to know when to hold 'em, know when to fold 'em,
Know when to walk away and know when to run.
You never count your money when you're sittin' at the table.
There'll be time enough for countin' when the dealin's done.

There was an edge of hysteria to it. Both men felt it, but neither cared. It felt better to be shouting a song like crazy men than lying mute, listening to water trickling and dealing with pictures in their heads that veered from their families to what might happen when the walls and the roof collapsed on them. Or listening for the drills that were bringing doom. And it warmed them up for the first time in . . . forever.

If you've got to go insane there was, Brant thought, a bit of comfort in this sort of insanity. They sang 'Coward of the County.'

That was about the breadth of Brant's repertoire.

They got back to singing 'The Gambler.'

Halfway through, Todd grabbed Brant's arm.

There was a voice. 'Shut up in there you blokes!' They both heard it. Faint. Muffled.

'I'm sure there's someone out there,' Todd whispered. 'What're they saying?' Brant demanded. Whispering too. Couldn't believe it.

'We're here! We're here!' they shouted together, desperate. There was some sort of reply but the meaning of it was lost to the two men in their cage, the words swimming around with the maddening cascade of water on the footwall. They hardly dared believe it, but this time, there was no mistaking what was happening. There were men out there, and they knew Todd and Brant were alive.

The mine foreman, Steven 'Salty' Saltmarsh, and Pat Ball decided to take a look at the 925-metre drive. No one had been in there since the night it collapsed.

Saltmarsh still believed there was a chance Todd and Brant were alive and he wanted to see for himself whether there was any way a rescue could be launched through the fall of rock covering the telehandler.

Everyone associated with the search recognised that the new tunnel being blown up from the decline towards Todd and Brant was nearing a tipping point. It had been driven more than 20 metres through solid rock, and there were still almost 16 metres to go. The rescue coordinators wanted one more explosive cut. One more nerve-shredding blast. It would take the tunnel 24.5 metres. They would drill probe holes then. Probe for life. Push a light, the heat-seeking camera and a microphone through. They had to hold out the chance that the two men had managed to cling to existence.

Saltmarsh wanted to explore every possible contingency before any more blasting took place.

None of the men who were in the mine on the night of the earthquake was supposed to be called back in to the rescue, but Saltmarsh needed an expert driller and he was running out of available hands. He called Mick Borrill's mobile phone. Found him at the Launceston markets with his wife Sandra.

'Mick,' he said, 'I need you for a special job.' The mine had found a thermal camera from somewhere – the NSW Fire Service – and he needed Mick to operate the Simba drilling rig to bore a hole big enough to push the camera through the wall. A thermal camera reacts to heat. If the men were still alive, the camera might be able to detect their body heat.

Mick Borrill agreed and Sandra knew she couldn't protest. She was torn by the very idea of her husband going underground again, but she recognised he couldn't refuse to help. He was a hard-rock miner, had been one ever since she had met him, and he wouldn't be able to live properly with himself if he didn't lend a hand to mates in trouble.

Neither Mick nor Sandra had slept well since Anzac night. Unspoken fears roamed the darkness, put them both on edge. Truth be told, Sandra felt a creeping suspicion that the threads binding them could fray at the far edges if Mick didn't go back down and do this task that was being set for him, whatever it was. It could drive a wedge into their relationship. Sandra called a friend, Cheryl, to sit with her during the long hours to come. She wept all day.

Mick kitted himself up, rode the shaft down and climbed aboard the Simba. Drove it to the 915 level and waited. Dennis Newson was in the new drive fired from the decline towards the 925, using a jumbo to drill the pinholes for bolting and meshing to secure it.

Saltmarsh and Ball headed off on foot down the access to the 925, stepping over the ropes that had fenced it off since the tele-remote bogger was pulled out on Thursday.

They had an idea that it might be possible to set a thermal camera on the remote bogger's blade, get it in behind the telehandler and see if it could detect anything.

In minutes they rushed back, screaming for Newson to turn off the jumbo and for the men to close down the fans and every machine in the place.

'They're alive,' Saltmarsh bellowed. 'We heard them. One of you blokes has got to come with us right now and verify it.'

It was 5.45 pm. Sunday, 30 April. The silence was unnatural, creepy.

All the men in the decline ran for the 925 tunnel: Mick Borrill, Dennis Newson, Garth Bonney and Dave 'Johnno' Johnson.

They gathered behind the telehandler.

'Can you hear us?' Saltmarsh called.

Indistinct voices came from the rock piled over the telehandler. The hair prickled on the backs of the necks of each of the men standing in the drive. They elected Johnno to make the next call because he had the loudest voice.

'We're coming to get you,' he boomed.

'All right!'

This time, they made out the voices of Todd and Brant crying in unison.

The men stood stunned. They held a hurried conference and decided to compile a list of crucial questions. They couldn't make a mistake here. Not now.

A tragedy at the Sago coalmine in West Virginia, US, on 2 January 2006, had spooked the world's mining community. The ghastly fiasco had been playing on the minds of all those taking part in the search and rescue at Beaconsfield.

Twelve men asphyxiated after the underground gas explosion in West Virginia and one man was injured. But the tragedy was hideously compounded when someone got the details reversed and family members and friends gathered in a church were told that only one man had died and 12 had survived. Celebrations and prayers of praise lasted for three hours before the families learned the dreadful truth.

The Beaconsfield mine management and the rescuers working underground were determined to prevent any repeat of such a debacle. They had to ascertain proof of life before a single word seeped out of the mine. Couldn't simply *believe* they had heard both Todd and Brant.

Saltmarsh and Johnno Johnson returned to the drive, right up close behind the telehandler.

'Todd,' shouted Johnno. 'Are you there?'

'Yes, I am here,' came the distorted reply.

'Brant, are you there?'

'Yes, I am here.'

'Todd, are you injured?'

'No.'

'Brant, are you injured?'

'No.'

'Do you have water?'

'Yes.'

'Do you have food?'

'No.'

Inside their cage, Brant and Todd were delirious with relief and joy. Those blokes out there wanted the proof of life. Now they had it. They were coming!

Still Saltmarsh and Pat Ball couldn't allow news of the extraordinary discovery to reach the surface. Mick Borrill needed to phone his wife to assure her he was safe. He had promised. Four hours had passed since he came down the mine. Sandra would be worried half out of her mind. He was granted permission, but he could not say a word about Brant and Todd. Saltmarsh stood alongside Borrill as he made a quick call, telling Sandra he was fine and there was no reason to be anxious.

The men of the night shift came down the shaft around 6 pm. Pat Ball met them as they alighted from the cage at the 375 Plat.

'They're alive,' he said. 'We've talked to Todd and Brant. You can't leave and you can't say anything to anyone.' Radio silence had to be observed so no word leaked to the surface.

'We didn't know what to do or what to say,' Daniel Piscioneri remembers. 'It was just amazing.'

Corey Verhey could hardly believe his ears. His friends Keno Tatto and Dean Mackrell ran to him and slapped him on the back. 'Mate, you were right. You were right all the way along.'

Nobody had believed Corey's story about a psychic laying out his destiny, that he would be responsible for two men being alive. He felt dizzy. 'It turned me into a bit of a believer, I can tell you,' he said later.

Dale Burgess, a shift boss highly regarded by his men, had the task of setting up more reliable communication with Brant and Todd. He rounded up Daniel Piscioneri and a few of the other fellows. The mine had a microphone provided by the fire service specialists.

They found a long stick of conduit – the stiff plastic pipe electricians use to protect cables – and connected it to the bucket at the front of the remote bogger. The microphone was attached to the furthest length of the conduit extending 3 metres from the front of the big loader.

They rolled the bogger into the 925 drive until the microphone sprouting from the blade was nestled as far as possible into the scree covering the telehandler.

A long cable trailed from the microphone, 80 metres down the length of the drive and out through the access tunnel to the decline where the men set up a loudspeaker balanced on the concrete block previously used by the tele-remote operators.

Burgess, a handsome man with dark hair parted in the middle and swept back, picked up a megaphone, strode down the access and stood at the crosscut, the T-intersection with the 925 drive. He felt vulnerable. The roof above his head, somewhere up there in darkness, was unsupported and fractured. Rex Johnson stood with him.

Daniel Piscioneri and Dean Mackrell hovered by the loudspeaker. An official from the mines inspectorate, Fred Sears's offsider Mark Smith, prepared to record every word.

This was not only a moment that everyone in the mine knew was about to become an Australian legend.

There would be an inquiry. Every step of the search and rescue would be subjected to microscopic examination. Careers, the future of the Beaconsfield mine, the whole Tasmanian mining industry and the regulatory bodies charged with overseeing the industry were all on the line. Everything had to be recorded.

Dale Burgess shouted into the darkness, his megaphone amplifying his voice, the power of it echoing down the access.

'Can you hear me, Todd?' he called.

No response.

Piscioneri and Mackrell had already worked out a system of signalling Burgess. They shook their heads and the beam from their cap lamps swept from side to side.

'Can you hear me, Brant?'

No response. Piscioneri and Mackrell, bent closer to the loudspeaker, willing a voice, any sound of life at all, to reach out to them. Nothing. Shook their heads.

Burgess tried again. 'Todd? Brant?' he hollered.

Piscioneri and Mackrell heard it together. 'Yes.' The voice was faint; almost too faint to discern. But it was a voice. Todd, they thought.

Relief washed through Piscioneri. He had found Larry's body. Was still rocked by it. Now he was hearing the voice of a man he was sure had died, too. A voice from the dead.

'Yeah, it was brilliant,' he said later. 'It was pretty hard to hold back the tears. We were pretty glassy-eyed. Hard to describe, really.'

Burgess, standing more than 30 metres away down at the crosscut, could see two cap lamps nodding back in the decline. Two thin light beams zipping from the floor to the roof and back. Someone in there had acknowledged his amplified questions. Burgess had had to deal with his own rattled emotions after he had spent Thursday overseeing the removal of Larry's body from the mine. Talked to his wife Carolyn on the phone for an hour to try to soothe the jagged boundaries of his mind. Now it felt like redemption despite the danger of the roof falling on him.

Burgess went through the proof-of-life procedure. He had a script, a long series of prepared questions that would help the rescuers understand the depth of the predicament facing them and Brant and Todd.

Was either of the men injured? Was there blood? Airflow? Water? Food? Did they have cap lamps? Oxy-boxes? Was their mental state okay?

Todd had a louder, deeper voice than Brant. But he was further away from the microphone, scrunched up behind Brant, even if it was only a few centimetres. Piscioneri and Mackrell had to strain to hear every word. They got a message to Burgess. Could Brant respond instead of Todd? The switch worked. Brant's voice travelled much more clearly to the microphone.

Burgess's questions were often difficult for Todd and Brant to understand, however. The words merged with the sound of running water. Brant often had to ask that a question be repeated.

The questions became more complex, too. Burgess asked if the men had any messages they would like passed to their families.

'Tell them we're all right and we're coming home,' Brant yelled.

One of the more pressing problems for Burgess was to find out exactly where the men lay trapped. Brant told him they were in the steel basket and that when the roof collapsed, it was resting on the bund. What he didn't know was whether the floor beneath was part of the bund, or whether the basket had been hammered towards the original floor of the drive. It would take days for the rescuers and Simon Arthur, the surveyor, to establish that the weight of the rockfall had smashed the basket from about 2 metres up the side of the bund to just 50 centimetres above the original floor. As to the exact distance the basket sat from the telehandler, Brant could not tell. Everything was obscured by fallen rock.

Burgess's interrogation revealed mighty problems for rescuers. The great positive was that Brant and Todd were alive and relatively uninjured.

The thought of the two men huddled behind the rock without food fairly ripped at the brains of the miners. Brant and Todd could be no more than 6 metres or so from the back of the telehandler and it was within sight.

By 7 pm, the men of the day shift were finally free to leave the mine. Their tremendous secret could be released to the world.

First, Rex Johnson had to tell Carolyn and Rachel that their men were alive.

CHAPTER 16

JUST ONE CHANCE

Carolyn Russell, once she had regained a measure of composure after the first shock of hearing that Todd was missing underground, felt a physical need to be closer to him.

In the evenings she drew a beanie over her hair and organised a friend or a member of the big extended family around her to drive her to the mine.

She chose a different car each night because the route meant driving through the pack of journalists camped outside the mine gates. She didn't want to be recognised.

She felt free, almost cheeky as she cruised past the reporters and the camera crews, no more than another anonymous face in a procession of vehicles heading to the mine.

Her family and friends had protected her ever since Anzac night and somehow the media had never cottoned on to her appearance. One of the papers had run a picture of two women in the street and the caption said one of them was Carolyn Russell. It wasn't her. Another paper said she was hunkered down at home, never leaving the house. One day she was in the street talking to Todd's brother Stephen and they were approached by a journalist. The reporter asked Stephen if he would agree to an interview. 'No,' said Stephen. 'What about your dad?' the reporter asked. 'No, he won't be interviewed either.' And then the newsman walked away. He hadn't recognised Carolyn.

It was liberating. Carolyn had always been a private soul and she saw no reason why her suffering, however it was presented, should be stolen and beamed to a world of strangers.

Kaye Russell took a different approach. No one could miss her distinctive white hair. It caught the light and radiated her presence. This was her town. She had walked its streets most days of her life. All the microphones and cameras did not belong; they were a mere transitory phenomenon. And so she steeled her nerve and marched along Weld Street any time she felt like it; visited the baker, the newsagent, the butcher and the credit union. Chatted to friends. Brushed past reporters. Pretty soon the media recognised that Kaye had right of passage and let her be.

The family took some delight in stories they knew to be wrong appearing in the papers. One day Todd's labrador Harley got out of the yard and wandered around to the mine. The dog gambolled unnoticed among the news cars and vans parked outside the mine gates and finally found his way into the grounds of the mine. One of the security guards eventually recognised Harley and called Carolyn. The dog was locked up after that, but days later stories appeared in newspapers claiming Harley was so distraught at Todd's disappearance that the faithful animal had spent every day pining for its master outside the mine.

What might those journalists give to know that Todd Russell's wife was driving to the mine right under their noses every evening just to be closer to her man?

The dull light of day fading through twilight, she stepped through the security gate into the grounds of the mine. Familiar. She knew the guards and they were happy to have her sit on the steps inside the gate, lost in her thoughts.

A song had slipped inside her head a day or two after the first turmoil and it had taken up residence, playing over and over. She welcomed the tune. It soothed her. Kept her sane, really. It was Nickelback's 'Far Away.'

Just one chance
Just one breath
Just in case there's just one left
'Cause you know,
you know, you know
I love you
I have loved you all along
And I miss you
Been far away for far too long
I keep dreaming you'll be with me
and you'll never go
Stop breathing if
I don't see you anymore.

Most nights Carolyn sat there above the mine for two or three hours, cold dark settling around her. The windlass turned and she knew men were coming and going, trying to find her husband. She chatted easily to the guards. She belonged there. Close to Todd. Her children would be asleep by now, settled by her parents or her sister.

Trent had gone quiet after she sat him down and explained the accident. He hovered by her side all day, serious, whatever he was thinking buried deep. Maddison, normally effervescent and loud, had withdrawn, too. Carolyn wondered whether little Liam quite understood what had happened. He kicked his football and played with his friends and seemed to enjoy all the restless movement of people coming and going.

Carolyn didn't have the burden of cooking for her guests. Peter Gill from the Foodworks supermarket filled the boot of a car with frozen meals, cooked chickens, boxes of tea and coffee, crates of milk. All sorts of things. Just sent it around. Slammed the boot. Off you go. No cost. Gill just kept re-stocking the larder. Friends and strangers turned up at the door carrying casseroles and containers of soup. Spoke kind words. Drove away. All the kindnesses left Carolyn dazed.

By Sunday, Carolyn felt strong enough for a real outing. The whole family was invited to attend an Australian Football League match in Launceston. St Kilda and Fremantle. The Australian Workers Union was to take the bucket for its fund for the victims of the mine disaster.

Addison, the 10-year-old son of Larry Knight's partner Jacqui, was given a treat boys of his age could only dream about. He ran onto the oval at Aurora Stadium with the St Kilda team, the big crowd cheering.

Carolyn wasn't much interested in the game. Couldn't concentrate anyway. She and her sister Vicki wandered about, watching Liam kicking the new football his uncle Stephen had given him.

Around 14,000 people had packed the stadium and as they walked in, attendants ripped their tickets in half, returning the stub to the ticket holder and tossing the other half on the ground. Liam, bored after hours at the stadium, began thrashing around in the pile of tickets and picked one up. He handed it to his mother. Stephen glanced at it and could hardly believe his eyes. It was Liam's own ticket. He had the stub in his pocket. It matched. Ticket number Q129. It seemed to Stephen to be beyond coincidence. A chance in 14,000. It was a portent.

'Carolyn,' he said. 'I have to tell you I've never been able to believe you when you say Todd is alive. But I believe you now. I do.'

Stephen took the two halves of Liam's ticket home and had them framed. Hung it on his wall.

That evening, Nobby Russell retired to the little shed in his back yard he called the office. Had a fridge in there stocked with beer, a TV, a few chairs. It was his retreat, but no one was about to let Todd Russell's dad sit there alone, thinking. Stephen dropped in for a beer; Nobby's son-in-law, Tim Scott, arrived; a close friend of the family, Tim Williams, turned up. Pretty soon the shed was filled with men.

And then they heard screaming.

Kaye Russell had charge of her youngest grand-children, Liam, Logan and Callum. The day at the footy had tired everyone out. Kaye cooked dinner for the children and took them for a walk down to Carolyn's. As she turned the corner, a utility roared down the street. Screeched to a stop outside Carolyn's house.

It was Rex Johnson.

'Quick, Kaye, come inside,' Rex called. 'Quick.'

Kaye marshalled her grandchildren and hurried.

Rex stood in the lounge-room, panting, and the words rushed out.

'We've found them. Todd and Brant are alive. I can't tell you any more. I've got to get to Rachel's. But they're alive.'

The house exploded in shouts and cheers. Everyone, it seemed, was kissing and hugging everyone else. Carolyn felt the room sway and it seemed she was in the middle of a storm.

Kaye couldn't contain herself. She left Liam with Carolyn and ran out of the house, clutching the hands of her other two grandchildren. She screamed and couldn't stop. 'They're alive! They're alive!' But her voice was ahead of the words and it came out as a long shriek. She kept shrieking as she ran to her house. Noel had to know. Noel had to know now.

Noel and the boys in the shed were horrified. Christ, what now? Nobby's first thought: Logan, the three-year-old. Where was he? Gone down the driveway, someone's backed over him! All the men in the shed, six or eight of them, bolted for the doorway and hit it at the same time. They were wedged, couldn't get out and the screaming was getting louder.

'Noel, Noel,' Kaye cried. 'They're alive!'

Rex Johnson hunted his ute to Beauty Point, speed limits forgotten. Pulled up outside Rachel's house, ran inside.

Rachel had a bowl of soup, flowers on the plate, and was on the phone to a friend in Melbourne, Kym

Sadler, sister of one of Brant's best mates from his days in Bowen. Rachel had been crying, her eyes puffy, but she was mesmerised by what Kym was telling her. Kym had visited a psychic who had drawn her a picture. Oblong shapes. A crystal out the back. Two figures in the oblong out the front. The crystal had to represent Larry's soul and the two figures in the oblong box had to mean that Brant and Todd were still alive, they agreed.

Rex Johnson shouldered his way through a crowd of Rachel and Brant's family members and friends, charged through the house.

'Where's Rachel?' he shouted. People pointed to her small lounge-room. 'Hold on, Kym,' Rachel said, holding the phone away from her ear, trying to understand what all the fuss was about.

Rex burst through the door, took two steps, fell to one knee and gasped: 'Rachel, we've found them. They're alive! They're fine.'

Rachel had the impression of people flowing like water through the door behind Rex. She felt a rumbling energy rolling through her body, from her feet to her head. 'You could feel this power, this great roar from all the people in the room and all through the house,' she described the sensation.

It was one of the rare occasions that Rachel's parents and both Brant's parents were all in the house at the same time. Parents, brothers, sisters, friends hugged and kissed and danced jigs.

'I've got to get back to the mine,' Rex said. Kym Sadler was still on the phone. Had listened to the whole thing sitting in her little house in Melbourne. Couldn't believe it.

The news shot through the district like a jolt of electricity.

The switch from fearful waiting to cacophonous joy rolled across Beauty Point. Zac and Zoey and their partners Kimberley and Richard; Brant's brother Shaun, their parents John and Christa, with partners Val and Don; Rachel's parents Julie and Mike and her sister Natalie; Brant's aunties Corinna and Allyson; old mates Tony Sadler and Vinnie Tunks – everyone cried and screamed at once. Greg Crowden's partner Jodie Curran, hardly knowing what to do with herself with Greg down the mine, had dropped in to comfort Rachel. Suddenly she found herself in the middle of a maelstrom. She wanted to cuddle someone, but apart from Rachel and Vinnie, she didn't know anyone in the house.

'Let's get into Brant's bar,' Rachel's mother Julie suggested. The party went all night and into the next day, a trailer out the back filling with emptied bottles and cans, the stocks in Brant's sacred bar depleting rapidly as more and more friends rushed to the house from all around the district.

In Beaconsfield, Kaye Russell ran directionless from her home after bringing the tidings to Noel and the boys. A friend, Ute Hillard, was on the street and Kaye shouted to her. She almost danced. 'Come on, Ute, I'll have to tell Frances down at the church. Come with me.'

Kaye was a one-woman commotion. People stuck their heads out of doors and windows to see what all the fuss was about. When they discovered what was going on, they ran to tell neighbours and hit the phones. By the time Kaye reached the Uniting Church 300 metres from her home half the town was shouting.

'Frances,' Kaye called as she ran into the church. 'Frances. Todd's coming home. The boys are safe. They're alive.' Frances Seen reached for Kaye. A miracle. Of course it was a miracle.

The town's fire siren wailed. Skinny Williams couldn't help himself. The siren was the quickest way to get Beaconsfield's attention. The fire station was just across the road and around the corner from Kaye and Noel's home. He sprinted over there and got the thing howling.

By some kind of small-town telepathy the streets filled with citizens yelling in astonishment. Cars roared up and down Weld Street, horns honking, lights flashing and passengers hanging out the windows.

Within 20 minutes, 300 people crowded on to Nobby's and Kaye's front lawn, cheering, pouring beer down their throats and hugging each other.

Larry Knight's partner Jacqui came from Launceston. Kaye Russell threw her arms around her, burst into tears and said, 'If I could give a part of my miracle to you, Jacqui, I would.' Nobby thought Jacqui's visit was the bravest and saddest thing he'd ever seen.

Larry's daughter Lauren came, too. She had spent the weekend with Larry's brother Darren in Launceston. She climbed into a car with another uncle, Shane, and two cousins, Katie, 22 and Cory, 25, and drove to Beaconsfield.

Lauren cried when she reached the Russell's home and saw the party spilling on to the street. Happy for the Russells, broken-hearted for herself. All these people were celebrating a victory. She had lost a father. Someone handed her a Vodka Cruiser and she drank it so fast she couldn't remember swallowing.

Carolyn, still stunned, experiencing a storm of emotion, received a phone call from Brenda Johnson, Rex's wife away in Launceston. 'Get yourself ready, Carolyn,' she said. 'I'm coming to pick you up. We're going up to the mine.'

It was a relief. Carolyn's home was pandemonium. The phone rang off the hook, visitors came bearing boxes of beer; family and friends cavorted around as if there were no tomorrow. But Carolyn still had no information beyond the refrain shouted up and down the street: 'Alive! Alive!' She needed facts and the space to digest them.

Brenda arrived in not much more than half an hour and the two women drove up Weld Street. The town appeared to have gone mad. Noise, screaming, whistling, car horns blaring. The ABC had reported by now, shouted it across a disbelieving Australia, that Todd and Brant had been found breathing. People from out all around the valley had bundled their kids in pyjamas and driven to Beaconsfield just to be there on this night. Kaye and Noel Russell's house was under siege. Cars were parked at all angles. A seething crowd marched up West Street towards the mine. TV reporters stood bathed in lights babbling at cameras.

The grounds of the mine heaved with activity, too, though in comparison with the main street, the place felt like a quiet sanctuary. Every man who could wear a hard hat hurried through security, hoping to help underground.

Mick Borrill faced a stream of traffic in the decline as he tried to leave the mine's depths, anxious to get home to Sandra with the story of the most extraordinary day in his life. He climbed into a work vehicle down by the 925 and had to reverse all the way to the 860-metre level, more than half a kilometre, before he could find a hole in the wall to turn around. Every tunnel and cuddy was full of vehicles already driven down by rescue workers, senior members of the mine's hierarchy, fire service personnel and miners arriving for the night shift.

Carolyn was not content merely to sit quietly by the gates this time. She wanted to talk to men who had been in the mine when her husband had been found. Had Todd passed any message? What was his state of health? How soon might he be released?

Slowly, she pieced together the story. Men drifted over, sat with her, murmured. Carolyn felt strengthened by being at the mine, all these people taking her into their confidence. It gave her a sense of being part of the effort to bring her husband home.

She had often felt frustrated during the week by her inability to be involved in the search. Most nights she had been at the mine the men who knew what was happening were either deep in the earth on night shift or had gone home to sleep. But there was electricity in the air tonight and people hung around, passing on what they had learned.

She had proof now, at least, that her belief that Todd was still alive had been no dream bathed in a wish.

What she could not know were the astounding efforts that Todd and Brant's colleagues would make this night – acts of daring and bravery that would have set the townsfolk's hearts on fire if only they had been allowed to know. But the exploits that would take place 925 metres below Beaconsfield on the night of 30 April and the morning of 1 May would be covered up, the telling of them reduced to whispers.

Carolyn and Brenda stayed only a couple of hours. They drove away. Carolyn dropped in to Kaye and Nobby's home, fought her way through a boiling crowd of revellers spilling from the house and across the front and back yards, wearied of the hugs and kisses, and walked to her own home where the scene was hardly different.

It would be a long night in Beaconsfield. The pubs stayed open serving more beer than anyone could remember being drunk in the town. The crowd at the Club spilled out across the verandah and onto the street. The boys would be out of their hole by tomorrow, enthusiasts predicted.

Matthew Gill issued a media release at 2.30 in the morning trying to hose down such optimistic expectations.

'We have established contact with Todd Russell and Brant Webb,' Gill announced. The devil, though, was in the detail.

'After we found that they were alive, our first priorities were to establish communications and assess their conditions and needs. We are currently examining all the options to get them out as quickly as we possibly can. These options include continuing to push through a smaller probe hole in the new tunnel to the area where they are located. We are also looking at a number of other mechanical and other means to allow us to gain access.

'Conditions in the area are very dangerous and rescuers must proceed with extreme care. People should not underestimate the difficulties in getting them out safely.

'Safely accessing the trapped miners is paramount and this will take some time, so I would like to urge people to be patient.'

The truth was that no one had a clue how to reach the men without bringing the whole roof down on them. The control room was in a frenzy.

Nobby Russell shooed the last guest from his front lawn at 5.30 am. Kaye is a non-drinker, but she remembered tumblers of champagne being thrust into her hands. Most of the guests took care to remove boxes of empty bottles when they left, but Nobby still had to cart away 16 cartons of empty stubbies and a pile of bourbon and cola containers.

Carolyn received a gift the next day. Dale Burgess came to her home and told her he had spoken to Todd. Her husband had made him promise to visit Carolyn and tell her he loved her.

CHAPTER 17

THE ANGLE OF REPOSE

The old-school miners could not contemplate leaving Brant and Todd to their fate, chilled to the bone and starving. Why, they were no more than 6 metres the other side of a rockfall.

Brett Cresswell, a shift boss, wouldn't hear of it either. All the men in the mine knew by now what Brant and Todd had shouted down the microphone. Dale Burgess had asked exactly the right questions and the miners could imagine the horror those blokes had endured. Shit, six days of it.

Cresswell slung a pelican pick over his shoulder and set off down the 925 tunnel. Pat Ball followed him.

Cresswell climbed the small mountain of broken earth covering the telehandler, rocks tumbling in his wake, and set to burrowing through the mess at the top, using a narrow space between the piled dirt and the smashed roof. In minutes his companions, their cap lamps trained on him, could see nothing but the soles of his gumboots. He went at it like a rabbit, one of them said later.

To say that Cresswell and Ball's excursion was dangerous is to seriously understate it.

They were taken by that wild energy that wins men Victoria Crosses in war.

Cresswell scrabbled and dug and picked his way through the unstable mess, and Brant and Todd heard him coming. Long minutes passed before he and Ball reached an area beyond the telehandler, right above the tiny chamber in which Brant and Todd lay incarcerated.

Cresswell had a length of conduit with him. He tied a glove to the end of it and carefully threaded it through smashed rock and mesh below him. Todd reached up, touched the glove. He believed he was grasping Cresswell's hand. He still swears he touched the warmth of another man's flesh, the first tactile contact with the world beyond his cage in more than six days.

Neither Cresswell nor Ball has ever spoken to outsiders about this moment. Probably never will.

The two men brought water to the captives. Bottles of fresh water. They had a rope, a bottle taped to the middle of it. They got a packet of Teddy Bear biscuits down to Brant and Todd the same way. It was the only food they could find.

Cresswell withdrew the rope and he and Ball tied a new bottle to it. Repeated the process.

After six days of drinking coarse mineralised groundwater, the contents of those plastic bottles tasted sweeter than anything Todd and Brant could remember.

Cresswell reversed his journey and gathered whatever he could find that might make the existence of Todd and Brant a little more endurable. Dry disposable overalls, thermal blankets and cartons of Sustagen, a nutritional drink.

The second time Cresswell made the slithering trek he carried bolt-cutters. He needed to cut a hole in that mesh if he was to get blankets and overalls to the men. Part of the rock above Brant and Todd was, it turned out, supported by two sheets of mesh brought down from the roof in the initial collapse. It was tangled and twisted within the rock, as important to the precarious and random balancing act that had somehow refused to tumble as any of the myriad keystones jammed above the men.

When Cresswell applied his bolt-cutters to a single strand of this steel mesh, it parted with the high-pitched twang of a rifle shot. Brant and Todd froze. Terrified.

'Christ, Cres!' Todd cried. 'Stop! Don't do it!'

The two men in the cage almost stopped breathing. They were as attuned to the tiniest movements of the collapsed roof as a great symphonic conductor might be to a semi-tone from his orchestra's third clarinet. The sharp report of the wire parting told them of the fearful stress pressing upon the mesh. Another strand and there would be no hope for them.

There was no way down to them. It was obvious now. Todd and Brant understood it and so did Cresswell. If they were to be rescued, another way would have to be found.

It was a disappointment beyond description, but Todd and Brant had grown accustomed to disappointment. They could deal with it because they were no longer utterly alone.

The packet of Teddy Bear biscuits had jam in the centre. Todd and Brant fell on the sweets, ravenous. But then one of the blokes out in the drive realised that a rush of sugar to systems denied food for six days wasn't the smartest nutritional move.

Brant was already into his second biscuit and Todd had wolfed another when they heard a voice screaming 'Don't eat the biscuits! Don't eat the biscuits!'

The two men were nonplussed. Were the bloody things contaminated?

Soon enough, Brant understood. His stomach cramped, spasms roiling around down there, doubling him up with pain. He groaned and cursed. Todd escaped this new suffering but the near-full packet of biscuits sat down the end of the cage, tantalising but forbidden.

The two men rode waves of gratitude to the miners delivering them sustenance. Larry had made sure they would be found; they had told themselves so many times that Larry would bring help, and now they knew it.

They did not know, however, that another group of miners was trying to get to them through a different route. Garth Bonney, Robbie Sears, Dave Johnson and Daniel Piscioneri believed it might be possible to reach Brant and Todd, not from over the telehandler, but from the west, down in the open stope. They set off determined, heading uphill to an access they knew would lead them back down to the hole. But their trek was in vain. They would be prevented because the man in charge of workplace safety, Fred Sears, decided to put a stop to all the unsanctioned expeditions.

Sears was vastly unimpressed when he discovered the impromptu rescue effort. He ordered that it stop and that the 925 tunnel be cleared. Sears then roped it off and declared any man who ventured there again did so under pain of prosecution. He threatened Cresswell with a fine of $20,000, and Cresswell stopped the other party from trying the back door.

Such a penalty was absurd, of course.

No fair-minded arbiter would cripple financially a miner who put his own life at risk for no reason other than to assist two men trapped in such unthinkable circumstances. It would run counter to every measure of justice and, anyway, would cause a public outcry. Such a fine would be paid twenty times over by the mere process of handing around the hat on a Saturday night at pubs across the country.

Sears, though, had the responsibility of ensuring there were no more tragedies in the mine. The whole thing was a dreadful mess and he – an experienced miner himself – operated under the requirement that the rescue operation be undertaken without making things worse than they were already.

The first rule was that every move had to be assessed for risk before any action was authorised. Sears was doing a tough job, shouldering a weight that no one man ought to have to bear, and he had no alternative but to enforce rules.

In a perfect world, dispassionate rescuers from other mines with no attachment to Brant and Todd might have been brought in and the men of Beaconsfield kept out because they were emotionally involved. Perfect worlds are a bit thin on the ground, however.

Brett Cresswell and his colleagues were reacting in a manner that most observers would judge heroic.

They couldn't bear to see their mates suffer and they did everything in their power to alleviate that suffering. If they had been able to achieve a snatch and grab, hauling the two men out of their hole and bringing them back to the surface quickly, they would have been showered with medals for courage. Their names surely would have become household words rather than whispered in awe among a few mates around Beaconsfield who learned the story.

In time, sketchy details leaked to the media, but the full impact of the exploits of tough men with soft hearts 925 metres below the ground never captured the national imagination as it might.

No press releases about their efforts were ever issued. Instead, the managers of the mine and their spin doctors omitted all reference to these events.

Other courageous adventures occurred that night that have never been publicly revealed.

Gavan Cheesman couldn't stay away once news swept town that Brant and Todd were alive. He tossed on a hard hat and rode the shaft.

Cheesman arrived a couple of hours after the initial excitement and no one in authority paid him a second glance. Everyone was too busy.

Anyway, it was Cheesy. A shift boss. He belonged.

He found his way to the 925 drive, grabbed the megaphone previously used by Dale Burgess and approached the back of the telehandler.

'Todd, Brant. It's Cheesy,' he called.

The two trapped men were still high on the knowledge they had been found. Brant's sense of humour had returned.

'Cheesy,' he yelled. 'Really sorry, but we haven't finished this wall you wanted yet.'

'Get us out of here, will you?' Todd shouted.

'Don't worry, we'll get you out,' replied Cheesman.

He had to find a way. He told the men around him he knew a route that might get him closer to the boys. Dale Burgess heard about it and decided he couldn't allow Cheesy to go alone.

The two shift bosses collected sturdy rope and chose a scary path. They would go in from above the 925 drive. In through the great echoing black space of the open stope that Brant Webb had tried to reach by tunnelling.

The tunnel immediately above the trapped men, the 915, was blocked. It had suffered a rock fall six months previously, choking it off, and on Anzac night it collapsed even more. Since October 2005 the Beaconsfield miners had simply bypassed it, using the access above at 900 and building a ramp to the west that led down to 915 metres.

Cheesman and Burgess wound their way through this track to the far end, the western end of the stope blown clear up to 900 from the 925 a little beyond the spot where Brant, Todd and Larry had been building their bund and wire wall.

It was an intimidating hole. Vast.

They began climbing down, picking their way over loose rock – mullock – dumped over the side in an early effort to fill the space left after the ore had been blown away. The rill, miners called it, lying at an angle of around 40 degrees. There was a lyrical term for it. The angle of repose. Poetry, though, was distant from the minds of Cheesy and Burgess.

Burgess shone his light around, found an old split-bolt poking from the wall and tied his rope to it. The men clung to it as they descended the rill. When they reached the bottom, they shone their lamps to the ceiling.

Way up there, 20 metres through black space, they could see the bottom of a 5-metre thick concrete and rock pillar installed by the mine to replace the original ore blasted away in the search for gold. This artificial pillar supported the tunnel at 900 metres.

They walked east across the floor of the stope, their steps echoing. Right above them now was a bridge of ore suspended in nothingness. It was nothing but a mighty chunk of rock; part of the earth that was left hanging when the ground failed and fell in.

They were close to Todd and Brant and their lamps revealed a hopeless state of affairs. The roof of the tunnel leading into the stope, the brow, had collapsed leaving nothing but that bit of a bridge hovering above, a part of what had been the floor of the 915-metre level.

Brant and Todd were under hundreds of tonnes of broken rock and shattered ore. A waterfall tumbled from a water table beneath the concrete rockfill pillar at 905 metres.

The water, then, was falling 20 metres, splashing onto the scree entrapping Todd and Brant and running as a stream along the footwall.

Burgess suddenly understood what Brant and Todd had been telling him when he was out there in the drive and they complained of being wet and cold. The poor buggers had to be suffering badly. Burgess called free-flowing water in the mine 'the holy water' but there was nothing holy about this.

Cheesman was shocked by the scene. He decided he would not call out for it might simply give Todd and Brant the impossible hope that rescue lay this way.

The two men retreated, dragging themselves back up the rill, hand over hand on the rope.

It seemed pretty clear to Burgess what had happened.

The geology below Beaconsfield is unusual.

In most gold mines, the gold-bearing quartz seam is stronger than the rock surrounding it. But at Beaconsfield, the conglomerate rock encasing the gold seam is tougher than the quartz ore body.

Stress within the earth is complex – essentially, it is created both by gravity exerting its vertical pull and great energy trying to shift the ground at infinitesimal rates sideways.

All mines interfere with this process.

Miners remove rock and ore. In great quantities. It is their business. But it is a vanity, for the ground is ancient – beneath Beaconsfield, as we have mentioned, it settled itself during the Ordovician period some time between 445 and 510 million years ago – and does not take kindly to dis-turbance. Its internal stresses, suddenly irritated, have been granted space to vent their annoyance.

Stress in the ground normally distributes itself perfectly unnoticed unless its energy is interrupted by, say, a fault line. At such places it grinds away until something gives. The result is an earthquake.

A gold seam is by its nature an ancient fault, which is why the fluid containing dissolved gold flowed through the rock in the first place, until it cooled and crystallised, tempting humans brave and foolish enough to try to dig it up.

All the digging, all the blasting of tunnels and all the removal of great pillars of ore equate, thus, to something approaching the reopening of a fault.

Meanwhile, a few hundred millions of years of water coursing through the earth on its relentless journey from the Tasmanian highlands towards the Tamar River had done its work, too. Water is a powerful solvent and it niggled away at the natural agents binding rock to the crystals of gold-bearing quartz.

Stress has to expend its energy somewhere. Travelling through hard-bound earth, imagine it discovering a hole of nothingness. Or nosing along and suddenly finding itself tearing along a pillar of cement and rock that some human imagined was as solid as siltstone and sandstone that had been sitting there squeezed tight forever.

In such circumstances stress tends to shake itself a bit and search out a more convenient path.

Geoscientists employed by mines know all about this sort of behaviour and keep a close eye on it. Miners know about it and become accustomed to the ground coughing up stones, spurting dust.

At Beaconsfield, the mine's managers stuck seismic monitors everywhere underground to scrutinise the earth's moods. Employees kept watch on the computerised readouts, and at any sign of trouble, men were pulled out of tunnels and ordered to the crib or the surface.

But the ground has its own rhythms and agendas and does not always telegraph its punches.

Troubled and confused, the earth's vertical and horizontal stresses can lean heavily on that hard conglomerate rock as if seeking respite. Recall Brant's relief when he went into the 925 tunnel and discovered it was perfectly quiet, peaceful. The ground, however, was foxing.

The rock yields a little, but refuses to break. If it happens to lie next to a body of quartz, things can go awry. The quartz is brittle, neither as elastic nor – thanks to all the water nagging away at the elements binding it together – as solid.

Something has to give. Picture, if you like, placing the head of a baseball bat against a pane of glass and exerting steady pressure.

It is, of course, the quartz ore body that shatters, just like the glass. When that happens, the quartz expends its pent-up energy in all directions, a bit like the exploding star, the supernova, that deposited gold into the earth's structure in the first place.

Even the tough rock encasing the body of quartz cannot contain such a blast. It peels off in slabs and breaks apart. And because miners always tunnel beneath a quartz ore body, the lode, the whole catastrophe tumbles down.

Dale Burgess could see it all out there in the stope. Stresses building up above Todd and Brant, nowhere to go because they were beneath the brow, which simply stopped in midair. And boom.

He couldn't drive the vision from his mind. Couldn't forget all that water tumbling down on Todd and Brant's prison, either.

Later, he returned to the stope, this time with Corey Verhey. They climbed down the rope Burgess had fixed earlier to the bolt sticking from the wall. Verhey's heart thudded so hard he thought Burgess could hear it through his chest. Massive slabs of rock hung from the walls supported only by a few bolts and torn strips of mesh.

They brought picks with them and dug a trench along the footwall close to Brant and Todd's cell, hoping to drain away at least some of the water flooding down. They took note of the numbers written on lines stencilled on the walls. These strips marked at regular intervals are known as eastings and they contribute to the three-dimensional map of the underground essential to mine surveyors. Perhaps, Burgess and Verhey figured, their recordings could assist in determining with some precision the location of Brant and Todd.

Burgess felt too that if the rescue hit a serious snag the miners would have to attempt an emergency 'snatch and grab' through any means possible. He had already been asked to assess the potential for burrowing to the trapped men, gaining access beneath the telehandler. He had ruled it out. Too risky for rescuers. Too dangerous for Brant and Todd. It could cause an even more serious collapse than had already occurred. If all else failed, he had to know whether it might be possible to go in from the stope. It didn't look good. Not good at all.

The critical management team up in the control room settled on a less hair-raising plan. They ordered that a hole be drilled from the end of the drive the miners had blown from the decline clear through to Todd and Brant. It would establish communications with the two men, and the thin pipeline could be used to send water, food, medical aid and more.

Daniel Piscioneri was chosen to operate the Simba drill. He would be required to drill through 15.5 metres of rock wall. His aim would have to be true. Too high, low or wide and he would miss the space in which the men were confined.

The surveyor, Simon Arthur, had to employ every skill of his profession for this exercise to be successful. Every calculation he made now was crucial. No longer was he able to rely on the sort of margin of error that a drive 4.5 metres square allowed. His charts and graphs had to gauge a small point the other side of a wall 15.5 metres thick in which two men lay.

He lined up the path that Daniel Piscioneri would have to follow as he drilled a hole 54 millimetres in diameter.

A Simba is a powerful wheeled drilling rig normally used to bore long vertical holes. But Piscioneri's job was to bore a hole that was closer to horizontal, sloping only gently up. It meant the controls he was accustomed to employing were out of whack. The young man pointed his drill at the rock face at precisely the angle the surveyor had calculated and dug it in.

A Simba drill uses a series of rods, each 1.8 metres long sitting upon a carousel. As the first rod winds the drill bit through the rock and reaches its depth, a new rod swings from the carousel and couples on, driving the bit deeper. On and on, new rods joining the effort. Water pumps through the series of joined steel pipes to the bit, spraying the face of the hole and washing rock shavings out of the way. The operator needs experience and expertise to 'feel' the rods, ensuring the bit does not waver from a direct path or become jammed and stall the machine.

Piscioneri was under enormous stress. Behind him, 10 to 12 miners stood willing him to drill with care. Their cap lamps burned in the dark. Piscioneri's greatest fear was to drill too far. If he broke through the distant wall into Brant and Todd's confinement, he knew he could kill them. Bring rocks down upon them or – and he did not want to think about it – spear them with the tungsten drilling head.

Adrenaline surged through him. Sweat popped from every pore on his body.

He felt the earth's texture way down the hole begin to alter. He knew he was close to breaking into the cell holding Brant and Todd. Eased off. Not too much, for he did not want to stall.

He jiggled the rods back and forth a bit and suddenly he felt the ground go loose. Piscioneri could bring himself to push no farther. He reversed the whole process, pulling his rods out one by one.

As the drill was withdrawn from the hole, Piscioneri jumped from his machine, got down on his hands and knees and put his ear to the hole. He could hear the voices of Brant and Todd, clear as day.

Back in the drive, the gathering of miners stared down their light beams at Piscioneri, silent.

Dale Burgess called from the dark. 'What's going on?'

And Todd Russell's voice roared from the hole.

'For fuck's sake,' he cried. 'You near drilled me. You've saturated us!'

Piscioneri, following Simon Arthur's calculations, had drilled clean through the wall to the side of the basket, his drill bit after 15.5 metres of progress through solid rock aimed precisely between the heads of Todd Russell and Brant Webb. The whirling drill head, still spewing water, had rained all over them. Another centimetre or two and the effort would have ended in disaster.

Daniel Piscioneri had within the space of four days found Larry Knight's body, listened to the first words of Todd and Brant back from the dead, and now he had come within a shadow of killing the two survivors while drilling a lifeline to them.

For weeks afterwards he would lie sleepless in his bed at night, soaked in perspiration, trying unsuccessfully to rid himself of his memories.

Above: Glenn Burns, the miner who broke through to Todd and Brant's underground prison. **Right:** Todd and Brant celebrate with family and friends after returning to the surface, 9 May 2006.

VOICES FROM OUTSIDE

There was a voice. 'Shut up in there you blokes!' They both heard it. Faint. Muffled.

'I'm sure there's someone out there,' Todd whispered. 'What're they saying?' Brant demanded. Whispering too.

'We're here! We're here!' they shouted together, desperate. There was some sort of reply but the meaning of it was lost to the two men in their cage, the words swimming around with the maddening cascade of water on the footwall. They hardly dared believe it, but this time there was no mistaking what was happening. There were men out there, and they knew Todd and Brant were alive.

Above: Todd (left) and Brant wearing the first warm, dry clothes sent to them down the PVC tube. The picture shows how close they lived for 14 days, their space so cramped that one always had to be on his shoulder if the other was on his back.

Above: The rescuers' end of the 90 millimetre PVC tube that was Brant and Todd's lifeline. Food, clothing and medical supplies were passed through this tube, as well as torches and glow sticks to give the men light. A video camera sent down the tube revealed horrifyingly cramped conditions, and a telephone (sent in pieces and reassembled) provided the men with a vital link to the world outside their prison.

OPEN
HOLE

Previous page: Freedom! Todd Russell (left) and Brant Webb emerge from the Beaconsfield mine after almost 14 days trapped 925 metres below. At right is Corey Verhey, a mines rescue team member and one of the men who kept vigil, watching Todd and Brant on a video screen through the days after they were found alive. **This page:** Out safe, the boys snatch their tags from a board declaring them 'In Underground'.

Above: Family reunions. Brant (left) and Todd in the arms of Rachel and Carolyn after being rescued from the Beaconsfield mine, 9 May 2006.

Left: Todd celebrates newfound freedom with family and friends. **Top:** Todd embraces his father Noel and speaks with his son Liam as his mother Kay (right) is overcome by emotion. **Bottom:** Brant (left) and Todd, about to be taken to Launceston hospital by ambulance.

TODD

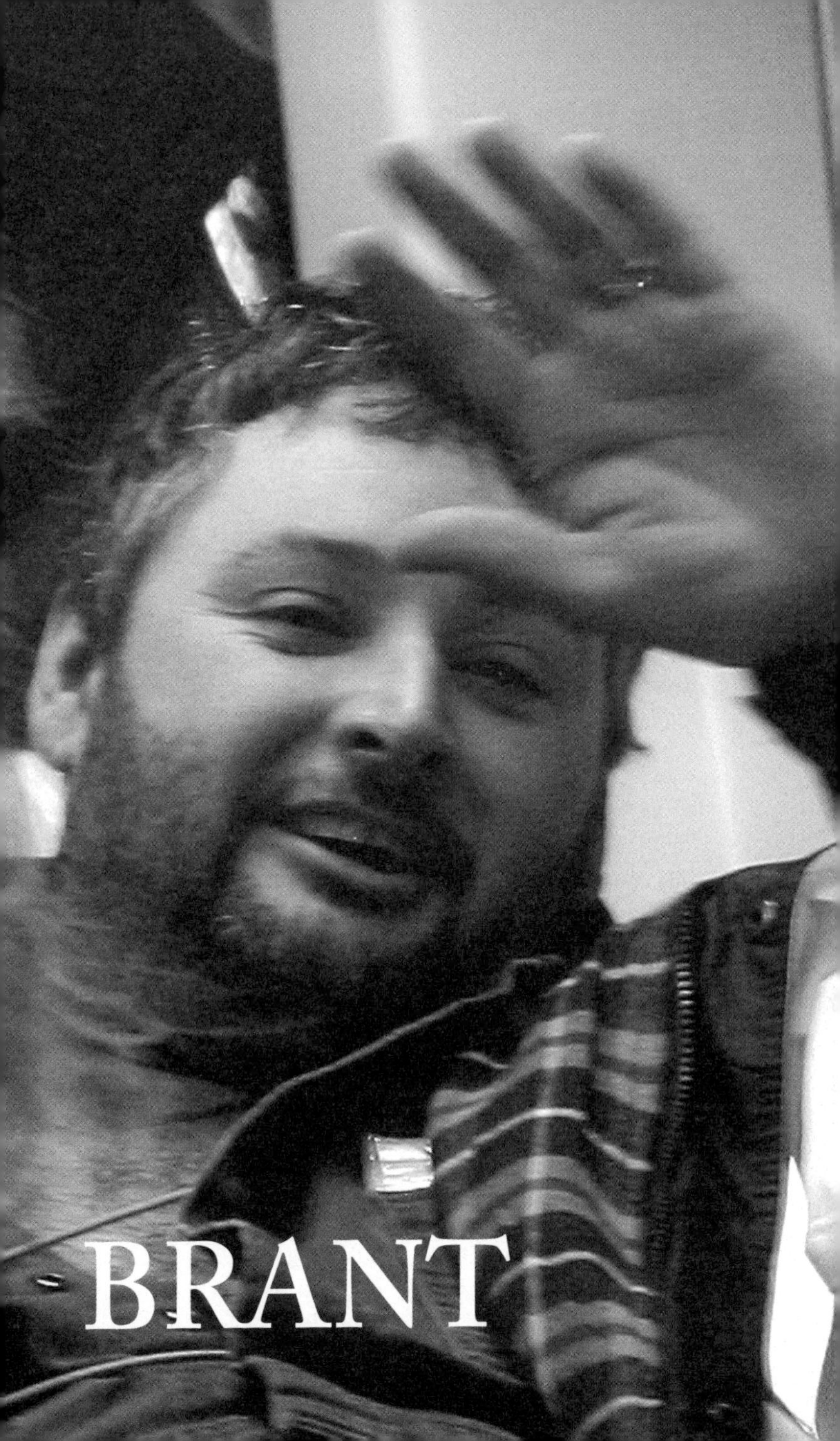

BRANT

TODD

I would like to dedicate this book to all the mining communities around the world who have suffered and grieved at the loss of their loved ones. To the people involved in our rescue and to mine rescue teams around the world: your skills and perseverance even at the risk to your own lives will not be forgotten. To my wife Carolyn and children Trent, Maddison and Liam, and to our wonderful families: you are the reason I would never give in. To our friends Mark and Natalie, Steven and Elizabeth, Michael and Julie, for being there.

Being trapped and buried in a black space that appears to have no boundaries is a frightening place.

BRANT

I would like to dedicate this book to Rachel, Zachary and Zoey, and to everyone who made it possible for me to reunite with my family. And for those who gave support to family and friends: my health and mental stability are due to you. I'd love to mention all your names as recognition, but would have to write another book to do this. You know who you are, and I thank you from my heart.

Thinking of you all.
Brant

CHAPTER 18

HATSY TO THE RESCUE

■ ■ ■

Peter Hatswell was standing outside his room at the Town & Country Motel in the dusty mining town of Cobar, far western New South Wales, when he got the call.

It was Donna, Dean Mackrell's wife, down in Beaconsfield.

'They've found Todd and Brant,' she said. 'They're alive.'

Macka, a young miner from the Beaconsfield rescue team, couldn't come to the phone. He was in tears. Just wanted Hatsy to know. It was a bit after seven o'clock on Sunday, 30 April.

Peter Hatswell is about the most experienced search and rescue man in Australia's mining industry. The Training Coordinator for NSW Mines Rescue, he has 25 years' mining experience, and has spent the last 10 years training teams all over Australia, which was why he was in Cobar, a long drive from home base in Lithgow, on the western slopes of the Blue Mountains.

Hatswell had kept in close touch with the Beaconsfield gold mine ever since Rex Johnson had phoned him – woke him up at three o'clock on the morning of 26 April – to tell him three men were trapped in a rock fall.

One of the men was Todd Russell. Hatswell had trained Russell ever since he went underground at Beaconsfield years ago and they had become friends. Both of them were country boys – Hatswell grew up in the Megalong Valley in the Blue Mountains – and often they used Nobby Russell's garage for accident scenarios. Nobby serviced Hatsy's truck when he was in town.

Rex had urgent requests that morning. He wanted to know where he could get a tele-remote system for a bogger. Hatswell knew mines at Henty and Rosebery in Tasmania used tele-remote gear. He'd make some calls.

Hatswell had to go to Cobar for the week to run a rescue-training course, but he kept the phone on and later put Rex in touch with the NSW Fire Service when he called in search of special cameras and high-frequency wireless gear. Within a day a NSW urban search and rescue specialist, Andrew Haag, was flown to Launceston with the equipment. As the week wore on, things didn't sound promising for Todd and Brant, but Hatswell's motto is 'you never give up hope'.

Donna's call on Sunday night just about floored Hatsy. He wasn't a superstitious man, but something weird had been happening.

Every time he left his motel room at the Town & Country, he'd turn off the TV. And every time he returned, it would be playing. Annoyed hell out of him. Couldn't fix it. In the next room was Gary Smith, the former superintendent of NSW Police Rescue. The ABC-TV show *Police Rescue* based one of its characters, Nugget, on Smith, whose career would make a good movie itself. Hatswell and Smith, now retired, often worked together and part of their work in Cobar was to carry out a car-accident training course. Vehicle extrication, they called it. Hatswell thought Smith's TV remote might be leaking through the walls and responsible for the strange behaviour of his television, but no matter how they fiddled with the set they couldn't work out what was happening. It kept switching itself on and most of the time, it blared with news updates from Beaconsfield.

'But you know, soon as they found those boys, the TV stopped playing up,' Hatswell said. 'I don't believe in that sort of unexplained stuff, but it's a fact.'

Within a day, he was on a private jet chartered by the Beaconsfield mine, bound for Launceston. Rex had called. The Beaconsfield incident management team was exhausted and needed relief.

The jet flew hither and thither collecting rescue experts. To Bathurst to pick up Russell Giles, the manager of the Western Mines Rescue Station. To Williamtown near Newcastle for Ken Enright from the Hunter Valley rescue station.

The jet landed in Sydney for re-fuelling and a party of medical experts boarded – Dr Richard Morris, a retrieval specialist attached to FlightCare, and ambulance paramedics Paul Featherstone, Dominic Morgan and Superintendent Keith Williams. (Peter Croft and Tony

Bishenden were dispatched to Tasmania on a different flight.) They were all members of SCAT – the Specialty Casualty Access Team, which has the often horrendous job of getting human beings out of the sort of jams that most of us could barely imagine.

Hatswell walked into the Beaconsfield gold mine incident room at 2.30 am on Tuesday, 2 May.

It was the same room he had used 12 months previously to run his training course in Emergency Preparedness and Incident Management. The same table, the same whiteboards. The same faces. Matthew Gill, Pat Ball, Rex Johnson. Geotechnician Peter Hills; mill manager Richard Holder; engineer-in-charge Chris Newett; chief accountant Toni Griffiths. A bank of typists recorded and transcribed every word of every conversation. It was obvious to Hatswell that everyone was worn out, needing sleep.

The discovery of Brant and Todd had changed the whole nature of events at Beaconsfield. What had been a search and rescue, with the emphasis on search, was now a full-blown rescue operation. A rescue facing mind-blowing difficulties.

The hole Daniel Piscioneri had punched through 15.5 metres of rock to Todd and Brant had been reamed out with a wider drill head. The hole was now almost double its original size to allow the miners to hammer a round 90-millimetre PVC pipe clean through the wall to the little prison holding the two men.

The process was fraught with danger – the wider drilling head on the reamer threatened to push slabs of rock from the fractured footwall on to Todd and Brant as it reached the end of the hole and had to be withdrawn before it completed the job. The result was that when the PVC pipe was pushed through, Todd and Brant were forced to rip away at the rocks to fashion a path that allowed the pipe to be driven the last few centimetres. The effort tore Todd's hands because he had no gloves, leaving Brant to finish the job, cursing the wet, confined conditions, his body cramping.

Finally, though, rescuers had a tube with a smooth surface through which they could talk to the imprisoned men and feed them essential supplies.

Brant's first words down the tube were straightforward.

'Send smokes! I'm out and I need a smoke now! Got packets of the fuckin' things in me crib bag. Bring 'em down.' Brant's nervous tension levels were peaking, his emotions swirling, all mixed up. Frustrated by the effort of clearing a path for the pipe, he'd yelled and cursed at Steve Saltmarsh, one of the men trying to assist out there in the drive. Brant felt bad about it. Saltmarsh was the man who had found them in the first place and like everyone else out there he'd only been trying to help get the bloody pipe through. Anyway, it had finally worked. It gave Brant and Todd the ability to communicate with the outside world. But to Brant it simply emphasised that he and Todd were caged rats. He really, really needed a smoke to calm him down.

But no one was about to feed him cigarettes, now or later. Doctors and paramedics were about to take over the medical and nutritional care of the two men and no miner dared compromise their treatment.

Karen Pendrey from the Tasmanian Ambulance Service, based at its northern regional headquarters in Launceston, was the first paramedic to speak to Todd and Brant. She had been involved in all sorts of difficult retrievals during her career, but she had never been down a mine before.

So when she went underground at Beaconsfield at 10 o'clock on the night of Monday, 1 May, she took a deep breath as the cage dropped down its shaft, her legs turning to jelly and the dark rock flashing past. But when she reached the pipe leading through a rock wall to the 925 drive, she was all business.

She was forced to kneel in mud and water and call down the tube poking from the wall about 60 centimetres from the floor. Karen grew up in the Tamar Valley and had met Todd.

'Hi guys,' she said. 'Todd, I'm Justin's sister.'

It established a bond from the start. Todd and Brant told her their most urgent requirement was saline solution to wash out their eyes, which had been full of dust and grit and dirt for days. Karen learned Todd had many scratches on his body, but Brant said he didn't believe their wounds needed stitching.

A system had to be devised to send supplies down the narrow lifeline. The solution was makeshift, but effective. Small plastic mineral-water bottles were the answer. The bottom of each bottle was sliced away, whatever was needed was placed inside and tape applied to seal it.

Then the bottle was taped to a stick of plastic conduit 16 metres long and a miner pushed it through. The tapering head of the bottle acted as a guide. Todd or Brant drew the bottle from their end of the tube, removed the contents and taped the bottle back to the conduit so it could be withdrawn and used again.

It was fine for small containers of saline solution and the next supplies sent to the men – baby-wipes so they could scrub filth from their hands and faces and give themselves a crude bath. Karen was not keen on antibiotic creams and instructed Brant on how to swab Todd's wounds with saline solution.

Brant continued to demand cigarettes, but Karen was firm, trying to talk him down with a little humour.

'Sorry, Brant, don't you realise I'd get my arse kicked if I let you smoke?' she said. 'Anyway, don't you remember signing a form before you went down agreeing to go on a Quit program?'

'I didn't sign nothing,' he gruffed.

'Oh, you mustn't have noticed, but we've got the papers here. You're on a Quit program,' she responded. The last thing she or the doctors or the other paramedics needed was any chance of the men contracting a chest infection. No one knew how long Todd and Brant might be forced to stay almost 16 metres from any physical help.

Over the next hours, Brant and Todd received fresh water, small cartons of vanilla-flavoured Sustagen, vitamins and medical supplies in a stream down the tube. They also received needles and syringes and were told they would have to inject themselves with an anticoagulant designed to prevent deep vein thrombosis. Brant hollered down the tube that he wasn't keen on injections. Karen told him not to worry. If he fainted, he wouldn't have far to fall.

In fact, Brant was terrified of needles. Todd simply uncapped his syringe and plunged the needle into his stomach, but Brant hesitated, touching the needle to his stomach, drawing back, touching it, drawing back. Little pinpricks.

'For Christ's sake,' Todd growled at him. 'You'll tattoo yourself before you're finished. Just shove it in.' Both men would be required to inject themselves every day.

They had to become accustomed to orders. The first note they received down the tube set the tone: 'There are two tablets: thiamine, multivitamin. Take one of each immediately. One hour after taking tablets you can commence to take one 250 ml pack of Sustagen each. Sustagen should be taken one pack every eight hours. One of each tablet should be taken every 24 hours. Once you have commenced the Sustagen do not drink any more mine water.'

For two men who had lain in darkness on rocks in a terrifyingly confined space for more than six days, the instructions were confusing. They had to read them again and again before they could decipher precisely what they were being told. The only words that made perfect sense were 'do not drink any more mine water.' They had no problem with that.

By the early morning of Tuesday, Dr Richard Morris and the SCAT team arrived with Peter Hatswell and Karen went to the surface to brief them all. She returned with Paul Featherstone, the NSW paramedic who became famous across Australia for his role in the rescue of Stuart Diver at Thredbo. Featherstone travelled down the mine with Karen and had a long discussion with Todd and Brant, assessing their condition. He assured them that if Stuart Diver could be rescued, so could they.

Upstairs, Hatswell had much to get his head around.

This was going to be a long haul. It was all very fine that Todd and Brant had been found alive and that they were receiving nourishment, medical assistance and the mercy of human contact. But they remained in dreadful danger.

They had to be released, but they were behind a barrier of solid rock, 15.5 metres wide. The whiteboards in the control room were a great scrawl of options considered and rejected.

Already, though, one choice had risen to the top of the pile.

In the hours after the two men were found, Dale Burgess had mentioned to Pat Ball that he believed a raise bore might have to be considered. It seemed possible to Burgess that such a machine could bore a rescue tunnel to the men.

That same night, the team in the control room had made frantic calls across Australia for expert help. One of the calls was to Jeremy Rowlings, the underground mine manager at a deep gold mine at Stawell in western Victoria. Bill Colvin, the chief executive officer of Beaconsfield Gold, knew Rowlings well – they had worked together previously at Stawell. 'How are we going to get these blokes out?' Colvin asked.

'Have you thought of turning a raise bore on its side?' Rowlings said.

The idea took hold.

There was only one problem. A raise bore is a massively powerful machine designed to drill large vertical holes. No one anywhere in the world had ever used a raise bore to drill a tunnel on a horizontal axis.

Normally, the drilling motor is placed on its expanding legs in a drive above the hole to be bored. It then drills a long pilot hole vertically below, heading down into the earth until it reaches a tunnel where its big circular bore head is fitted to the end of the probe. It then draws the drilling head back up through the earth, opening a perfectly round shaft to whatever width is required, depending on the size of the boring head. The head is fitted with a series of revolving wheels that grind away at rock.

In short, it *pulls* the drilling head vertically up towards the machine sitting above.

In Beaconsfield, the rescue management team was proposing to reverse the operation. The machine would be required to *push* its drilling head, which itself would be reversed, through tough rock. Not only that, but it would have to swing its weight and power behind a drilling head that would drill almost horizontally.

Just such a machine was being used in a mine at Henty in Tasmania's west.

It was owned and operated by a company based in Adelaide called RaiseBore Australia. With the entire Australian community riveted to the story emerging in Beaconsfield, phone calls flew through the night.

By Monday, the raise bore – 6 or 7 tonnes of electric motors, hydraulic power packs and pure steel muscle, as big as a couple of Kombi vans – was on a truck, heading from Tasmania's west coast bound for Beaconsfield. But it needed a special borehead suitable for the hole proposed to be pushed through to Brant and Todd. This item of gear was in Adelaide, but no obstacle was about to be placed in its path. It was loaded on a truck bound for Melbourne.

The drilling head, weighing about 3 tonnes, had to get across Bass Strait as fast as possible.

A large passenger and car ferry called the *Spirit of Tasmania* makes the voyage from Melbourne to the

Tasmanian port of Devonport most nights. It leaves Melbourne at 8 pm.

But once the drilling head was located and loaded safely on a truck in Adelaide, it would not be possible to reach the *Spirit of Tasmania* by sailing time. The ferry operators, as caught up in the drama unfolding in Beaconsfield as the rest of the nation, agreed to keep the ship waiting at the wharf in Melbourne. Passengers would simply have to understand.

And so the *Spirit of Tasmania* sailed an hour late on Monday night, its cargo hold containing a truck carrying a weird circular piece of mining equipment that might – just might – help save the lives of two men sealed away from the world.

CHAPTER 19

'SEE YOU SOON, DADDY'

If Beaconsfield's citizens thought they had been subjected to a media circus during the long days Brant and Todd were nothing but ghosts in a mystery, they were in for a shock.

News that the two men had survived burst through Australia's news organisations like a shot of adrenaline direct to the heart.

Many of the journalists who had spent the days since Anzac night wandering the periphery of the mine in search of an angle – any angle – that might get editors off their backs boarded planes and flew home for the weekend. Confirmation that Larry Knight had died beneath the rock convinced them this was the story of a tragedy. An industrial accident with no happy ending.

When ABC-TV inserted a small report into its 7 o'clock national news on Sunday night, 30 April, it seemed barely believable. Todd Russell and Brant Webb had been found alive.

Many of the journalists still in Beaconsfield had retired to their rooms, and those with the fattest expense accounts were having dinner at the Tamar Cove restaurant, a fine eatery attached to a motel between Beaconsfield and Beauty Point. Their mobile phones suddenly began shrilling and they bolted from their glasses of red wine, confused and in urgent search of confirmation.

While cameras and lights were hastily set up outside the mine, Sky TV got the jump on them. Presenters John Mangos and Jacinta Tynan, sitting in a studio in Sydney, hit the phones and adlibbed a long and compelling report.

They lacked pictures, but their phone calls reaped gold – Kaye Russell and Frances Seen laughed and cried and declared they were witnessing a miracle. A general hubbub of residents shouted praise into the phone, and Mangos and Tynan simply allowed a festive stream of consciousness to take over their broadcast. It was talkback radio on TV.

Bill Shorten had flown home to Melbourne, but he wasn't about to allow himself to be stranded. Unable to get a commercial flight to Tasmania, he called a friend, the billionaire cardboard tycoon Dick Pratt, and begged a favour. Within an hour he was aboard Pratt's corporate jet bound for Launceston.

By morning, every major newspaper in Australia shouted the news. 'Alive', screamed Sydney's *Daily Telegraph* and the Hobart *Mercury*. 'Miracle,' declared Adelaide's *Advertiser*. *The Australian* had room for more words across its broadsheet: 'It's . . . cold and cramped in here. Get us out. Trapped miners found alive.'

It was a sensation. Editors and news directors across the land tore up their budget sheets and threw reporters, photographers, directors, producers and camera crews at the story.

Airlines from the mainland were besieged, hire car companies in Launceston and Hobart quickly ran out of available vehicles and media travel organisers hunted in increasing desperation for rooms to rent. Beaconsfield was about to become Australia Central.

By Monday evening, there was hardly a bed to be had from Launceston to Beauty Point and beyond. Hotels, motels, bed and breakfast establishments and caravan parks filled with newshounds frantic to witness a legend in the making. At the Exchange and Club hotels in Beaconsfield, reporters were crammed four to a room.

The TV networks sent in the big guns. David Koch and Melissa Doyle from Seven's *Sunrise*; Karl Stefanovik from Nine's rival *Today* show. Koch and Doyle scored rooms in a first-class hotel in Launceston, but Stefanovik and his producer Tom Malone wanted to be closer. They bought swags and rolled them out on the floor of a house at Beauty Point. Tracey Grimshaw from Nine's *A Current Affair* and her rival from Seven's *Today Tonight*, Naomi Robson, squared off from tents erected outside the mine for live broadcasts.

The little car park outside the mine gates took on the appearance of a large gathering of gypsy tribes. Many of the savvier media companies hired camper vans so their journalists could sleep and file stories on site. The wagons circled, crept into rows side by side and hooked their electrical systems to generators that purred all night. Big broadcast vans muscled in, satellite antennas perched at rakish angles like ladies' hats on Derby Day. Sound and video technicians took possession of a nearby council barbecue and headed to the butchery down the street for steak and sausages. Public toilets nearby came under heavy pressure.

Down West Street a bit sat a community meeting house used for bingo evenings and meetings of the historical society and the like. The council unlocked the room and it became a media centre. Journalists fought for space around a central table, snapped open their laptops and discovered there were exactly two phone connections available to dial up their email and Internet servers. The floor quickly became a spaghetti of electrical cables and phone extension leads too complicated to fathom. Next door, the ABC converted a St John Ambulance Base into a radio studio.

Tasmania's weather offered a chill reception. Beaconsfield sits at latitude 41 degrees 12 minutes south. It thus sits within that band at the bottom of the earth the old sailors called the roaring forties, where westerly winds, the breath of Antarctica within them, circle the earth with hardly a mass of land to block their path. The winds rushed in at the invasion from the mainland and brought with them frozen rain, lashing the waters of the Tamar and the streets of Beaconsfield.

The Foodworks store in Weld Street suddenly began doing big business in waterproof work boots, gloves, scarves and knitted beanies. John and Penny Farrar's coffee shop swarmed with reporters seeking shelter and hot beverages, Manion's Bakery could hardly keep pace with orders for pies and Kramer's newsagency increased its orders for newspapers twentyfold and still had trouble meeting demand.

The Club Hotel's chef Roger Broad could hardly keep pace with dinner orders and like others around town, he received rushed calls for meals to be sent up to the mine for rescuers. Out of nowhere one night, his dining room already full, Broad was required to knock up 40 extra plates for the mineworkers: fish and chips, Moroccan pork, spaghetti bolognaise and vegetables. He almost melted over his stoves.

Yet the story unfolding beneath the earth proceeded out of sight of the media maelstrom. It tantalised journalists, particularly those needing pictures to go with their words. A representative of one of the big TV channels sidled in to the Club Hotel and quietly suggested to the miners that big money was on offer to anyone prepared to smuggle a video camera into the depths of the mine. The sum of $10,000 was mentioned. The miners were affronted and threatened violence if the fellow didn't leave the hotel.

Journalists, mine rescue experts and paramedics from NSW weren't the only outsiders flying in to Tasmania.

In the hours after Todd and Brant were discovered to have survived, Michael Ryan, the Perth-based administrator of Allstate Explorations – the company managing the mine – phoned the sales manager of Johnson High-Tech Explosives, Darren Flanagan. Flanagan was sitting at home in Nowra, a town on the NSW south coast, watching with amazement TV news reports of the extraordinary events in Beaconsfield.

Flanagan had worked for 13 years in the blasting business, specialising in low-energy explosives. His company's product is known as PCF/RocKracker. PCF (which stands for 'penetrating cone fracture') does its work by blasting a 45-degree cone within a drill-hole. One of its attributes is that it does not create the sort of massive shockwave caused by high explosives.

Ryan wanted to know whether PCF could be used safely to break rock close to Brant and Todd. Flanagan said it would be a slow method, but yes, it could work.

By midnight, Flanagan was aboard a corporate jet sent by the mine company to pick him up at Nowra's naval base, HMAS *Albatross*. He was the only passenger, bound for Launceston.

The same jet was sent later to western Victoria to collect three senior miners from the Leviathan Resources Stawell gold mine – Jeremy Rowlings, who had suggested that Beaconsfield might try to use a raise bore, Brett Chalmers, a specialist air-leg driller who was familiar with PCF explosives and Scott Franklin, the Stawell mine's occupational health and safety manager.

The three men had no idea how far they might have to blast through the wall to Brant and Todd. PCF is an inefficient method of blowing a wall, and they calculated that if they were required to break through 16 metres of solid rock, it would take 16 days.

As for other rescuers from across Australia, the three men's partners – Ingar Rowlings, Linda Franklin and Scott's partner Ros Morgan – were left not knowing when they would see their men again. They supported each other, getting together in the evenings for red wine and dinner, and the Stawell mine management offered them anything they needed, from firewood to babysitters. The women knew the dangers, but Ingar summed up their philosophy: 'When you're a miner's wife, you worry, but you learn not to stress. When Jeremy goes underground, you just accept it – it's the only way of coping.'

Time quickly became an obsession in Beaconsfield. Every journalist wanted to know exactly when Brant and Todd might be released from their incarceration. Matthew Gill stressed that everyone would have to be patient.

'The condition of the guys in terms of their health and wellbeing has brought us time to do it right without rushing,' he said.

'And it's for exactly that reason I'm reluctant to give an end point [for a rescue] because this thing is so dynamic; we've had change of plan after change of plan as information has come to light. These guys are actually giving us a lot of information to allow us to work out the appropriate plan and as that changes, so too may the duration. But if that means what we do is still the safest option, we'll do safety over speed any day.

'I can't stress how difficult and dangerous the next phase is and this emotional roller-coaster I know the families are going through, I know the community is going through, we on site are going through, I'm sure a lot of the people are going through, we just have the keep our heads and work through it logically and carefully and sensibly.'

Bill Shorten nominated 48 hours as the most likely period for the rescue.

But he could not say when the clock might start ticking.

'The 48 hours hasn't begun to run yet,' he said, using a phrase that would become familiar and infuriating.

In Launceston, Larry Knight's family and partner Jacqui extended extraordinary generosity. They would postpone Larry's funeral until Todd and Brant were released.

Only those who have experienced the netherworld of grief that engulfs families between the death of one of their own and the final act, the ritualised goodbye, could understand the bravery of the act. The Knight clan had put on hold its own right to vent its anguish in solidarity with the hopes and fears engulfing the Russell and Webb families.

Lauren, Larry's daughter, spent much of her time sitting on the front steps of her grandmother Pearl's home, smoking cigarette after cigarette, trying to hold herself together. She was half a continent away from familiar surroundings, still grieving for her grandfather and sunk into the depth of the knowledge that she would never see her biological father again. 'I just wanted to crawl into a little hole and die,' she said later.

Down in the hole of the living, Todd and Brant wanted food. Bacon and eggs, preferably. The supply of vanilla-flavoured Sustagen and vitamin pills pushed down the tube lost its appeal quickly. On doctors' orders, they were forced to content themselves with other comforts.

Torches came down the tube so they might push away a little of the darkness shrouding them. Glow-sticks, too. They broke the seals, releasing a sickly fluorescence, and wedged the sticks in cavities between broken rocks above their heads. No chandelier had ever been so prized. When they slept, they would no longer wake to confusing blackness.

One of their more urgent requirements was to deal with the waterfall soaking them. They had been shaking with cold for days now. It was an agony offering no respite. Rescuers sent through a probe and discovered the temperature in the cavern was 24.5 degrees Celsius.

Anywhere else, it might have been a pleasant spring day. But both men lay prone, their clothes wet and chafing. Because air within the mine moved steadily, drawn down ventilation shafts by a vacuum created by big fans at the surface, those wet clothes were refrigerated. The movement of air, it was later ascertained, came from the big open stope to their west. It found its way through space within collapsed rock, meandered through their cell and wafted out through more collapsed rock into the 925 drive.

If Todd and Brant could only mop themselves dry and stay dry, they might rid themselves of at least one of their tortures. There could be no semblance of comfort while a torrent poured upon them.

Miners in the decline brought a sheet of plastic. Sending it down the tube presented greater difficulties than cramming pills and syringes and little boxes of Sustagen into a small water bottle, however. The plastic sheet was rolled tightly and a train of cut-down water bottles was produced. Each bottle had its snout and its bottom sliced off and was taped to another, fashioning a tube of plastic bottles into which the rolled makeshift tarpaulin was fitted. The arrangement was pushed down the pipe. Brant and Todd finally had some protection. They spread the plastic sheet above them and stretched it on an angle so most of the water falling from the roof drained into the little void by the footwall.

Todd and Brant's families sent tracksuits and shirts. The clothes were stretched and rolled into long sausages, packed into the chain of taped bottles and pushed through the wall.

In the world beyond, the Russell and Webb families felt an overwhelming desire to send messages to the two men. The Launceston psychologist, Bev Ernst, in consultation with doctors, paramedics and the incident management team, felt that a wave of emotion could prove an assault too difficult for the men to handle. Rachel Webb recorded on tape a deep-felt voice message to Brant speaking of her love and her need to see him and hold him. It was judged too raw, and was never sent down the hole.

Carolyn Russell was told she could write no more than a straightforward letter informing Todd that all was well with the family. She felt cheated, but went along with it.

Rachel could not bring herself to write at all. Instead, her twins composed letters, and so did Brant's mother and father. When they were delivered to the mine, they were censored and re-written, the jagged edges of the messages chiselled away.

Brant knew immediately that Rachel had not written the first letter he received. As he shone torchlight upon the sheet of paper, he recognised the words were not in her handwriting and anyway, someone had misspelled Rachel's name. It began:

> Rachael's messages to Brant,
>
> Vinnie talked about sending in an empty ciggie [cigarette] packet. Rachy isn't frowning now. Vinnie's putting a red Corvette in the blender. Zac cleaned the car today. You left the mower out – it's now in the shed.
>
> Rachel says she loves you but can't find the words because you are the writer.
>
> Can't wait for you to lose at Yahtzee, Zilch and Pigs.
>
> Rex keeps turning up and eating the pizza.

He's like Father Christmas 'cause he always brings good news.

Your bar is more than fine – everyone is impressed with it.

Brant read and re-read the letter. It might not be in Rachel's hand, but it spoke of his world outside, a world where board games could while away an evening, cars were washed, Vinnie – good old Vinnie – made cocktails in the blender and joked about tormenting him with an empty packet of cigarettes. Yes, and Rachel loved him and clung to good news brought by Rex Johnson.

Todd had his own letter – a letter so precious to him he would never allow an outsider to read it. He would, he vowed, keep every word he received from his family private. Only Brant, the man with whom he had survived, would be granted the right to share the messages that came into their prison.

Both men laughed and cried, big sobs wracking big bodies, bereft of the touch of their families.

Zac and Zoey wrote their own letters.

Dear Dad.

We never gave up hope! Mum was beside herself with joy when we received the news, and laughed when they told us you or Todd swore, hah ha. [A reference to an early report published in *The Australian* that the first words to come out of the cell were 'It's fuckin' cold and cramped in here. Get us out.']

Mum can't put into words what she's feeling, only she loves you so much and she'll let you know just how she feels when she sees you.

We love you so much, Dad. Can't wait to see you. Mum will be the first of us you'll see. She's so emotional and we had a rushed job writing this, but she has been so strong for you, and always believed.

That's why I'm writing this for her; she can't find the words to express her love and everything. See you soon Daddy.

Oodles of love, Zoey, Zac and Rachel.

The letter was in Zoey's handwriting and right below was a personal note from Zac.

Dad, I've missed you mate. I've been holding strong and we've been keeping the house in some sort of order, ha ha.

We'll be waiting for you, oh, and if you check your pockets, you'll find some gear to make it to the end. Keep strong, it's not long now.

Somehow the letters on a single sheet made it through the censors. Zac's suggestion that Brant check his pockets led to more gold. When the family sent tracksuits, they recognised a smuggling opportunity: little notes of love were secreted in the pockets. Brant's mother Christa wrote:

To my darling Brant,

Cannot wait to see you and Todd.

Love you so much. Mum, Don. Love you – Allyson, John Shaun and Val aren't here to sign.

Brant's aunt Corinna signed with kisses and hugs. Zoey's boyfriend Richard slipped in a tiny letter:

Hey Brant can't wait to crack a can with you when you get out.

Zoey added:

> You're going to have the hugest party when you and Todd are out. Tell Todd we're thinking of him, too. We love you.

Carolyn Russell hit on the same idea. She and the children scribbled words from their hearts on post-it stickers and hid them in the warm clothes they sent to Todd. These, too, he carefully folded and tucked away.

Todd and Brant read each other's letters again and again, the words from that place and those people beyond the darkness they had come to believe they would never see again a treasure beyond price.

CHAPTER 20

PICTURES FROM THE DARK

As the mine management, rescue workers, miners, doctors, paramedics and all the rest of the throng gathered to keep Todd and Brant alive and to grapple with the perplexing question of how they might release the men safely from their incarceration, Mark Lopez knew Carolyn Russell needed help.

Lopez, a policeman from Hobart, had kept in touch with Carolyn by phone every day for the long week the men were missing. He and his partner Natalie, a detective, had become close to Todd and Carolyn after Lopez was posted to Beaconsfield as the town's police sergeant in 1995. The four of them spent evenings playing cards, Lopez introduced Todd to deer hunting in the Midlands, and the two men often took to the bush after kangaroos or simply practised their gun skills on clay pigeons.

He saw beyond Todd's bluff exterior, recognising a sensitive man with a strong sense of humour who rarely smiled simply because he was self-conscious – he felt his teeth had never grown properly and were too small for his face. He also knew Todd as a man who made few close friends, but who was capable of immense loyalty to those he allowed himself to trust. Lopez even performed the role of marriage-counsellor and sounding board when Todd and Carolyn hit a rocky patch years ago.

Lopez and Natalie hauled themselves free of work responsibilities on Sunday, 30 April, and headed from Hobart to Beaconsfield. Around 7 pm, still driving, Lopez took a call on his mobile. It was Carolyn. Todd and Brant had been found. He had to pull his car to the side of the road to deal with the emotion of it.

The Russell home was in an uproar of joy and relief when Lopez and Natalie arrived. Todd and Carolyn's eldest son Trent, recognising the strength of this old friend of his family, finally let himself go. He sat with Mark Lopez and sobbed – the first time he had allowed his fears and tears to bubble to the surface. The boy had believed for almost a week that his father was dead and as the eldest child, he had been determined to stay strong for his mother.

Lopez watched the children closely. He recognised the strain was eating at Maddison, exhaustion turning the sweet girl fractious. Little Liam seemed unaffected – until Lopez found him one day in the back yard using his Tonka truck to excavate a hole deep in the sand beneath his swing. 'I'm going to dig Dad out,' he declared. Rex Johnson had previously tried to explain to Liam that he and the miners were trying to bring his father out of the mine. The boy understood too much. He sat down and drew a picture of a man buried, a cross above and a child standing alone. 'My Dad's died because he's buried,' he cried to his mother. Carolyn tried to ease his alarm through metaphor. Liam often buried his toys in his sandpit. He always found them, Carolyn reminded him. It will be like that with Dad. And there he was, digging a great hole, searching for his father.

Down the road at Beauty Point, Rachel Webb had Vinnie Tunks as her gatekeeper. Now Carolyn Russell had Mark Lopez.

The policeman had dealt with the media many times and understood their need for information. He knew Carolyn was an intensely private person reluctant to show any emotion to outsiders. Even among her family and closest friends she rarely allowed herself to break down. He established himself as the point man for Todd Russell's family, handling every phone call. Over the next days, he made and received more than 1,000 calls, released a photo of the family to try to ease the clamour and became negotiator with those who wouldn't back off. And he decided Carolyn should not be bothered with the confusing blizzard of news reports, some of which were plain wrong. An ABC radio news reporter claimed at one point that Todd and Brant were out of their cage, *walking around,* as if they had enough space in the cavern for a stroll! The report infuriated a big mine worker who dropped in to John and Penny Farrar's coffee shop just in time to hear it broadcast. 'Bullshit!' he thundered.

At the Russell home, Lopez switched off the TV and radio and banned newspapers.

Lopez and Natalie moved in to a caravan in the Russell family's back yard. In the evenings, they sought to give Carolyn a little relief by dressing the children against the cold and taking them for a walk down the street to collect pizza. Sometimes, too, Lopez drove Carolyn to the mine at night, leaving her to sit on a bench beside the security office so she could be closer to her husband.

They both knew there was going to be no quick resolution to Carolyn's misery. They had to sit tight and watch and hope, like the rest of the country.

■ ■ ■

Never had an obscure piece of mining equipment received such attention. The vast majority of Australians had never heard of a raise bore, but within hours of it being dropped down the shaft at Beaconsfield it was the subject of excited discussion on the airwaves from one side of Australia to the other.

It quickly assumed the status of a lifesaver.

Few of the journalists at Beaconsfield knew anything about such a machine and many of their first reports referred to a 'raze bore', which was not a bad guess considering its job would be to demolish solid rock.

Peter Hatswell, the incident controller during the day, and the mine's mill manager, Richard Holder, who controlled the operation at night, needed to ensure that once the machine began drilling towards Brant and Todd – assuming such an exercise proved possible – it didn't lose power. It could be disastrous. The big drilling head could bog itself, possibly damaging it and forcing its operators to withdraw it from the hole before it could resume drilling.

The Tasmanian government-owned Aurora Energy provided electricity to the mine. Perhaps for the first time in history, a power supplier pledged to place a single machine ahead of all its other customers.

Aurora executives assured Hatswell that the company would alert all its substation staff to stay at work and report immediately any circumstance that might conceivably lead to a power interruption. The foul autumn weather across northern Tasmania was to be taken into account – any hint of an electrical storm would have to be monitored closely. Aurora would not switch excess capacity across Bass Strait to feed the national grid during the emergency at the mine lest the process cause problems.

Hatswell was told also that if it became necessary, the power company would deny electricity to households rather than disrupt supply to the mine. First the *Spirit of Tasmania*'s sailing schedule. Now the electricity supplier. The rescue effort came first.

Every day at 4 pm, an Aurora executive phoned Hatswell and provided an update. And every day, the news was good. There would be no disruption to the massive amount of electricity needed to run the raise bore.

That didn't mean the big drilling machine, its hydraulic system containing hundreds of litres of oil, was about to shudder into action or even that it could do the job required. Once it was reassembled after its journey in parts down the mineshaft, it had to be hauled down the decline and set up within the drive.

It was no simple task. The raise bore had to be bolted securely to handle the great thrust it would exert upon the rock wall – the equivalent of about 80 tonnes.

Those overseeing the exercise had a more urgent problem. Where, precisely, should it be directed?

As Hatswell and the team sifted through the options, modelling and assessing each for risk, it became clear that the metre-wide drill-head could not be used to break through the final wall entrapping the men. It could bring catastrophe, pushing the wall clean on top of Brant and Todd. And because the rig would be drilling on an angle upwards, only part of the revolving wheel would enter first, possibly causing it to shudder. A few tonnes of juddering steel in such an enclosed space, rocks poised to plummet from the ceiling, was a prospect not worth contemplating.

An early plan involved directing the bore towards a small enclosure cut into the footwall near the rear of the telehandler, a cuddy previously used by remote bogger operators in the 925 tunnel. If the raise bore could drill into that cuddy, miners might be able to crawl through the cylindrical hole created by the borehead and tunnel by hand along the footwall to the men. But the idea was ruled out for fear the tunnelers might cause Todd and Brant's tiny hole to collapse.

Once all the options had been argued, the team settled on a scheme to bore to a point *under* the basket.

It had several advantages. The raise bore would not be required to break the wall protecting the two men. It would also mean the bore's trajectory would be at a gentle angle, close to horizontal rather than climbing relatively steeply, therefore reducing the distance it would have to travel. And once it had completed its task, miners could break through the last metre or two, perhaps using nothing more than hand-held drills without causing too much violent vibration.

There were still plenty of unknown variables and great dangers associated with the task, not the least of which was whether a raise bore – designed for vertical drilling – could accomplish a horizontal hole. The only vaguely comparable exercise anywhere in the world, it seemed, was the use several years ago of a smaller Cubex machine to drill a roughly horizontal tunnel at the Stawell gold mine. The Cubex wasn't exactly a raise bore and its tunnel wasn't built to rescue two men trapped deep in the earth. But the fact that it was accomplished gave Jeremy Rowlings the idea of suggesting that a raise bore might be tried at Beaconsfield.

The first task was to bolt down the great bulk of the bore's power pack. The stone floor of the drive blasted the previous week was rough and uneven. The miners considered using planks of wood to prop the machine on the correct angle, to bore bolts deep into the floor and to anchor it with chains to the rock face. But when they considered the huge stress and pressure that would be brought to bear, they feared the bolts could simply shear off.

They had no choice but to drag the massive machine out of the drive and pour a concrete platform. Tonnes of concrete were sent down the shaft in a stream of kibbles – conical buckets – decanted into the agitator cylinder of a truck and transported down the decline.

The frustration within the mine and on the surface grew almost unbearable.

It was one thing to fashion a concrete platform, but another altogether to stand around and watch it dry, knowing that every minute was a new age that could bring disaster upon the two men forced to await rescue in the most appalling circumstances.

A quickset chemical was poured within the concrete, but the material had to be allowed to reach its greatest strength and hardness before it could be trusted to withstand the grunt of the raise bore. It took more than a day.

Indeed, it was late Wednesday afternoon – more than four days after Todd and Brant had been found alive – before the big drill finally began pushing a long thin hole into the rock wall. The hole, 220 millimetres wide and around 16 metres long, was required to guide the main drill head. Paramedics, unversed in mining techniques, watched in awe as the pilot drill bounced off the rock and wandered across the surface, trying to get purchase, before it finally sank into the stone at exactly the spot defined by the surveyor, Simon Arthur.

Once the pilot hole was completed, the bore head, measuring 1070 millimetres across, had to be lifted over the top of the drilling machine, scraping the roof, so it could be fitted to the rods that would push it against the rock face to begin its thrusting and grinding journey into the wall.

By then, a strict routine had been established to ensure that Todd and Brant were never out of communications.

The mine's electrician, Tony Woolhouse, a New Zealander with a flowing beard and John Lennon eyeglasses, fed a video camera down the tube. He had purchased the camera some days before, believing it might aid the search for bodies. It was simply a cheap light-intensifying camera about the diameter of a 50-cent piece, a cylinder not much bigger than a lipstick. Woolhouse – known to his mates as Bubbles because nothing was too difficult, he'd always rise to the surface – had spent hours modifying and testing it in his workshop at home. It could capture pictures in the dark and transmit them by cable to a TV screen.

The scene it revealed left rescuers transfixed. Speechless. Not in their worst dreams had they imagined anything as horrifying.

Two men huddled squashed together on their sides within a space no bigger than a rabbit hutch. Todd held the camera, pointed it at Brant's dirt-encrusted face, a pair of eyes staring, and swept the lens over a tangle of rocks above their heads hanging as if by some magical force that defied gravity.

Two mine rescue workers were assigned to watch the video screen. Corey Verhey and Dean Mackrell. Each was required to sit on an upturned milk crate, 12 hours at a time, never taking his eyes off Todd and Brant.

After the first rush of enthusiasm, fooling around and making faces at this strange little instrument that linked them with a world that had lost its meaning to them, Todd and Brant wedged the camera in a corner of their cage, granting those outside a continuous view of their monotonous existence.

'Just looking at their faces,' Corey said later. 'They were absolutely exhausted.

'You couldn't help but feel how utterly helpless they were. It was like you were watching over two young kids, trying to protect them from being hurt.'

Peter Hatswell had a more pragmatic need to peer closely at the video screen. He had to know the conditions within the cavern so he could figure out how rescuers might be able to break in without killing the two men.

Woolhouse also sent a telephone in pieces down the feeding tube and gave the men instructions on how to reassemble it. The phone was connected by cable to another telephone out in the decline and two paramedics were required to be on hand at all times. The paramedics, on a rotating roster, were relieved every twelve hours by two of their colleagues. Todd and Brant could speak to these people at any time of day or night for however long they felt like conversing.

Hatswell called up Todd and asked him to use the camera to map the prison. They agreed on a system that would use the face of a clock to denote each position. Todd started by aiming the lens at the roof. He raised one finger in front of the camera. One o'clock. He angled it a little forward. Two fingers. Two o'clock. By the time he had finished and the camera was again pointed at the roof, 12 o'clock, Hatswell had formed a mental picture that left him shaken.

'We're going to get you out,' he told Todd and Brant.

'I want you to be here at the end, Hatsy,' Todd told him.

'I'll be here. Don't worry,' said Hatswell.

Todd told Brant that he was deeply relieved that Hatsy was on the job.

'I'm happy to put my life in that bloke's hands,' he said.

Hatswell came down the decline often after that and stood staring at the video screen, inquiring of the team monitoring the men how Todd and Brant were bearing up mentally. But he did not speak to the trapped men during these visits. He had said he would be there at the end, and that would be enough. He watched miners pushing drinks and pills down the feeding tube. As the strip of conduit with a bottle taped to its end was withdrawn, the miner had to walk backwards down the drive and out into the decline – for almost 17 metres. Each time it happened, it impressed upon Hatswell just how far away were the men he had promised to save.

Each night, he went to bed in a camper van in the mine's grounds, his stomach churning. He had no idea whether he and the rest of the team could pull this off.

Todd and Brant's ability to speak with people who were free to leave the mine, to joke, to whisper their fears and to explain the horrors of their captivity proved therapeutic beyond any previous mercy save the moment they knew rescuers had found them alive. 'The power of speech,' Bill Shorten told reporters on the surface, understating the intensity of it, 'is obviously a tool to survival.'

The communications system, however, served to emphasise the depth of the dilemma facing those trying to organise a safe rescue.

A wall of solid rock almost 16 metres wide still stood between Todd and Brant and those trying to break them out. Above, a mountain of earth threatened to bury them all. No one knew if the ground might shake itself again.

Brant's mate Greg Crowden sat in front of another screen monitoring sensors capable of picking up the smallest tremor within the mine. Every sensor in his own body was attuned to the readout, for a jump in seismic activity meant every rescuer would be ordered to run from their work and to scramble for safety.

Unspoken was the gut-wrenching fear that at any moment, those on the telephone and in front of the video screen might hear the screams and witness the last dreadful moments of Todd Russell and Brant Webb.

CHAPTER 21

'FIGHTING VERY HARD'

'Speech,' Thomas Mann once wrote, 'is civilisation itself. The word, even the most contradictious word, preserves contact. It is silence that isolates.'

Todd and Brant were almost delirious with pleasure when a thin telephone wire was poked through the long tube connecting them with mates and strangers out there in the decline.

Each recognised privately he would have gone mad if he had been alone in the hole, unable to share his thoughts during six days of darkness and hopelessness. But Todd and Brant's conversations in the dark had been about pure survival. Now it was quite different. Now they could talk to people who were *coming to get them*. Their little world was suddenly altogether more tolerable.

They even had music, granting them the extravagant gift of private reverie when the effort of talking or thinking about their predicament became too much. A couple of electrical stores in Launceston donated four MP3 players and mine employees loaded them up with Todd and Brant's favourite music.

Todd had country and western to soothe him: Alan Jackson and Lee Kernaghan and Kenny Rogers and the like.

Brant requested the Seattle rock band Foo Fighters and Canada's Nickelback. His sense of humour had entered a black phase: one of Foo Fighters' best-known songs is 'DOA' (the abbreviation for 'dead on arrival'). Part of the song's chorus is:

What a way to go, but have no fear
No one's getting out of here, alive
This time.

Alternatively, of course, he might have been thinking of some of the words in the first verse:

Waited and I waited the longest night
Nothing like the taste of sweet decline

The rescue team outside could not tolerate the thought of the two men lying on sharp rocks and sent them small self-inflating cushions. Each man received four of these little squares of kindness. It was impossible to send them larger mattresses. They were no more than pads, the sort of thing you might fit to a camping chair, but they formed a layer between the men and their bed of rocks, which had worn pressure sores into their flesh.

As the mad activity of the first days since they had been found began to settle, it came time to write letters.

The effort of writing anything that might make sense was very nearly the toughest challenge Todd and Brant had faced since they had been trapped. Neither of them wanted to do it – they wanted to see and touch their families. How could they offer their wives and children hope from a place like this? They wished to avoid adding to the anxiety of those they loved. It seemed an insurmountable task. Their families, surely, would want to know at least something of the conditions in which the men had survived, but if they were to tell the truth, it might prove too alarming.

Todd chewed at the end of a pen. He settled on a tender message that spoke of the future – a better future for Carolyn and him – that did not allow a chink of doubt that he would be rescued. Part of the letter would be chatty: his gratitude that Mark Lopez and his partner Natalie had come to help Carolyn, his happiness that his oldest friend Michael Piscioneri and his wife Julie were to visit from Western Australia and how he was looking forward to seeing another couple of mates, Ant and Pedro, security guards at the mine with whom he often went hunting.

> To Dear Carolyn
>
> This is not the best way that I want to talk to u babe. Fighting very hard, keeping our spirits high. Shouldn't be long now and we will be together again forever.
>
> A lot of things are going to change for u and the kids. Had a lot of time to reassess things. All the kids are good please give them a big kiss and hug for me and tell them that dad loves them and thinking of them all the time. It has been their thoughts that have helped me.
>
> It was good of Mark and Nat to come up for u, Mike and Jules will be home on Monday. Can't wait to see you all and kiss and cuddle u all. It's not much of a room we have up here can't wait to get

into my own bed. Tell Ant and Pedro looking forward to seeing them.

Oh by the way babe the two years that we said we would wait for our new Hilux has just came forward. Going to get it when I get out of here after what has happened. Not waiting anymore. Well hun say hi to everyone from me and we will party hard when we get out. Ok babe love u so much keep your chin up and hold u soon.

Love Toddles

p.s. say Hi to Mark and Nat

Todd decided also he would write short notes to his children that reassured them he was still the same old gruff Dad who hadn't changed a bit since he'd been away.

To Trent

How are u mate they tell me u have taken over the man of the house role, great to hear that. When we get out Brant has offered to give up his MP3 player so that u can have it. Already has Foo Fighters music on it keep looking after mum and see u soon.

Love Dad

p.s. clean up your bloody room

XXX

To Dear Maddison

Hope u are well thinking of you all the time won't be long now and dad will be home to take you motorbike riding Love dad.

p.s. same goes for u clean up your room

XXX

To Liam (Shit head)

How has dad's shadow been going? They tell me that u kicked 3 goals on Saturday and led St Kilda onto York Park. Will go motorbike riding when I get home.

Love dad

p.s. clean up your bloody room too shit for brains.

Brant tried for a mixture of levity and a little information about his health. He tried, too, to explain to Rachel why he had ventured so deep into the mine in the first place.

Morning Thurs. 4-5-06

To all in the Webb residence,

A surprise to hear you are all down in Tassie. You all look great; well, hope you all do. They say John Francis the media star does. [A reference to Brant's father, John Francis Webb, who had given an emotional TV interview.]

They will not tell us much about the outside even when the boys phone out of drill rig bore hole.

You will probably all be gone by the time we get out of Alcatraz.

A million-to-one chance, they say – will be a story to be told.

I have no injuries @ this stage. There is no space in cage – losing muscles. Still strong. A lot of cramps.

They found us Sunday; accident 9.30 pm Tuesday.

Sorry Rach. Was heading up to backfill plant 11 pm Tuesday night; didn't make it. Larry and I went to help Todd @ a job and now writing to you.

They are throwing everything and every resource @ getting us out, time has no meaning only safety to get us out in one piece.

It may take a while yet – options limited.

Spirits good – have a lot of good people here, the best rescue people in Australia.

Dad met Peter Featherstone at the Riviera I was told – Peter a big support. [Brant was confused – he meant Paul Featherstone, the NSW rescue paramedic.]

Had our first solid food – egg sandwich today – looking good for the piss-up. Protocol is being held and is best if done right.

Our fellow workmates have been great. Todd's been excellent and I've given up the smokes.

Hope you are all well and hang around.

Brant.

Almost a day later, Brant felt up to writing a few more personal notes. He wrote them all on one page.

Friday 5-5-06

People of the Webb residence @ Beauty Point.

All's well @ 2 am.

Hope Zac is looking after everyone and Zoey helping. I know you will. Thanks, Dad.

Rach, Love and miss you xxxooo.

The rest of you lovely people. I hope the weather improves for you all.

Rach PIN no. on phone I think??

Could you pick up my car from mine – locker no. 62 the keys in pocket.

When we get out could you bring clothes and shoes to L'ton Hospital as ambulance will take Rach and I there. Need car to follow later will call you when out.

Thanks for note Mum, I needed that a lot. To keep going. It hasn't been easy.

Love, Brant.

⁂

It was the egg sandwiches that did it.

As the days wore on, the doctors and paramedics began weaning the two men off their monotonous diet of Sustagen and vitamin pills.

Gradually, more solid food was allowed, and egg sandwiches were on the menu.

Brant couldn't hold out any longer.

'Mate,' he told Todd, 'I'm gonna have to take a crap.'

Neither man had moved his bowels in 10 days. Todd could not face the idea and was furious that Brant was even thinking of weakening.

'You're not going to take a shit in here,' he declared.

'I can't help it. I've just gotta,' said Brant.

To Todd's mounting disgust, Brant phoned out and asked for a plastic bag to be sent down the tube. The miners in the decline had no idea why a plastic bag was required and sent a super-sized garbage bag, the sort of thing gardeners use for clippings.

'You're gonna have to help me,' Brant told Todd.

'Pig's arse,' Todd bellowed. 'I'm not having anything to do with it. For fuck's sake, can't you just hold it in?'

Todd rolled on his side, facing as far away from Brant as he could.

Brant called for packing tape to be sent.

He was forced to tape the bag to his buttocks, back and thighs. There remained a major problem: room to move. He couldn't so much as kneel. The best position he could achieve was to stick his head out through the little door into the void and elevate his behind a few inches, rocks digging in to his knees.

When he finally completed the operation, Todd exclaiming every now and then that he was a filthy bastard, there remained the question of the garbage bag.

'You're not leavin' that fuckin' thing in here,' Todd proclaimed.

'What? You want me to send it back down the tube? That's our feed tube. What if the bag breaks? What happens if it gets stuck and we can't get any more food sent down?' Brant protested.

Todd wasn't having it. He wanted the bag out of the cell. Now.

No parcel had ever been so tightly bound by packing tape. Brant used what seemed miles of tape, crammed the whole thing into a drink bottle, sealed the bottle with more tape and bound it to the end of the conduit. It disappeared down the tube.

'What's this?' a voice hollered from the other end of the pipe.

'That,' yelled Brant, 'is shit.'

There was silence, followed by cursing.

A kilometre above, the incident management team, exhausted by days of intricate planning, was becoming frustrated. Helicopters carrying television camera crews hovered, the clatter of their blades so loud the planners could hardly hear each other in their tin-roofed conference room. They sent out a request that choppers fly higher or at some distance from the mine.

Kaye and Noel Russell were unimpressed by all the media attention, too. A reporter from one of the women's magazines approached both Kaye and her son Stephen wanting to write a story about Kaye's 'first miracle.' Stephen had been struck down when he was 13 with Ewing's sarcoma, a rare bone cancer. The family believed the boy would die, but after a year's treatment, he survived. When Todd was found to have survived the rock fall, Kaye declared it her 'second miracle.'

Kaye told the magazine reporter she didn't want to give any form of interview until Todd was released from the ground. A day later, the reporter returned.

Kaye tells it like this: 'First of all she came, the first night it was raining, she came and she said, "Look, can I just talk to you? I want to know what a mother feels, how a mother feels." She said, "I won't ask you about Todd." I said, "Look, I'm sorry, no. Until we get Todd out we're not doing anything. We don't want to do anything until we've got him home, until he's safe."

'So she went. The next day she came back, that's when she asked Stephen. She had a quiche and a loaf of bread. "Oh, I've walked past this nice little café on the way. There's a nice quiche and a loaf of bread." Stephen said, "I'm sorry, I don't want to give any story, not until we've got Todd home."'

The reporter offered to pay a fee, but Kaye and Stephen sent her on her way. They didn't want quiche or money.

Noel, almost out of his mind with worry about his son, threatened one day to run over photographers staking out his home. He believed that once he had made his appearance before the cameras and microphones outside the mine in the first week he had a bargain with the media. He couldn't understand why cameramen continued to point their lenses at him whenever he ventured out. Kaye was furious one day when she was hanging clothes on the line. She looked up to see a camera poking from a helicopter filming her.

Two media personalities were, however, perfectly welcome in the Russell home: David Koch and Melissa Doyle of Channel Seven's breakfast show *Sunrise*. Todd was a huge fan of Koch and sent a message down the tube: 'Tell the fat bastard I want him here when I come out – I've got something for him.' Todd had resolved that he would hand his identification pass to Koch – a reasonable exchange, he felt, for all those mornings when he arrived home from a night's work in the mine and sat before the TV, roaring with laughter at Koch's antics on the screen. Koch isn't particularly fat, but the message got through. Koch and Doyle often wandered down to Kaye and Noel's house and sat around, chatting. It sent a chill through the Nine Network, because the Todd and Brant story was the biggest news in the country, and both Seven and Nine wanted the right to interview the two men when they finally emerged.

There was, though, an ambivalence in the relationship between the massive media contingent and Beaconsfield's townsfolk. While many locals expressed annoyance at the invasion of their streets, they relied heavily upon the news reports these journalists prepared hour by hour to keep informed about what was happening at their own mine.

Many residents, too, were fascinated by the media encampment and trooped up to the park across the way to indulge in a little celebrity spotting.

A small group of women took pity on the visitors and offered the sort of country hospitality that left many reporters humbled. It began in the first week when a woman approached a reporter in Weld Street. 'I feel so sorry for all you people working so hard,' she said, and handed the reporter a large shopping bag. The woman would not give her name and scuttled away. Inside the bag was a bundle of hand-cut sandwiches, a big carton of orange juice and a container of sweets.

During the second week, with frozen rain sweeping the town, several women took to visiting the makeshift media centre bearing hot soup and casseroles. In the evenings they returned and set about washing dishes, tidying the room and replacing the casseroles with fresh meals as reporters tapped away on their laptops and chattered on mobile telephones. When the women discovered there was a vegetarian among the media contingent, they brought meat-free quiches. Each day, too, a truck bearing the brand name Tasfresh pulled up and crates of crunchy Tasmanian apples – royal gala – were delivered with no fanfare.

The women would not give their names and said they represented no organisation. They simply wanted to help. It took their minds off what might be happening deep in the mine, one of them explained. The journalists were left only with the knowledge that in kitchens across Beaconsfield, anonymous women rose early and boiled up steaming pots of soup and filled their ovens with baking dishes and sliced sandwiches for strange visitors they would never know. Such an elegant display of community and big-hearted kindness. The reporters took to calling these generous women 'the angels.'

Handwritten notes appeared on a pinboard in the media centre, too: if anyone needed a bed, they should phone this or that number. Not one of these notes suggested there was a fee attached. Mark and Lorraine Kramer from the newsagency made available their caravan to Tracey Grimshaw and her crew from Nine's *A Current Affair*. No charge.

Nine hundred and twenty-five metres beneath the town, two men were preparing for the final assault upon their tiny world. Miners fed lengths of sturdy chain, shackles and bolt-cutters down the tube. Todd and Brant set about replacing the flimsy net of cab straps above their cage with a stronger web of steel chain. They were not particularly concerned about the rumbling head of the raise bore as it chewed its way through the rock wall towards them – the methodical sound of it actually lulled them to sleep and the paramedics and miners watching them on video were cheered when Todd and Brant snoozed for four hours. It was the longest slumber either of the men had allowed himself in the whole saga.

But the men knew they had to be prepared for what happened once the raise bore reached its ultimate depth. The rescue miners had to find a way into the cavern. It would be the most dangerous phase of the entire operation.

CHAPTER 22

BAD GROUND ABOVE AND BELOW

Never in Australia's long history of underground mining had there been such a drawn-out rescue attempt.

Historians trawled through the records and came across the story of Modesto Varischetti, a 33-year-old Italian immigrant who was trapped by rising water in the Westralia gold mine at Bonnievale near Coolgardie, Western Australia.

On the afternoon of 19 March 1907, a freak storm sluiced millions of litres of water into the mine and Varischetti was caught alone in an air pocket 300 metres below the surface.

Two deep-sea divers on holiday from the pearl grounds of Broome and specialist diving equipment were raced from Perth by steam train – only the engine was used and the journey took 13 hours instead of the usual 17, a record that stood for 50 years.

The two pearl divers were joined by two others who, incredibly, happened to be in Kalgoorlie. The first attempt to reach the men failed when air hoses became tangled.

Eventually, one of the divers who was working as a miner in Kalgoorlie, Edward Hughes, found his way through the black water to Varischetti, bringing him in sealed containers a lamp, candles, matches, food, drink and tobacco. The Italian, seeing a creature in a brass helmet rising from the water, is supposed to have screamed 'Il diavolo stesso – Jesu Cristo' ('The devil himself – Jesus Christ').

But Varischetti could not be rescued. Not yet. The water was still too high, despite the frantic efforts of men on hand-operated pumps at the surface. Day after day Hughes returned, but Varischetti despaired, believing he would eventually be consigned to a lonely death, reduced to eating the stubs of candles.

Nine days after the Italian miner had been trapped, Hughes decided he could tarry no longer. He hoisted the exhausted Varischetti on his shoulders and carried him out through the mine's flooded tunnels. Pumping had reduced the water level, but Varischetti still almost drowned. The story was flashed around the world, carried by newspapers from London to New York.

Todd and Brant's incarceration stretched beyond 9 days before the great drill-head of the raise bore had dug a metre into the rock wall entrapping them.

The story unfolding in Beaconsfield captured the world's attention, too.

A correspondent from the CNN network, a bear of a man named Hugh Williams, set up camp in Beaconsfield and his reports flashed across the globe. The big

Australian television networks packaged reports for their affiliates in the USA, and newspapers from London to Moscow featured accounts from special correspondents and the wire services.

Beaconsfield's three churches blazed with candles and held special prayer services, but so, too, did churches across Australia. Brant Webb's mother Christa and her partner Don had built the altar and fashioned beautiful candlesticks for St Clare's Catholic Church in Tully, far north Queensland. Tully's parish priest, Father Kerry Crowley, ensured that candles were lit and prayers offered every day for Brant and Todd. Rachel's mother Julie Kelly placed rosary beads blessed by the Pope around Rachel's neck, and they stayed there throughout the long ordeal.

Beaconsfield's residents became accustomed to the sight of TV news and current affairs anchormen and women in the little town, but they knew they were on the map when Richard Carleton of *60 Minutes* sailed in. Carleton, a tall man with a talent for infuriating politicians and shaving the edges off complicated stories and presenting them in easily digestible, highly entertaining chunks, was easily the best-known television journalist in Australia. He had a splendid arrogance about him that caused viewers to either love him or loathe him. He was, in short, a star.

Beaconsfield's miners had spent the best part of two weeks giving the cold shoulder to most journalists in town, but there was no resisting Carleton's charms. Not long after he arrived, he disappeared down the road with a tight bunch of the mine's most respected old-school miners.

Around a table outside a café at the seaside resort town of Greens Beach, about 20 kilometres from

Beaconsfield, Carleton gleaned some handy information about the Beaconsfield mine.

On Sunday, 7 May, it became clear just how good his information was.

Shortly after midday, Matthew Gill emerged from the mine and walked to the park across the road to give journalists the latest news on efforts underground to release Todd and Brant. The raise bore had completed its work successfully, drilling a cylindrical hole around 1 metre wide deep into the rock wall. But it had stopped about 1.5 metres from the area where it might be possible to break through to the men.

The miners involved in the rescue attempt, Gill said, had reported the rock they now faced was among the hardest they had experienced. A technique of using low-impact blasting was being used, and other rock-breaking methods employing specialised drills were being considered.

Gill could not say how long the rescue might take – it was possible the men could be released within a day, but it was unlikely.

'If we were able to apply the same patience as Todd and Brant are showing, it would be great,' he told the impatient media throng.

Carleton used his height and his distinctive voice to break through the tumult of questions raining on the unfortunate Gill.

'On the 26th of October last year, not 10 metres from where these men are now entombed, you had a 400-tonne rock fall,' he boomed. 'Why is it, is it the strength of the seam, or the wealth of the seam, that you continue to send men in to work in such a dangerous environment?'

Gill responded that it was not the time to be discussing such matters, but most of the journalists had ears only for Carleton's follow-up question.

It never came. His face reddened and he stepped back, walked about 10 metres from the press conference and fell to the ground.

A Tasmanian Government media adviser, Shaun Rigby, followed Carleton from the media scrum, intent on tackling him about his confronting question to Gill. 'He's down,' Rigby yelled as Carleton toppled over. Police Constable Phil Pike and a Hobart radio journalist rushed to apply cardiopulmonary resuscitation but it was obvious in seconds that Carleton was dying.

Beaconsfield's ambulance screamed up the road and another roared out of the mine's grounds carrying two paramedics from NSW. Dr Andrew Hughes, the director of the Tasmanian Medical Retrieval Service from Launceston, worked on Carleton as he lay in the park. There was no more convenient place in Tasmania to fall ill. Expert medical assistance was no more than a whistle away.

Carleton was a skilled magician – one of his party tricks was to remove guests' wristwatches and produce them from behind his ear before anyone knew what he had done – but he could not conjure himself out of this appalling stroke of fate, no matter how many medical experts were on hand.

Journalists, Carleton's *60 Minutes* colleagues and emergency service personnel erected a wall of blankets and towels to try to grant him some dignity and to shield the ghastly scene from the eyes of children who had come to the park with their parents to watch a media circus and enjoy the first weak sunshine for a week. A few minutes before, Carleton had signed autographs for some of those children. 'Have a healthy life,' he had written.

Soon Carleton's body was placed in an ambulance. The ambulance driver set his siren wailing as he sped off down West Street. But as soon as he wheeled into Weld Street, heading towards Launceston, the driver turned off the sound and throttled back. Richard Carleton, 62, a journalist for more than 40 years and a man who had reported from some of the worst places in the world, was dead. In one of the most peaceful places on earth, covering the most dramatic story in the land. A few minutes after asking the toughest question anyone had dared or known to ask. And, of course, he died on camera. Many of the photographers in the park kept clicking. It is the nature of journalism: never look away, never turn off the camera. Carleton himself turned the cameras on his body in 1988, producing a documentary on his first heart bypass operation. He had another heart attack in 2003 and more surgery. When he came to Beaconsfield, he was recovering from treatment for prostate cancer. A glutton for punishment and a rattling good yarn.

His *60 Minutes* colleagues swallowed their shock and grief and completed Carleton's report so it could go to air six hours after he died.

It began:

> You see that mine head down there? That's just 500 metres away. In your mind, double that distance and then go straight down. You think of this – where were you last Anzac Day, last Tuesday week? Because it's since then that the two have

been down there. Let me ask you another question. What caused this disaster? We all know the answer. It was an earthquake, wasn't it? Well no, it wasn't, in the sense that you and I would use that word. This disaster was entirely man-made. On Anzac Day, the earth beneath Beaconsfield rumbled, but not for the first time. Back on the 26th of October last year, a 400-tonne rock fall caused another massive rumble. That fall was just 10 metres from the site of last week's disaster.

And there it was. Richard Carleton's reason for travelling to Beaconsfield. To declare the event that had killed Larry Knight and trapped Brant Webb and Todd Russell was no natural earthquake, but a man-made disaster.

His evidence? His quiet chat with miners at a café in Greens Beach.

If Carleton had been granted more time, he might have discovered that any number of the most experienced miners felt deep frustration because they believed their complaints about the dangers of mining at Beaconsfield were going unheeded. Men like Mick Borrill and Garth Bonney and others had complained openly at their weekly toolbox meetings that too many natural pillars were being removed, leaving the mine unsupported at deep levels. There was hardly a man underground who did not believe that the rock fall at 915 metres on 26 October 2005 – the 400-tonne fall that Carleton spoke about, just 10 metres above the Anzac Day fall that killed Larry Knight – was a sign of worse things to come.

And there were those words: *bad ground*. Virtually every man who had worked in the 925 level spoke of it as bad ground, and no one disputed that the level immediately above was bad ground. It was so bad that no one could enter 915 metres directly from the decline. The miners had been forced to build a new access from 900 simply to avoid the bad ground that had collapsed.

Younger miners like Daniel Piscioneri, Greg Crowden, Darren Geard and Corey Verhey and their friends had no doubts about the ground around the 925 either.

'It was a shit of a place to work,' Piscioneri declares. 'It was nothing for the walls and backs to crack and pop all day. It was nothing to get a windblast – when the ground moves and pushes the air. You get used to it.'

And Verhey: 'I'd worked in that area [the 925] so many times and it was horrible ground. There was that much ground support in there to hold it together, but it was loose. It felt dangerous. No one liked working in there and it was always making noises.'

Crowden: 'Bad ground? Yeah . . . Down in that area, the pillars had got smaller, down from 20 metres between the levels to just 10 metres. When you get pillars with so much weight on them, you're getting areas sheared off. Most levels were fractured. You'd have to get your scaling bar to pull loose rock off the walls before you could work. It was very nerve-wracking.'

And there was Darren Geard, who only 24 hours before the Anzac night disaster had worked in the precise area that had fallen on Brant, Todd and Larry and was so concerned about 'drummy' walls that he had chosen to drill pinholes in a different spot.

Todd Russell himself had planned to leave the underground, citing fears of an accident, and Brant Webb had promised his own wife he would not venture deep.

Seismic events of late 2005 and early 2006 had spooked just about all the miners.

Bill Shorten was getting the same sort of alarming information from members of the AWU in the mine. Recognising there would be an inquiry into the Anzac Day rock fall, he and his union colleagues began collecting statements from miners. These statements would eventually form the basis of a long submission to that investigation.

Meanwhile, Brant and Todd remained trapped.

Richard Carleton's death, the accusations central to his *60 Minutes* report, the anguish felt by his closest colleagues, the long-held concerns of miners and the debate about the timing and the taste of Carleton's question to Matthew Gill – all these were swept aside as the rescue effort maintained its momentum. Beaconsfield was united in a single effort. Those boys had to be released safely. Everything else could be discussed later.

Wind-driven rain swept back down the Tamar Valley, and the little park where a reporter had died lay deserted.

CHAPTER 23

5.59 AM: THE DAWN

As the days and nights wore on, each blurring into a long dusk for the men trapped far from the moods of the Tamar Valley's wide sky, Todd and Brant rode waves of high humour and deep melancholy.

Their worst moments came soon after the rapture that accompanied the sound of human voices calling them. Shortly after their lifeline was drilled through the rock wall, they summoned up the courage to inquire of Larry Knight's fate. The news that Larry had perished struck them sharp as a knife to the throat.

Brant, who had worked all the shifts of his years at the Beaconsfield mine on the same roster as Larry, slumped into dejection. He had believed so strongly that Larry had escaped the rock fall and was working to save his mates that sometimes in the agony of his confinement Brant had felt an extra presence in the cavern.

An image, perhaps a hallucination, had lodged itself in his consciousness – a golden sphere of light wedged between his and Todd's bodies. He became fixated on the mysterious orb, believing it represented salvation. Now, it was gone. Brant experienced the physical sensation that there was suddenly a little more room in the chamber. Larry's spirit, he decided, had protected him and Todd. Now it had fled, leaving the responsibility to rescuers.

There was not time enough to grieve properly. Brant and Todd had to attend to the serious business of continuing to survive.

The paramedics, anyway, were not about to allow either of the men to lapse into extended depression.

Over the phone, they set about finding ways to keep the two men busy, drawing them out of themselves. There was the job of teaching them to inject themselves, to eat and drink at regular hours in an attempt to ease them back into the patterns of normal life, to tend to each other's wounds. The paramedics gave the men exercises to try to rebuild lost muscle and movement. Because of the lack of space, these could be no more than the most basic of isometric exercises, in which they were instructed to push their feet against the mesh of their cage and to lift their pelvises from the bed of rock. The men had to capture urine samples and send them up the tube daily so their medical condition could be tested.

The paramedics and rescuers were relieved to discover quickly that the men were breathing clean air. Peter Hatswell sent bags for Todd to fill with air from within the cavern and tests proved it was as fresh as anywhere else in the mine.

The phone conversations revealed the men's personal interests. Magazines were rolled and pushed down the tube – hunting magazines for Todd, boating journals and a book of sudoku puzzles for Brant. Todd, only half-jokingly, asked for a Saturday edition of Launceston's *The Examiner* – he wanted to study the job advertisements. No way was he continuing to work underground, he declared. And he sent word that he had been keeping track of the hours that he and Brant had spent underground, and both would be demanding full pay for the time spent underground, calculated to the hour.

A close relationship built quickly between the two trapped men and the paramedics out there on the phone. Todd and Brant were entirely dependent on the paramedics and the paramedics became, in a strange sense, dependent on the men. They wanted, *needed* Todd and Brant to survive and to remain as healthy as possible in body and mind, and the long 12-hour shifts on the phone slowly transformed from affiliations between strangers to deep bonds between humans.

One of the Launceston-based paramedics, Peter James, who was working at an ambulance branch station at Deloraine when he was called to the mine, felt his time on the phone with the two men was therapeutic. James had been thrown into despondency after a hideous period 10 years before when he was required to supervise the removal of 35 bodies from around the ruins of Tasmania's Port Arthur prison colony. On 28 April 1996, a 28-year-old creep named Martin Bryant used an arsenal of rifles to carry out the world's deadliest and most abrupt one-person murder spree. Peter James not only had to supervise the removal of bodies, but to counsel traumatised emergency service workers. There was no chance of any form of happy ending at Port Arthur, and the 10th anniversary – just three days after Larry Knight, Brant Webb and Todd Russell were lost beneath Beaconsfield – brought all the dreadful memories back.

The opportunity to help save two men trapped deep in the earth and to keep their spirits from sinking seemed to Peter James like a shot at redemption. Besides, he found the mining activity around him in the decline and in the drive fascinating. The boggers reminded him of scorpions, scuttling from holes in the walls, diving into piles of rock and reversing at speed back into their dark nests. He watched as miners built a wall to stop the concrete pad they were building for the raise bore slipping away down the decline.

James and Todd, it turned out, shared two passions: David Koch of *Sunrise* and country singer Alan Jackson. He delivered to the Seven Network's Chris Reason Todd's demand that 'the fat bastard', David Koch, should not leave the state until he was out of the hole. And he delivered to CNN's Hugh Williams a message that Todd would like Alan Jackson to know he was a big fan. Williams managed to have the message conveyed across the world through CNN's office in Atlanta, Georgia.

Karen Pendrey, the first of the Launceston paramedics to speak to Todd and Brant, was married to another paramedic called to Beaconsfield, Daryl Pendrey. Their lives were consumed by the mine. Karen spent nights in the decline and Daryl's roster took him to the mine during alternating days. They had three sons, and the family's existence was turned upside down. The journey to and from Beaconsfield and their home in Launceston and the requirement to change into miners' gear added hours to each 12-hour shift. They woke, they worked, they went to bed, often exhausted. Daryl woke sometimes in the night, haunted by the knowledge that his wife, the mother of young boys, was a kilometre beneath the earth in a place that had already collapsed.

Karen found herself terrified only once. On Thursday, 4 May, sensors attached to the walls detected renewed seismic activity. Everyone in the decline was ordered to retreat to higher levels and all equipment, including a huge fan pumping fresh air into the drive, was switched off.

When the all clear was given, miners and paramedics trooped back to their stations, the sound of dripping water and their boots tramping on hard rock lending a ghostly atmosphere to the dark surroundings. Karen was quite unprepared for the resumption of activity. Suddenly, an almighty roar filled the air. She thought the roof was collapsing and began running. It was simply the great fan whistling into action up the decline, ramming air down a large pipe to cool the miners at their drills in the drive.

Todd and Brant couldn't visualise the various paramedics manning the phones, and asked for photos. The ambulance officers agreed to send their identification tags bearing their pictures down the tube.

The two trapped men amused themselves by giving each of the paramedics a nickname. Karen had a broad grin and they dubbed her Smiley. Daryl, whose photo was taken when he wore a beard, became Sparky – Todd and Brant decided he had a head like a Champion sparkplug.

The two men whiled away their time asking paramedics to tell them the worst stories they could recall about their colleagues. Someone related that Peter James had been subjected to an obscene ritual involving a vacuum cleaner when he was a young paramedic. He became Dyson, a popular brand of vacuum cleaner.

Another member of the team from Launceston, Matthew Eastham, was bald. Todd and Brant renamed him Monk. Greg Edsall had a sharply receding hairline. Morehead, naturally. Graeme Jones had a deep voice, and thus became Harvey after Channel Nine's rumbling Peter Harvey. Judith Barnes undertook only one shift in the mine, but it was long enough for the two men in the cage to discover she sported a tattoo of a panther. They called her the Pink Panther, with much ribald banter about precisely where the tattoo might be situated upon her body. Ian Hart copped the nickname Dimples and Nick Chapman was Chipmunk.

A football tipping competition was organised. Anything that might take Todd's and Brant's minds on an excursion from their entrapment. Brant tried to make a wry joke out of his surroundings. When he picked up the phone, he had a signature answering technique. 'Hello. The Rock.' Sometimes it was more to the point. 'Alcatraz here.'

The only subject that was off-limits was the question of just how long it might be before the men were released. If they asked, paramedics and miners alike were instructed by management to blur the answer. Greg Crowden, Dean Mackrell and Corey Verhey, who occasionally had a chat down the pipe or on the phone with Brant and Todd, all learned to skirt the subject by responding along the lines of 'Guys, you know mining – it's hard to say, but everything's being done safely and as fast as possible.'

Todd tried to take his mind off his surroundings by thinking about the contentment he might have cruising free on the surface in a brand-new four-wheel-drive Toyota Hilux, the vehicle of preference among Tasmanian outdoorsmen. Daniel Piscioneri had just such a machine. Piscioneri dropped by one day to shoot the breeze down the tube.

'Mate,' said Todd. 'The first thing I'm gonna do when I get out of here is take your bus for a drive, and then I'm gonna buy one for myself.'

As the raise bore inched its way towards the men, pulverising hard rock at no more than half a metre an hour, Todd's and Brant's nerves wore thin.

Dr Richard Morris came for a discussion about the manner of their eventual release.

Todd and Brant told him they would walk out of the mine. 'We walked in and we're walking out,' they declared.

'Unlikely,' Dr Morris responded. After all their days recumbent, their muscles simply wouldn't be up to the task and it would be inadvisable, medically speaking, to try to walk.

Todd flew into a rage.

'You just try to stop me, cock,' he hissed.

'We may have to sedate you,' the doctor replied.

'You'd need to be fast – you try to sedate me and I'll punch you in the head.'

The doctor took a look at the men on the video. 'Yes,' he said, 'you do look like a big boy.'

‘Fuckin’ oath, you just stay away from me, cock,’ Todd hollered.

The doctor tried a little humour. He had a tranquilliser gun, and he might just have to use it, he chortled. It was exactly the wrong thing to say to a rifleman like Todd.

‘Listen to me, Dr Dick,’ he said. ‘You point a gun at me, you better be a fuckin’ good shot because if you miss, I’ll ram that gun right up your arse!’

‘Well,’ said the doctor. ‘It happens that I have two tranquilliser guns. If I miss with the first, I’m sure to get you with the second.’

Todd, just about beside himself, handed the phone to Brant.

‘Have you been hunting lately, Doc?’ Brant inquired. ‘Because Todd’s going to run at you like a rhino.’

The doctor and the paramedics were concerned Todd’s blood pressure might be rising to dangerous levels. Dr Morris thought it best that he withdraw from the discussion and allow Todd to calm down.

The raise bore operation proved agonisingly slow – it began on Thursday evening and was not completed until 6 pm Saturday when it finally reached the point at which the rescue coordinators estimated it could no longer safely proceed. It had bored a perfectly round hole, becoming slightly oval as its head wandered a little on its rods, 14.5 metres from its collar on the wall of rock in the drive.

Peter Hatswell and one of Australia’s best air-leggers, Glenn Burns, a nuggety man known as ‘the Fox’ because he craftily discovered gold in the West Australian fields where no one else could find it, crawled down the tunnel.

Hatswell struck the smooth rock at the end with an iron bar and it ricocheted back, not a flint breaking from its surface.

'Burnsy, you better take a look at this,' Hatswell said. The rock was about the hardest he had encountered. Mine experts later rated it at 180–200 mega Pascals – a measure of compressive strength. Concrete slabs used in construction projects are usually rated at 30–35 mega Pascals. Matthew Gill and Bill Shorten later used the equation to explain the problem: the rock was more than five times as tough as concrete. When Burns and other drillers tried attacking the material with jackhammers, Shorten had the perfect radio grab: 'It was,' he said, 'like throwing Kleenex at rock'.

The miners, working on their hands and knees with heavy air-leg drills cut down to dwarf size to deal with the cramped space, simply couldn't break the rock. They were only 1.2 metres from their goal, which would place them directly below Brant and Todd's cell, though they would need to blast 1.7 metres to provide space below the basket for drillers to work on breaking through to the men. Their drills hammered holes in the compressed laterite sandstone, leaving it like a Swiss cheese, but it still wouldn't break apart. It was infuriating.

The coordinating team upstairs finally reached the conclusion that jackhammering would have to be replaced by tougher measures.

■ ■ ■

At 3 o'clock on Sunday morning, 7 May, Darren Flanagan received a call from Pat Ball to explain that the jackhammers had failed to break the rock and there was no choice but to proceed with the low-energy PCF explosives. Flanagan and the three Stawell miners, Jeremy Rowlings, Brett Chalmers and Scott Franklin, were staying in a house at Greens Beach about 20 kilometres from Beaconsfield, but they reached the mine in half an hour.

The four men had already spent the past week testing, at the 630-metre level, high- and low-energy explosives in different patterns to determine which product and what method would produce lower levels of vibrations but still be productive.

Bruce Fagan and Mike Lovitt from Orica blasting services worked alongside the team using special monitoring equipment to record vibrations produced from every blast. The data identified exactly what level of vibration would be produced by each product tested in the extremely hard rock. Bruce and Mike also recorded vibrations produced by the raise bore machine and drilling equipment.

The video footage that Todd had taken earlier shocked the blasting team – the conditions within the cavern were far worse than they had imagined. If just one of those keystones above Todd and Brant were to give way while the blasting took place, both men would die.

Pat Ball told Flanagan that he was to take as much time as he needed to ensure the blasting was done safely. Ball's view, according to Flanagan, was that as long as Todd and Brant could be given food and medication through the communication pipe, time was not an issue. He believed they could be kept alive for a month if necessary.

Ball also said that even though the mine had given permission for the PCF blasting to start, the final decision rested with Todd and Brant.

Flanagan crawled up the tunnel to see what he and the Stawell miners were up against before talking to Todd and Brant. The face of the rock was a mess – there were drill holes everywhere. Blasting is a precise science that requires the correct hole placement, hole depth and angle to produce the best results.

The fear of bringing Todd and Brant's world tumbling down, combined with vibration reports from the test blasting, meant only a single 30-gram PCF cartridge would be allowed to fire at a time. The method would be painfully slow.

Flanagan had never met or spoken to either Todd or Brant. He picked up the phone to explain how PCF RocKracker differed from high explosives, and how testing earlier in the week had produced such encouraging results.

Todd said he and Brant, shot-firers themselves, would discuss it and call back. After about 10 minutes, Todd rang to say he and Brant were very worried, but they would allow one firing and then they would decide whether blasting could proceed.

Flanagan crawled the length of the 14.5 metre tunnel on his hands and knees to load the PCF cartridge with an electric firing match into a drill hole, followed by several sausage-shaped stemming packs of malleable aggregate (raise bore cuttings and clay, tamped in behind the cartridge to stem the release of explosive gases) and crammed them in with a tamping stick. Brett Chalmers was right behind Flanagan, passing the equipment. Chalmers and Flanagan then retreated from the tunnel.

When Flanagan declared the shot was ready to fire, Pat Ball ordered everyone except the paramedics to move

20 metres away in the decline. Flanagan's reflective overalls glowed like a Christmas tree – all those miners in the decline had their cap lamps trained onto him. Each had the same thought: would the vibrations from the explosion bring everything down on top of Brant and Todd?

If the whole process turned to shit, Flanagan thought, he would have to live with it for the rest of his life.

Todd and Brant put in ear plugs, pulled safety glasses over their eyes and wrapped their bodies in a blanket. Flanagan handed the phone to a paramedic and held on to the shot-firing box. Todd intoned a countdown over the phone. 'Three.' The paramedic held up three fingers. 'Two.' Two fingers. On 'one' Flanagan pressed the button. Boom!

He grabbed the phone. 'Are you there Todd? How was that?' Todd replied that Flanagan was a big girl and that he had a shotgun at home that made more racket.

Hatsy had fitted two 90-millimetre poly-pipes to the roof of the tunnel, and these were connected to fans outside the tunnel. Immediately after a shot was fired, the fans had to be switched on to blow all of the noxious gases created by the explosives back out of the tunnel.

Flanagan and Brett Chalmers returned to the long burrow. Jeremy Rowlings had fashioned a busted chair as a make-shift bogger for the blown rock. The mine also provided a rectangular tray that had a handle on either end, and each handle had a length of rope attached to it.

The men took to loading the explosives and stemming packs into the tray and dragging it up to the end of the tunnel, unloading it and filling it with broken rock. When it was full they yelled to a miner known as

Dutchie who pulled his end of the rope, hauling out the tray full of rock and emptying it into a wheel barrow. And then Flanagan and Chalmers pulled the tray back up the tunnel to do it all again.

At the very end of the tunnel, the water fell in sheets through cracks in the rock. Those loading the shots could not avoid lying directly under the water.

Once they left the tunnel, they were blasted by cool air the mine had directed to the work area, causing violent shivering.

Chalmers and Flanagan, with assistance from Rowlings and Franklin, continued the process until Steve Saltmarsh asked Rowlings to brief the management on progress and coordinate a roster so the four men could continue around the clock.

The men split into pairs to make sure the blasting could continue over several shifts. Jeremy Rowlings joined forces with Flanagan. Brett Chalmers and Scott Franklin formed the other team. The men had been on the job for 12 hours, and went to the surface for a break. Chalmers and Franklin would resume firing in a couple of hours, and Flanagan and Rowlings would rest in preparation for the next shift.

* * *

The men snatched coffee, a bite to eat and a hot shower. Eight Winnebago vans sat parked on the surface for rescuers to lie down in and get some sleep. Flanagan says he tried to sleep, but found it impossible.

Flanagan found himself haunted by a memory from his youth of a friend who had tried to swim through a concrete pipe beneath a road. The boy became trapped, unable to swim backwards or forwards, and drowned on a hot summer's night.

The memory played over in his mind as he tried to sleep in the Winnebago. He imagined himself stuck in the tunnel underground, caught around the shoulders, water pouring in.

After about seven hours – at one o'clock in the morning – it was time for Rowlings and Flanagan to get back underground and finish this thing.

The shift boss, Nigel Webb, a man who looks as if he could turn a bulldozer over if he lost his temper, told the men there had been a few problems during the night. There had been a few misfires because the firing line in the tunnel had been damaged by hand-bogging and had to be replaced.

The job had been made even more difficult because mine management hadn't allowed the men to fire the top half of the face – the part nearest to Todd and Brant – meaning Franklin and Chalmers were forced to persevere in an area that did not produce the results required.

Flanagan and Rowlings insisted that they be allowed to fire a hole in the top half of the face, or it would not be successful. They were granted permission.

Nigel asked them to stay until the blasting was finished. Flanagan and Rowlings agreed, and Flanagan picked up the phone. Todd asked who it was. Flanagan could hear Todd yelling to Brant, 'It's the gun, the gun is back!'

'Who are you talking about?' Flanagan asked.

'That's what Brant and I have nicknamed you,' Todd said. 'You're the gun and you're going to get us out of here.'

Chalmers and Franklin, exhausted and soaked after their night of attacking the rock, went back to the house in Greens Beach for a well-earned sleep. Flanagan and Rowlings returned to the effort of firing, bogging out, setting the charge, firing – repeating the effort over and over.

Slowly, slowly they forced the rock to fracture and yield.

Inside their cage, Todd and Brant simply endured, feeling the percussion of every shot. Brant felt the whole process was taking forever, and it wore at him. At one point, Todd screamed down the phone for the explosions to stop. Loose dirt streamed from the roof and he feared a large rock was about to come loose. But the emergency passed and he called for the men to press on.

Darren Flanagan's knees – like those of all the rescuers forced to crawl up and down the tunnel – were swollen with fluid. He could hardly tolerate the emotional pressure: after the close call, he was concerned about how much more of a pounding the ground above Todd and Brant could take. He had formed an emotional attachment to the two men within their cage, though the three miners from Stawell remained detached, feeling their judgment as miners could be affected if they grew too close to the men they were trying to save.

Dale Burgess oversaw the operation and became increasingly concerned about Flanagan's obvious turmoil. He asked Rowlings to stay close and keep an eye on the explosives man because he was not accustomed to the environment.

Shortly before 11 am on Monday, 8 May, the job was done. The team had blasted to within 300 millimetres of

Todd and Brant's cavern. Flanagan, emotionally wrung out, walked out into the drive and down into the darkness and wept. Todd Russell and Brant Webb had been nothing to him previously but pictures in the newspaper. During the long hours of firing and talking on the phone, they had become Flanagan's world.

Now, Dale Burgess approached him. He wanted two more shots fired to broaden the hole beneath the men's cage. Flanagan had trouble facing the task. He felt he had taken all the risks he wanted to take that day, but he and Rowlings did it.

The four men had blown through 1.7 metres of some of the hardest rock in the world, an operation that took, all up, 29 hours.

Far above, Beaconsfield seethed with impatience and worry and the rescue coordination team debated the best and safest method of taking the final step: breaking into Todd and Brant's cavern. All the finest surveying could not offer precise knowledge of where the cage sat in relation to the tunnel beneath. The planners knew what the cavern looked like thanks to the little video camera. They had even poured 1,500 litres of cement down the tube so Todd and Brant could grout unstable areas of the floor. The process had driven Todd to a rage, because much of the free-flowing grout had spurted into the cage itself, ruining their bedding and putting them in fear of suffering cement burns.

But knowing exactly where the cage sat within the rockfall was another matter altogether. Was it perched high on the bund, the ground beneath it simply collapsed earth? Had it been slammed closer to the original floor? And was the tunnel beneath the cage itself, or beneath the void? A wrong guess would almost certainly guarantee disaster, for if the ground beneath the cage was disturbed, it could crash down upon the rescuers and bring the roof down on Brant and Todd. The rescuers had to find their way into the void alongside the cage if they were to get the men out safely.

It was excruciating. The burden on the surveyor, Simon Arthur, could hardly be imagined. Option after option was considered and discarded. Finally, a decision. Drillers would go in, chip away a last section of hard material with hydraulic rock splitters and drill a probe upwards. If Simon Arthur's calculations were right, it should break through to the void alongside the cage.

Why was it taking so long, the media contingent and much of Beaconsfield's population wanted to know. All of Australia sat on the edge of its collective seat, television and radio sets tuned to the real-life drama. Reporters surged around the mine searching for any scrap of information that might give them a new angle. Emergency service workers and council employees erected temporary fencing and established media viewing points for the moment the men might be released from their captivity. Police made it clear they would enforce the rules.

A single TV camera and one stills photographer were to be allowed on a platform overlooking the mine to film the moment Todd and Brant emerged from the shaft, and their pictures had to be shared with every media organisation in the land. A hapless cameraman from *The Examiner* had initially been given the nod, but after a mutiny by other photographers, the job went to a snapper from the big photo agency Getty.

Rachel Webb and her family and the Russells were told to be prepared to be called to the mine in the dead of night.

Carolyn, Stephen, Mark Lopez and several other friends decided it was time to turn the tables on the journalists. They dressed for a cold night and strode towards the media camp, video camera at the ready. They filmed well-known journalists milling about, recorded caustic comments about the standard of Winnebago accommodation hired by rival media companies ('the ABC seems to have fallen short compared with Nine') and had a fine old time.

Not a single reporter recognised any of them, and Carolyn thought it was hilarious. They called their recording 'Wombat Cam'. It was their private video to show Todd when he came out. He would never otherwise believe just how much interest his disappearance had stirred up, Carolyn thought.

Below, a team of expert drillers set to work. Manfred Koshin, Dennis Newson and Heath Graauw took the first shift. Using a cut-down air-leg drill – an ingenious contraption designed and built especially for the task by fellow miner Royce Gill, who bolted an air-leg in tandem with a drill so it could be used vertically in such a confined space – they began probing. Water sluiced them and dirt fell in their faces.

Manfred Koshin eventually forced the first probe into Brant and Todd's world. The spinning drill bit sprayed water over the men, and they cared not a jot.

Todd and Brant, acting on instructions from outside, had plotted precisely where the probe should appear. It was 20 millimetres off bullseye!

'Call yourselves precision miners!' Brant yelled, laughing. 'You're 20 millimetres out.'

After blasting a drive for more than 20 metres, using a raise bore to drill 14.5 metres only three degrees off horizontal – a task it was not designed to do – and employing PCF blasting to crack 1.7 metres of the toughest rock in the mine, a driller in an impossibly confined space had pushed a probe into an area the position of which no one could be sure of, and it was the width of a man's thumb from perfect.

All those mine executives, search coordinators, geotechnicians, surveyors, drillers, shot-firers and miners of all sorts had pulled off one of the greatest engineering and surveying feats in underground history.

Brant and Todd were still hours away from rescue. Many hours. Two more probes had to be drilled to provide proper coordinates so the men below could understand exactly where they were. The third probe drilled straight through the PVC feed tube sticking out of the wall and severed the telephone wire. Frantically, technicians worked to re-establish contact. The last thing in the world the rescuers wanted was to be unable to speak to Todd and Brant as the project reached its most crucial phase.

Below, Manfred Koshin and the other drillers were ordered out of the tunnel. Koshin was furious.

'We've gotta get these boys out,' he cried. 'We're right there. We can get them out now.'

But coordinators, managers and safety officers weren't going to rush now.

Nigel Webb, one of the shift bosses, and Rex Johnson crawled down the tunnel to inspect the potential for a final safe breakthrough. All work stopped. Miners danced from one foot to the other in frustration.

In the early hours of Tuesday morning, 9 May, Glenn Burns and Donovan Lightfoot entered the long raise bore tunnel for the final assault. Every contingency had been checked. They had just 300 millimetres of broken rock and soil to drill directly above their heads and they would be able to break through to Brant and Todd's prison.

Water poured upon them, seeping through the floor of the cell and running down the probe holes. Todd had worried about this. All that water would be full of urine washed from the cage. He ordered disinfectant to be sent down the feed tube, and he splashed it everywhere. Todd liked order and cleanliness. He still hadn't moved his bowels. Almost fourteen days now.

Glenn Burns carefully levered rocks from the space above him, drilled a bit, grabbed his scaling bar and worked the earth. Behind him, the dirt he removed was hauled away down the tunnel in a little cart with splayed wheels built to travel the cylindrical tube. Above, Todd pulled a broken pipe from the soil and pushed aside stones lest they fall. Peter Hatswell watched the whole thing on the video screen, his heart in his mouth, separated from the performance by 16 metres of solid rock.

Suddenly, there was a gap in the floor of the void next to the cage.

'I can see your light,' Todd yelled.

'Yeah, I can see yours, too,' Burns called back. He dragged more dirt away, opening a hole. He looked into a pair of wide, staring eyes. Exactly like a possum peering down from a tree, he thought. He thrust his hand up and Todd grasped it. Burns hoisted himself up and was confronted by a sight that etched itself into his mind. Two men, with wild beards and wilder hair, each sprawled upon the other because there was no space. Glow-sticks sprouted from a roof of rocks a few inches above their heads. Junk everywhere – Sustagen cartons and water bottles and God knew what. And a stink that almost made him retch.

'You're coming out,' Burns said.

He hauled himself back down into the tunnel.

Pat Ball, Dr Morris and senior mine personnel made their way down the decline. Everything slowed down again. Word came from the surface that the miners should pretend to make themselves busy to ease Todd and Brant's anxiety. Burns picked at rocks that didn't need moving and Corey Verhey told Brant and Todd over the phone that he and his colleagues were getting equipment ready to take them out. Two stretchers lay ready at the mouth of the tunnel covered in blankets and coats, and first aid equipment sat nearby.

Pat Ball crawled into the tunnel, dragging a stretcher. Rex Johnson and Burns went with him.

Peter Hatswell had instructions for Todd. Brant would come out first, then Todd. He believed Todd would hold fast, but he didn't know Brant. He'd seen men panic and rush at the last minute and once he'd witnessed a miner so frenzied that the man had thrown himself headfirst into a narrow escape tunnel, his helmet becoming wedged. Nothing like that could happen here. Not now.

At 4.47 am, 9 May, Brant Webb lowered himself down the hole feet first, Pat Ball guiding him. He laid himself on the stretcher and was dragged away down the tunnel. Exactly five minutes later, Todd Russell followed. As he moved, someone kicked a cable powering the video, and Hatswell – who needed to watch every moment of the operation lest anything went wrong – suddenly found himself staring at a blank screen. Keeping his voice as calm as possible, giving no indication that he could no longer oversee what could be an emergency at this eleventh hour, he simply relayed to Todd that everything was fine, you're nearly there, slowly now. Hatswell could not see it, but Todd slid effortlessly and safely down the hatch.

Corey Verhey and Dean Mackrell – the two men who had watched Brant and Todd's every waking and sleeping moment on a TV screen for a week – and the man many of the miners considered the engine of the rescue underground, Dale Burgess, dragged the men to freedom, ropes attached to their stretchers. Paramedics and Dr Morris checked them quickly, lifted them on their stretchers into the mine ambulance and drove them up the decline to the 375 Plat.

Beaconsfield's fire station siren howled at 5.04 am. Two minutes later, Uniting Church community minister Frances Seen rang her church's old bell, which had not been rung since 1945. 'My brother-in-law rang this bell to mark the end of World War II, 61 years ago, and I am proud to be able to do it this morning,' Seen said. It continued tolling until its rusted old clapper fell out. Lights blinked on up and down the streets and a stream of townsfolk filed up West Street, gathering in the dark outside the mine's gates, faces aglow in television lights.

Carolyn Russell and her three children, her family, Todd's family and many of their friends were already in the mine's grounds, waiting with perhaps 200 rescue workers. Rachel Webb was there, too, with Zac and Zoey and Brant's father John and mother Christa.

Todd and Brant wanted to rinse away the grime and the stench of the depths before they were reunited with their families, and Hatswell had overseen the construction of a makeshift shower recess in the 375 crib. Hot water was brought from the surface and for the first time in 13 days and eight hours, Todd and Brant stood up. Their legs felt too weak to hold them, but they weren't about to show Dr Morris that they could not stand. They were walking out, and the doctor agreed. The business of tranquilliser guns was forgotten.

Clean for the first time since Anzac Day, the two men dressed in fresh miners' uniforms, placed helmets and cap lamps on their heads and were pushed on wheelchairs into the cage. Ceremoniously, Todd rang the bells signalling that they should be wound up the shaft.

The winder driver slowed the cage 80 metres from the surface. The two men stood shakily, stowed their wheelchairs out of sight and prepared to return to a world they had thought for too long was lost to them.

Waiting beneath the poppet were perhaps 200 men and women who had worn themselves beyond exhaustion in the wild hope they might witness this moment.

At 5.59 am, the two men stepped from the cage, punching the air, the moment beamed to television screens across the world.

Brant Webb and Todd Russell walked determinedly to the board still displaying their tags declaring them 'In Underground'. Each man snatched his tag away and placed it on a hook below the words 'Out – Safe'.

They turned and their wives ran into their arms.

Beaconsfield's cheers echoed from Cabbage Tree Hill clear across the darkened Tamar Valley.

Forty kilometres away down that valley, a family prepared to bury a man named Larry Knight.

EPILOGUE

ALL THAT PASSES...

A few weeks after Brant Webb and Todd Russell returned to the light, a visitor to the Tamar Valley might have ventured 6 kilometres north-west of Beaconsfield and found on a lonely rise above the river a small team of workers scrabbling in the dirt.

La Trobe University PhD student Adrienne Ellis and members of the West Tamar Historical Society were unearthing the remains of the first British settlement in northern Tasmania. Carefully they brushed aside 200 years of soil to reveal the crumbling brick foundations of the house once occupied by Lieutenant-Colonel William Paterson, a hard-drinking fellow sent by his masters in Sydney town in 1804 to establish a settlement he called York Town. The hard, often starving village of convicts, soldiers and free men, designed to lay claim to northern Tasmania before the French could do it, lasted only a few turbulent years before it was abandoned and its inhabitants moved up the river to what became

Launceston. From 1808, its remains slowly succumbed to the earth and the bush.

Things disappear in Tasmania: its Aboriginal people, the Tasmanian tiger (or thylacine), old-growth forests and convicts who simply walked into the bush and were swallowed by its ageless indifference. Whole settlements, too, have been consumed by time.

All that passes sometimes reappears, too. History wrote Tasmanian Aborigines from its script when Truganini, 'the last Tasmanian Aborigine', died in 1876, but a century later, maybe 15,000 Tasmanians claim Aboriginal heritage. Old-growth forests were once simply trees to be chopped, but in recent years they have re-emerged as heritage to be saved. The thylacine is officially extinct, but many Tasmanians believe the tiger still slinks silently in remote valleys. Plenty of those old convicts who fled their bonds materialised as bushrangers. Yes, and places like York Town are being conjured from the soil.

Brant Webb, Todd Russell and Larry Knight disappeared. Against all odds, two of them came back. The day they emerged, Larry Knight was returned to the earth forever.

Larry's funeral at St John's Anglican Church in Launceston was conducted by Chris Brooks and Graham Mulligan of God's Squad Christian Motorcycle Club and there were eulogies by Larry's daughter Lauren, his last shift boss Gavan Cheesman, a mate named only as Scruff and Beaconsfield Mayor Barry Easther. The 'Miner's Prayer' was recited: 'When that whistle blows each morning/ And I go down in that cold dark mine/ I say a prayer to my dear saviour/ Please let me see the sunshine one more time.'

Todd Russell checked himself out of Launceston hospital to attend the funeral wearing a suit a local clothes shop ran up for him. He had lost so much weight – 10 kilograms despite being fed for the last week – that his own clothes would no longer fit. A battery of TV cameras lined up on the street across the road from the church, rain falling. More than 60 motorcycles led the cortege away to the Carr Villa Memorial Cemetery, Larry's partner Jacqui mounted pillion on Larry's Harley. Lauren went to the cemetery as a passenger on another bike, feeling the funeral had been turned into a circus. There were so many journalists, photographers and camera crews that police closed the street and erected barriers.

Brant could not bring himself to attend the funeral. His mother Christa had to fly home to Queensland to meet a long-postponed appointment with an eye doctor – she suffers diabetes, with consequent damage to her sight. She and Brant had only one and a half hours together between the time he left Launceston's hospital and his mother's departure, and Brant felt his mother, after so many days of trauma, deserved his attention. He needed the comfort of family around him, and his family needed him. He would say goodbye to Larry from within his heart.

Brant and Todd were no longer quite the same men who went down the Beaconsfield mine on Anzac Day.

Every now and then, even now, demons crawl from the earth below Beaconsfield to torment the two men, reminding them of the days they were lost to the world.

Three months after they were released from purgatory, Brant fled from an osteopath's rooms in the old Queen Victoria Hospital building in Launceston. As he sat in the waiting room, a builder using a hammer drill began working on a wall outside. The sound of it – an echo from those horrifying hours when other drills bored into another wall – was intolerable.

Todd tried to confront his own terror by returning underground less than two months after being rescued. The familiar scent of ancient, dank earth sickened him as he rode the shaft and he grew more apprehensive as he approached the entrance to the tunnel blasted and drilled to the cage in which he and Brant had lain trapped for almost 14 days.

Todd, overwhelmed and fighting nausea, had to withdraw, vowing he would never venture down the mine again.

The men appeared so much more healthy than had been expected when they walked from the mine shaft that a myth arose that they had avoided injury altogether.

It was not so. Neither man has been able to return to work or search for employment: the mere business of walking remains painful for both.

Bone fragments float around Todd's left knee and he has three crushed discs in his back. He will undergo surgery on his leg in January 2007.

Brant suffers badly bruised bones in his lower legs and he, too, has four crushed, bulging discs in his neck and lower back. He also suffers a painful build-up of stomach acids that stems from six days of starvation, and he has trouble eating.

Other wounds are more deeply embedded. Todd wakes often in the night, sweating, fighting off fearful dreams. During his waking hours Carolyn watches concerned as he roams, unable to sit still, as if pursued.

Brant is powerless to predict the occasional onset of panic attacks that leave him gasping for air, his stomach knotted and tears in his eyes. The emotional trigger, bizarrely, is often nothing more than a 'feel-good' movie or a moment of happiness.

Todd and Brant are among more than 50 workers who have accepted redundancy offers from the mine. Most of the 14 men who escaped from the tunnels on Anzac night have no intention of returning to the mine, and several of them still require medication to ease them into sleep.

Many of the rescuers, a lot of them senior miners, have left Beaconsfield and its district to find work, heading to other mines in Tasmania, Victoria, South Australia and Western Australia.

Corey Verhey is working underground in Bendigo, just as the psychic predicted in early 2005. Dale Burgess has moved to Papua New Guinea. Daniel Piscioneri is working on a fly-in, fly-out basis at Roxby Downs. Mick Borrill has gone back to his hometown, Broken Hill. Greg Crowden has returned to his trade as an outboard mechanic at Port Sorell Marine. Vinnie Tunks has established his own metal fabrication and welding business, v-tec industries, and has a contract on a sea-going drilling rig.

Gavan 'Cheesy' Cheesman, however, surprised a lot of Beaconsfield's residents by returning to the town more than four months after his confrontation with the forces of the earth. He had travelled north, all the way to Darwin, but the mine called him back. He has accepted a new job underground at Beaconsfield, and his daughter Renee was due to visit from Ireland in late October.

The three miners from Stawell, Victoria, who with Darren Flanagan from New South Wales used low-impact explosives to blast the last of the hard rock in the rescue, received awards for bravery. Brett Chalmers, Jeremy Rowlings and Scott Franklin were invested with the bravery awards in the Melbourne *Herald Sun/Sunday Herald Sun* Pride of Australia Medal awards. Brant has declined nomination for a similar award in Tasmania, and has instead nominated Pat Ball and Steve Saltmarsh, the men who found him and Todd.

Brett Cresswell, the shift boss who was threatened with a $20,000 fine for burrowing through the rubble over the telehandler to reach Todd and Brant, received in August the Hobart *Mercury* Pride of Australia Medal for bravery. The citation said the medal was 'for an act of bravery that helped save a life'.

Todd and Brant appointed an agent to handle their affairs after they emerged into a blaze of national and international publicity.

Sydney-based Sean Anderson, of 22 Management, negotiated an exclusive, multi-million dollar TV contract with the Nine Network, with a percentage to be returned to Beaconsfield community organisations through the Russell Webb Legacy. Brant and Todd rejected the approaches of several of Australia's leading celebrity agents, choosing Anderson because he suggested a legacy arrangement that would grant benefits to the community in which both men wished to continue living. Anderson also negotiated a contract with the publishers of this book to allow the story of the men to be told, and part of the proceeds will also be distributed through the Russell Webb Legacy.

The Australian Workers Union raised about $800,000 to support distressed mining families. At Todd and Brant's request, the majority of it is to go to the family of Larry Knight. The fund, authorised by Bill Shorten before he flew from Canada to Tasmania to support AWU members, received a massive boost when Brant and Todd appeared on the Nine Network's *The Footy Show* only days after they were brought out of the mine. Prime Minister John Howard later announced a $25,000 donation from the Federal Government and saw to it that the AWU fund received tax-free status.

One of the more extraordinary events in the Australian Parliament's history occurred on Monday, 29 May when hundreds of Beaconsfield residents and rescuers were flown free to Canberra for a reception to honour Todd Russell, Brant Webb and the memory of Larry Knight.

John Howard declared: 'We gather in this Great Hall of the Parliament of Australia as a united nation to pay tribute to people who were involved in a remarkable Australian achievement, an event which has touched the hearts and brought forth the inspiration of millions of Australians and indeed had an enormous impact around the world. What we saw in the rescue of Brant and Todd was the Australian character at its very best. We saw all of the things that we pride ourselves on as distinctively Australian characteristics at work. We saw guts, we saw resilience, we saw courage, we saw strength and we saw enormous endurance.'

Opposition Leader Kim Beazley saw the power of mateship at work. 'Everybody became a citizen of Beaconsfield, every single Australian became a citizen of Beaconsfield in the course of those two weeks,' he said.

Brant and Todd denied they were heroes.

'All the people in this room today, they're the true heroes, they're the ones that risked their lives to free Brant and myself,' Todd said. 'They're the ones that left loved ones at home knowing the dangers were there.'

And Brant: 'We're not heroes, of course. People that saved us are the heroes, but at the end of the day we're just really glad, really happy to be here, and I think we'll just go for the ride if that's all right, Todd.'

Larry's daughter Lauren sat on stage next to Todd and Brant during the reception, and later they all went off to dinner at the Governor-General's residence at Yarralumla.

The Federal Government gave $1 million to establish a mining and engineering scholarship at the University of Tasmania in memory of Larry Knight, and contributed a further $8 million to a Beaconsfield Community Fund. More than half of it went to the mine operators to deal with the financial disaster and to try to keep the enterprise under maintenance in the hope that it might reopen. The West Tamar Council wants some of the money to build an interactive display showing the efforts to rescue Todd and Brant, and local traders and community representatives hope the remainder will go to non-profit community organisations.

The Tasmanian Government appointed Sydney barrister Greg Melick SC, a former member of the National Crime Authority, to undertake an inquiry into the design of the mine, operating standards, corporate managerial and administrative arrangements, and whether previous seismic activity in the area was properly taken into account. He was also to investigate whether the mining work was likely to cause or increase seismic activity at the mine.

Melick's investigation has been behind closed doors – for legal reasons, according to Tasmanian Premier Paul Lennon – and at the time of writing his findings had not been published.

The only official explanation for the Anzac Day disaster beneath Beaconsfield remains Geoscience Australia's recording of an earthquake officially designated as 2.2 on the Richter scale, which it places at Georgetown, right across the river from Beaconsfield. This is a very small earthquake, although 2.2 suggests an effect roughly equivalent to the explosion of three tonnes of TNT. In World War II terms, this would have slightly less power than a 'blockbuster' bomb, which could level a city block.

Since the disaster, the Beaconsfield mine operators have continued extracting gold from existing stockpiles of ore while pumps continued emptying the mine of water. One of the mine's owners, Beaconsfield Gold NL, issued share placements in an attempt to buy out the other partner, Allstate Explorations NL, although the effort remains in dispute. The betting around Beaconsfield was that mining would start again before the end of the year – there was just too much gold down there to imagine leaving it undisturbed.

Macquarie Bank, known as 'the millionaire factory', offered to turn over $47 million of Allstate's debts to a trust for every miner employed in Beaconsfield on Anzac Day. Macquarie several years ago bought $77 million of Allstate's internal debts for just $300,000. Many financial commentators saw it as the deal of the century, because it meant Allstate's share of the gold from beneath Beaconsfield went straight to the bank. Allstate remains under administration, so Macquarie's gesture in handing over its debts would put the mine manager in the curious position of being in hock to its own mine employees. All this, of course, is contingent on the mine re-opening, and remains a chapter yet to be written in Beaconsfield's history.

The township has returned to its easy-going rhythm. Colin Smee hoists his flags in the mornings and reels them down in the evenings. A few extra tourists turn up West Street to gawk at the mine and imagine the scene that played out on every TV station in the land.

Todd Russell has bought a 35-acre block down Bowens Jetty Road where he and his old mate Michael Piscioneri once staggered in the moonlight, and he's planning to build a new home there for his family. And yes, Todd drives around in a brand-new shiny black Hilux ute.

Both Todd and Brant travelled extensively in Australia and clear to the United States in the months after they became international celebrities. The changes in Todd's life clearly affected his daughter Maddison, who revealed her feelings when she entered a writing competition. The subject was 'If I could change anything in the world or myself, what would it be?'

She wrote: 'I would like my life to settle down and to be normal again. Before we used to be normal everyday people but now we are travelling everywhere. Dad has to go everywhere but he always used to be home. He used to be able to fight with us but now he can't because he is sore. Before we could go outside and there would be no cameras on us but now cameras follow Dad and everyone wants his autograph. When Dad goes away we miss him and he misses us. Usually he would just come home from work and we would do everyday things. We used to have 2 or 3 things in the mail but now we have at least 10 things. Now it takes hours to sort out the mail. I am a bit concerned what Dad might do in the future. And I wish the media would mind its business because they say things that are not true. Life is sort of starting to settle down.'

Brant and Rachel continue to live at their modest home in Beauty Point, looking forward to sunny days on the river and out on the ocean. Brant bought a second-hand V8 Holden. It lasted eight days before it was smashed beyond repair in a collision with another car in Beaconsfield.

Still, Brant has kept himself busy. He and Rachel have bought a house in Launceston for their twins, Zac and Zoey. Brant and his mates Vinnie Tunks and Greg Crowden brought out their toolkits to do a few renovations on the Webbs' Beauty Point home, and Brant and Rachel found the time to visit both of Brant's parents in Queensland. With summer beckoning, Brant recently splurged on matching jet skis – he and Rachel plan to carve up the waters of the Tamar River when his body is up to it.

Brant and Rachel's daughter Zoey has left Dr Tony Lyall's employ and is working with Rachel's parents at their café, Red Kelly's, in central Launceston. Her brother Zac is continuing his studies at TAFE, but also works part-time at the café. Rachel's father Mike Kelly is undergoing chemotherapy for cancer of the face.

Jacqui Knight declined to be interviewed for this book.

TRUST FOUNDATION

RUSSELL WEBB LEGACY

A DONATION FROM THE PROCEEDS OF EACH COPY OF BAD GROUND WILL BE MADE TO THE RUSSELL WEBB LEGACY.

The Russell Webb Legacy was established by Todd Russell and Brant Webb to give back to the Beaconsfield community in Tasmania by supporting the youth of this region.

This legacy perpetuates the memory of the events that shocked the world in April 2006 when a minor earthquake rocked the small town of Beaconsfield, collapsing one of the tunnels in a local gold mine and trapping miners Larry Knight, Todd Russell and Brant Webb.

It is a thank you to their home town for the support and encouragement they received during their rescue, and an opportunity to provide valuable assistance to the youth of Beaconsfield and surrounding areas, who continue to feel the effects of the disaster.

For more information about Trust Foundation – Russell Webb Legacy please contact:

Trust Foundation – Russell Webb Legacy
Telephone (03) 9665 0200
Freecall 1800 650 358
or visit www.trust.com.au/russell_webb_legacy

Genesys Wealth Advisors and Trust Company Limited are proud to support the philanthropic endeavours for the Beaconsfield community.

POSTSCRIPT TO THE ANNIVERSARY EDITION

New Year's Eve; 2006 about to tick into 2007. A velvety summer's night in the Tamar Valley, northern Tasmania; stars littering a wide sky.

Two men stand in the shadows. The tips of their cigarettes bore into the night and they upend cans and murmur to each other.

Not so long ago, Todd Russell and Brant Webb had reason to believe they would never make it to 2007. There were long days and nights when they hardly dared imagine any more Christmases or New Years.

But here they were. Brant Webb and his wife Rachel had come down the track to spend a little time celebrating with Todd Russell and his wife Carolyn, and to give thanks that — against all the odds — they had another year ahead of them.

There was quite a little crowd at Todd's bush block by the river. Tents were erected, a homemade firepot spread its warmth, country music spilled among the trees from a sound system. Todd's whole family was there — his and Carolyn's three children, his parents, brother, sisters, their partners.

It seemed perfectly natural when Todd and Brant took themselves off a little way into the night and shared a drink and the sort of secrets that still give them nightmares.

Todd and Brant were the most famous Australians of 2006. They did it the hard way, trapped for a fortnight in a minuscule hole almost a kilometre beneath the town of Beaconsfield, the whole country tuning in to their predicament and celebrating when they were brought out alive, the word 'miracle' tossed into the dawn. They appeared on the covers of magazines, gathered the year's third-biggest Australian television ratings (after the Commonwealth Games opening ceremony and the Australian Football League grand final) when they told their story on Channel Nine, flew to New York to be interviewed on *Good Morning America*, travelled around Australia addressing transfixed audiences, and signed first-edition copies of this book by the thousands. At a hugely successful fundraiser for 16 surf life saving clubs on the Gold Coast, two mining helmets and two copies of *Bad Ground*, all signed by Brant and Todd, were auctioned for a total of $22,500.

Slowly, now, they are retrieving the rhythm of normal lives, and New Year's Eve on Todd's bush block, far from autograph seekers and the curious, was a milestone. Within a few days, Todd would enter St Luke's Hospital in Launceston for an operation that would repair a little of the damage he had suffered when the earth collapsed upon him and Brant way back on Anzac Day, 25 April, 2006. Doctors grafted bone taken from his hip, fixing it with a metal plate and four screws to his left knee.

By Anzac Day 2007, he ought to be able to walk properly again, a mercy for a man impatient at enforced indolence.

The operation robbed him of one of those thrills that come with fame. He and Brant were offered the chance of driving in the celebrity race at the 2007 Grand Prix in Melbourne in March. Brant, like many Australian blokes utterly addicted to the challenge of speed, couldn't resist. He put aside the pain of crushed discs in his back to declare himself a starter.

Both men have returned to part-time work as part of their rehabilitation from the trauma of their entrapment. Though neither will return to underground mining, Brant — in thrall to the sea since childhood — is employed working on boats with Greg Crowden at Port Sorell Marine in Port Sorell. Todd packs and distributes safety gear at a company called Emergency Management Solutions.

A large new family home is rising from Todd's block on the Tamar River, the view from its windows across bushland, the sort of country that soothes his soul, takes him hunting. Brant and Rachel continue to live in Beauty Point, not far from the water that is their recreation.

At the time of writing, Beaconsfield Gold was buying out its partner, Allstate Explorations, with a view to resuming mining gold deep beneath Beaconsfield. Beaconsfield Gold bought $48 million of Allstate's debt from the Macquarie Bank for $2.85 million, passing on this amount as a gift to the 131 miners employed at the mine when it collapsed. An inquiry into the mine disaster was continuing, and a coroner's inquest into the death of Brant and Todd's colleague Larry Knight was incomplete.

Todd and Brant are left with rare knowledge of terror and survival. The mercy of it is they have been granted the time to whisper their shared knowing in the secret nights of their valley.

Tony Wright

First published in 2006 by Pier 9, an imprint of Murdoch Books Pty Limited

Murdoch Books Australia
Pier 8/9, 23 Hickson Road, Millers Point NSW 2000
Phone: +61 (0) 2 8220 2000 Fax: +61 (0) 2 8220 2558

Chief Executive: Juliet Rogers
Publishing Director: Kay Scarlett

Concept and Design: Reuben Crossman
Project Manager and Editor: Tricia Dearborn
Production: Tiffany Johnson

Wright, Tony, 1951- .
Bad ground: inside the Beaconsfield mine rescue.
Rev. ed.
ISBN 978 1 74196 005 1 (pbk).
1. Russell, Todd. 2. Webb, Brant. 3. Rescues – Tasmania – Beaconsfield. 4. Gold miners – Tasmania – Beaconsfield – Biography. 5. Gold mines and mining – Accidents – Tasmania – Beaconsfield. 6. Mine rescue work – Tasmania – Beaconsfield. I. Russell, Todd. II. Webb, Brant. III. Title.
622.890922

Printed by McPherson's Printing Group. Printed in Australia.